D0617048

Virtual Teams

Virtual Teams

Mastering Communication and Collaboration in the Digital Age

Terri R. Kurtzberg

 PRAEGER

AN IMPRINT OF ABC-CLIO, LLC
Santa Barbara, California • Denver, Colorado • Oxford, England

Library of Congress Cataloging-in-Publication Data

Kurtzberg, Terri R.
   Virtual teams : mastering communication and collaboration in the digital age / Terri R. Kurtzberg.
      pages cm
   Includes index.
      ISBN 978-1-4408-2837-9 (alk. paper) — ISBN 978-1-4408-2838-6 (ebook)   1. Virtual work
teams—Management.   2. Virtual reality in management.   I. Title.
   HD66.K874   2014
   658.4'022—dc23   2013047547

ISBN: 978-1-4408-2837-9
EISBN: 978-1-4408-2838-6

18 17 16   3 4 5

This book is also available on the World Wide Web as an eBook.
Visit www.abc-clio.com for details.

Praeger
An Imprint of ABC-CLIO, LLC

ABC-CLIO, LLC
130 Cremona Drive, P.O. Box 1911
Santa Barbara, California 93116-1911

This book is printed on acid-free paper ∞

Manufactured in the United States of America

To Charles Naquin,
who set me on this book-writing path

Contents

Preface

Rare is the job today that does not contain an element of virtual work. This is evidenced by this slogan found on a T-shirt: "I love the people I work with. Maybe I'll get to meet them someday!" Whether it be working from home or other off-site locations or working with others (near and far) in a non-face-to-face manner, interactions are becoming increasingly mediated by technologies. And of course, this gets easier and easier the more comfortable everyone gets communicating in ways other than face to face. Think of the image of someone in the 1940s making a phone call: shouting into the receiver, talking over the other side, as compared to a phone conversation today. But ease of use with the technologies alone won't make virtual interactions seamless. Instead, we need to understand how things change, and why they change, when conversations move from face to face to voice or text. And changes there are. Some are quite obvious, such as the increased trouble coordinating conversations and work, or the increased difficulty in getting to know other people on a more personal level. Some are not as apparent to the casual observer, like the changes in risk-taking propensity and evaluation decisions that can result when discussions are taken online.

The phrase "virtual teams" has two words, and indeed two potentially separate topics, contained within it. Understanding how *virtuality* influences people at work is the first, and understanding *teamwork* is the second. Thus, this book is written in two sections and with two purposes in mind. The first is explaining what is known about virtual interaction (primarily via text such as e-mail, but including any form of non-face-to-face interaction) and how behavior, interpretations, and decisions can be systematically different in these media. The second goal targets a deeper understanding of virtual teams.

In a nutshell, virtual teams have many of the same challenges and problems that traditional teams do, but they tend to experience them to a greater extent (more often, more intensely, more quickly in the process, and more deeply rooted/difficult to eradicate). Coupled with the changes in conversation, comprehension, and decision making that can result from virtual interaction, these teams have a lot to contend with in order to successfully operate. However, it is both possible and exciting to know that virtual teams can work as well as more traditional types—and sometimes even better. After all, virtual teams were created for a reason, and being able to take advantage of those benefits while sidestepping the pitfalls is the goal of the virtual team, for managers and members alike.

This book will explore the effects of moving each area of work, conversations, decisions, and interactions into the online forum. Part I, which includes the first four chapters, explores virtual communication in a general sense, and not necessarily just in the virtual team context (this places more emphasis on the "virtual" part of virtual teams). First, Chapter 1 takes an in-depth look at the negative tendencies that people tend to display in text that they don't typically use in other forms of communication. This chapter also examines the ways in which emotions are expressed and (mis)interpreted online. Chapter 2 delves into issues of the changes in pace that result when we communicate electronically, and policies that may help guide effective use. In Chapter 3, the all-too-common practice of electronic multitasking is analyzed, with a section especially devoted to conference calls. Chapter 4 looks at effective communication practices, with tips for making sure your messages get across (in terms of getting your information understood) when put into electronic text. Part II includes the last six chapters and delves into virtual team management more specifically (focus here switches to the "teams" aspect of virtual teams). Chapter 5 explores networking and team-building strategies, and Chapter 6 focuses exclusively on building trust in this setting. Chapter 7 examines what motivates people to want to do their jobs, and how these principles apply specifically to virtual teams. Chapter 8 looks at leadership practices that work in this domain. Chapter 9 looks into the realm of decision making, and how these processes can work most effectively online. Chapter 10 explores the increasingly common challenges provided by having team members who span different countries and thus bring different expectations and work processes to the table. Finally, the conclusion provides an overall summary.

The information in this book rests primarily on a compilation of findings from research studies in the field of organizational behavior. But the anecdotes and experiences that poured in from MBA students and working professionals alike are what brought the issues to light in a vivid way. For that reason, the book contains summaries and explanations of decades of research on the topic alongside comments and notes from those experiencing these issues in a day-to-day sense. Thus, sprinkled throughout the chapters are many "quotes from the front lines," which provide an opportunity to hear from real working professionals on the issues and topics covered in the book. These are the result of many interviews with people from a wide variety of industries and from organizations ranging from an enormous global firm to the small entrepreneur starting a new business with a handful of employees. The quotes afford the opportunity to hear descriptions of the problems people encounter in the virtual aspects of their work more specifically, as well as some insights into potential solutions. You will also find important points and lessons highlighted in the "Tip" boxes for easy reference.

It is hard to imagine a career path at this point in time without any involvement in digital interaction, if not multiple roles on virtual teams (sometimes simultaneously!). This book was written to address the growing need for better information about how to manage this change in work life. The digital age is here to stay, so the task now is to learn to adapt to the new forum—to understand and overcome the challenges and actually thrive in this environment.

Introduction

Before expounding on the problems found in many virtual teams and possible solutions for alleviating them, it first makes sense to address this question: Why have virtual teams at all? Like most other organizational innovations, virtual teams were created to solve a set of problems for managers and employees alike. In addition to the more straightforward benefits such as having access to a greater pool of talent and cutting down on the travel budget, there are some other, more subtle advantages. One category of benefits stems from the relatively new ability to easily create and use multinational teams. Not only can this provide access to less expensive labor, it also allows for a "follow the sun" approach in which work can be accomplished continually around the globe. Even for the local organization, the ability to have team members work together virtually can sometimes reduce the physical real estate needs as employees are able to work from home.[1] Virtual teams can also help accommodate the need for flexible work arrangements.

But of course, as with electronic communication in general, the picture is not all rosy. Employees are more than twice as likely to have teamwork problems when working in the virtual environment, and given that statistic, it is not surprising to learn that they tend to be less satisfied with the overall experience.[2] The most common problem themes that virtual teams tend to face will be introduced in the paragraphs below, and will be explored in more detail throughout the book. But before going forward, it is worth noting that sometimes the answer is to *not* use a virtual team. Sometimes the tradeoff between getting input from other areas is outweighed by the coordination and integration obstacles present in nearly every virtual team. Opting for a co-located team who occasionally checks in with interested parties in other areas might satisfy the team's needs better in some cases, and is worth thinking through before a virtual team is launched.

The same goes for the decision about who belongs on and can thrive on a virtual team. In addition to the work-based skills required, attention to both the communication skills and the degree of "tech savvy" each person has is also relevant. On this last point, it has even been suggested that a great deal of one's affinity for technology is not based on practice but is instead based on genetics! Some people may just naturally gravitate towards and feel more comfortable using technology as a communication tool.[3] While it probably goes without saying that the right people for the job each need to be "self-starters," relatively independent, and tolerant of some ambiguity on the job, it might come as more of a surprise to learn that those classified as "lone wolf" types actually seem to do *worse* in this setting. By way of explanation, some theorize that lone wolves become that way because they are actually *poor* communicators and collaborators, which will hold them back when interacting from afar.[4]

The rise of virtual teams in nearly every facet of organizational life speaks to the fact that (most of the time) the benefits are deemed to outweigh the setbacks, and so the task becomes one of smoothing and mastering these processes. But people are creatures of habit. Once used to a particular way of doing, or seeing, or thinking about something, it is natural to not only feel more comfortable with it, but to defend it as the best way to do things. And people are used to face-to-face interaction. Whether or not it is an objectively better way to accomplish a meeting is almost a moot question; virtual teams need to interact in new ways, and newness is a liability in and of itself. It is commonly understood that when a person loses the ability to see, other senses develop much stronger capacities to receive subtle signals and can help fill the gap. In a way, losing the ability to interact face to face is analogous. Other abilities need to develop and strengthen in order to accomplish the same goals. Some argue, in fact, that this process happens more easily if face-to-face meetings are *not* included in the virtual team's process at all, to avoid using them as a crutch.[5] Learning how to develop the skills needed to effectively interact, discuss, decide, and proceed with work, while not relying on face-to-face meetings, is the goal of every virtual team, and is the goal of this book as well.

Virtuality itself can also be thought of as a state of mind. There are some employees whose work is 100% virtual, meaning they have never met their colleagues, and they communicate only from a distance. And though it may already be hard to imagine, there are individuals for whom electronic communication or virtual work *never* plays a role in their jobs. These pure situations are few and far between; the vast majority of jobs contain some elements of virtual work and some elements of more traditional interactions. It is increasingly common for individuals to belong to multiple virtual teams simultaneously. A sample from one global technology company turned up these numbers: 60% of the virtual team members in the study reported being concurrently on three or more teams, with 28% being on *five* or more.[6] Clearly, it is hard to count on complete attention and responsiveness from anyone in this type of situation, which exacerbates the need to have the tasks, the norms, and the interactions well established.

Whether on multiple teams or not, most people can quickly estimate what percentage of their work is conducted virtually. However, it's important to realize that to some degree, the question may be open to interpretation. Imagine two workers, both of whom use e-mail with the same frequency objectively. The first one, however, considers e-mail to be the only option for getting this work done, and considers this a limitation to her work. The second one feels that e-mail is one choice among many for staying in touch, and he routinely chooses to communicate in this way. These two may have quite different impressions of how much of their work is virtual, based on the degree of "pain" they feel when they interact in this way. Similarly, imagine two colleagues working from afar—one might consider the relationship to be very distant based on the miles and time zones that separate the two, while the other considers them to be close, based on the past history and trust that the two share.[7]

THREE PROBLEMS, ONE SOLUTION

When asked about the biggest challenge faced in their virtual teamwork, a surprisingly few categories of responses surface over and over again. In fact, to illustrate this point, I personally collected responses to this question from over 150 people covering a broad range of industries and job types. This quick survey highlighted the main issues at the forefront of virtual work. They fall into three categories, listed here and then explored in turn:

A. **Coordinating the Content:** "Everything got slowed down. People went off in different directions for the work, and so we wasted tons of time and effort."
B. **Coordinating the Relationships:** "It was too hard to get to know and trust my team members."
C. **Coordinating the Schedules:** "It was difficult to coordinate everyone's schedules for meetings, especially when we were working in different time zones."

A. Coordinating the Content. The difficulty in coordinating the work was a globally acknowledged problem. In fact, of the 150 survey respondents, a whopping 45% of them reported this as the main problem that they faced. Here is a small sample of the responses that highlight this problem:

- "You can read the final document and clearly figure out that it was written by many different people."
- "The two parts of the team were unintentionally working on two different sets of data."
- "We couldn't see or touch the item in question. Pictures just didn't cut it."
- "We sometimes find ourselves duplicating each other's efforts by having more than one person begin work on the same part of the project without notifying each other."

Later in the book the topic of motivation will be addressed in detail, but it is not hard to imagine that the above situations can cause frustration and can lead to decreased motivation levels. It wouldn't take that many times of doing work only to find that someone else had done the same thing before your effort and energy for applying yourself to the work would probably diminish. Similarly, an imperfect sense of what you are supposed to be doing can make even the most conscientious employees falter.

B. Coordinating the Relationships. Nearly 20% of the respondents focused primarily on the difficulty associated with getting to know and trust others on the team.

- "To make matters worse, first-time 'virtual teamers' tend to be even more stand-offish, and may get defensive if you press them on their performance. I think this is because they are unfamiliar with the process and it can be very easy to be impersonal on e-mail."
- "Everyone is very disconnected. There's no emotional bonding between the team members since we rarely meet in person. No one has any intention of helping each other out."
- "I just don't get that sense of camaraderie that I used to have with my previous face-to-face team."

As noted by one quote, a lack of personal connection can also spill into the related problem of people not feeling comfortable enough to reach out to each other for help. Another respondent addressed this directly: "Given that my teammates are not around, I can't see what they are doing at the time that I need help, so I am always hesitant to ask for help, especially for something like troubleshooting that could take a long time."

Additionally, one participant above has introduced the problem of interpreting tone in e-mail messages, as direct or simple messages can sometimes be read as impersonal. Misread tone can certainly inspire distance as opposed to trust. Survey respondents mentioned this type of communication problem again and again, with comments like these:

- "The other people often seemed cold and demanding."
- "Tones seemed condescending and arrogant."
- "The note was written in all capital letters, which made everyone think the manager was really upset and angered, when in actuality it was later learned that she was just in a rush and hit caps-lock by accident."
- "People seem to be less likely to ask questions on virtual teams because it is more difficult to explain the confusion, and for the person delivering information to clarify their points."

Developing team relationships, at least to the point where members are willing to both seek each other out as needed and give each other the benefit of the doubt when messages feel questionable, seems paramount to effective virtual team interaction. Some teams swear by the more traditional "fixes" to these problems, which include occasional face-to-face get-togethers with emphasis on "hanging out and bonding" and setting aside some time in a regular fashion to force chit-chat and personal exchanges. While those remedies may help in some circumstances, they alone will not ensure a well-functioning virtual team. (If that were all there was to it, this book wouldn't be necessary!) The job of this book is to dig deeper, to look at what makes people like and trust each other from the first introduction onwards, and to explore what kinds of rules and norms can help encourage the type of interactions that result in a successful virtual team.

C. **Coordinating the Schedules.** Lastly, while geographic distance is not perfectly correlated with the use of electronic communication, it certainly makes it more common and comes with a unique set of concerns. (Sometimes distance is not the relevant factor. Compare a team whose members are very dispersed, but who primarily wait for their occasional in-person meetings to converse, with a second team whose members are all in the same building, but choose to e-mail or instant message each other instead of speaking face to face the majority of the time.)

Nonetheless, the cross-time-zone problem was also raised by over 20% of the respondents.

- "When our team first started, we were given a date for project deadlines, such as 'end of day Thursday.' With team members from the U.S., Europe, Asia, North and South America, this didn't work. For the guys in Thailand and Australia, I was late even if I finished on time, since for them it was already Friday morning."
- "I needed to contact the team members in China at 10:30 at night from home so I could get them at work. I work almost 12-hour days without this, and it was awful, but it was either this or lose a whole day to communicate with them."
- "LOL means Laugh Out Loud in the U.S., but one of our international counterparts thought it meant Lots of Love. Similarly, the phrase 'I doubt that' means you challenge the other person's viewpoint if said by an American, but in other places it is used to mean 'I don't understand.' You can imagine the memorable mistakes made until we all learned what each other meant by these things."

Distance doesn't have to make a project suffer. At least in one study, distance itself did not impair virtual collaboration. It does, however, increase the chances of miscommunication, delays, and collaboration challenges, often driven by a lack of shared understanding. This can come in the form of disagreement about which tools to use, which standards to use, or even how to track progress (for instance, do all people have a common understanding of the phrase "phase completion"?). These types of obstacles can leave the teams that face them significantly the worse for wear.[8]

One Solution to All Three Problems: Plan ahead. Provide more structure than you think you'll need, both on the tasks and with the relationships.

If the numerous and varied challenges presented by virtual teams were to be forced into a one-word summary, that word would be "misaligned." This misalignment can be the result of uncertainty about what to do, how to do it, when to do it, and/or whether and how to trust the other team members. In short, virtual team members need extra hand-holding, additional specific instructions, more frequent regular check-ins, and more opportunities to express their uncertainties than do other teams. In fact, a research study of over 400 virtual teams showed that those with more of a process orientation and with more of a tightly controlled leadership style outperformed those teams oriented towards results.[9] In other words, spend more time on the means than the ends—virtual teams need this extra structure. On the relationship side, many of our survey respondents spoke to the value of having regular check-ins scheduled, even if it seemed that there was nothing to say. Of course there will be much more detail on this theme throughout the book, but here are a few quick examples of experiences reported by the survey respondents that helped realign the team on various dimensions:

- "I organized a presentation with everyone's picture, brief summaries of their backgrounds, and fun facts about their interests, as well as comments (based on interviews with each) about what they saw as their role on the team. This boosted morale and improved both efforts and results."
- "When an 11-hour time difference caused us to have to stay late into the evening for conference calls, we made sure the agenda was set 36 hours in advance and inquiries were sent back and forth 24 hours ahead of time, making sure the call itself was streamlined and effective without the need for unnecessary, time-consuming questioning that can derail a meeting."
- "Having a weekly conference call where we all say 'everything is fine' seems like a waste of time while it is happening, but when people are used to hearing each other's voices, they are much more helpful when someone actually has a problem that the group can help with."
- "We set aside the first 15 minutes or so of each videoconference call to BS about life and gossip, share pictures of our families, etc. It seems silly to have to plan it, but it just doesn't happen otherwise."
- "Having a manager who specifically and publicly thanked those team members who had made themselves available for meetings at inconvenient times made a huge difference in the attitudes of those who might have been annoyed otherwise."

MORE ON THE MISALIGNMENT PROBLEM

It's not just virtual teams that have trouble aligning themselves and their work. In truth, any two (or more) human beings who are trying to collaborate will struggle with getting, and remaining, on the same page as each other in order to produce the best joint effort and outcomes they possibly can. Sometimes ideas clash, sometimes personalities clash, and sometimes schedules clash. Sometimes it may be as simple or as complicated as finding the day (or time of day) that both people feel energized and motivated to think about that particular task. Think of the outcome of a team's work together as explained by the following formula:

Team Output = Team Potential + Synergy – Process Losses

Each of these elements has complexities—but first, the definitions. *Output* is what the team produces, and *potential* is what they should be capable of. The team's potential can be thought of as the ideal case whereby all of the group's individual talents and abilities add together in a straightforward way. Think, for example, of a team of five members engaging in a game of tug of war (whereby all members pull on a rope as strongly as they can to try and overcome a team of five pulling the rope in the other direction). The team's potential should be the maximum force that person 1 can pull, plus the maximum force that person 2 can pull, etc., through person 5.

Synergy is defined as an interaction of elements that when combined produce a total effect that is greater than the sum of the individual elements, contributions, etc. This implies that the team might actually be able to perform *better* than expected by the simple additive formula used to explain the team's potential. Isn't it conceivable that in the spirit of the moment, pulling alongside one's teammates and hearing the cheers of the crowd, some people may be able to actually pull *harder* on the tug of war rope than they could when working alone? If this is difficult to imagine, think instead of a creative team whose members generate more new ideas when they brainstorm together than when alone, as each person's thoughts inspire the others to think of things that might not have occurred to them otherwise. In fact, the whole idea of synergies is most of the reason we use teams at all. We expect them to raise the level of performance of the individuals over and above what they could do alone.

Last and most problematic are the *process losses*, whereby teams get waylaid by complications in their interactions and end up falling short of their potential. Three common potential process losses include:

- **Coordination Losses.** Returning to the tug of war example, the idea that all five members will pull as hard as they can the moment the start whistle blows is not entirely realistic. People have an extremely hard time exerting their best efforts at precisely the same moment. Fortunately, in real organizational teams, it is rarely required for teams to have such precise and simultaneous effort. Unfortunately, other types of coordination problems can interfere with smooth functioning. As in the earlier example, time and effort get wasted when people don't know exactly what to do or when to expect inputs from others. Though this can be a problem for all teams, it is one that often rises to the top of the list of concerns for virtual teams. Luckily, some types of virtual interaction can bypass one of the common problems in face-to-face meetings, known as "conceptual blocking." This problem occurs in real-time interactions when people face the challenging task of both thinking and listening at the same time. Meetings are not paused while members catch up with their thoughts and plan what they want to say next. Instead, someone always has the floor for speaking and this can limit the ability of the rest of the group to think properly. Asynchronous communication, such as through e-mail exchanges, can avoid this coordination loss problem (though it would still exist in conference calls and other real-time meetings).

- **The Free Rider Problem.** Simply put, many people dislike team-work, and typically their single biggest complaint is the problem of being stuck with more than one's share of the work without recognition of these efforts (since the team may share the credit equally). Apprehension over this issue can cause people to wage a pre-emptive strike and stop giving their best efforts. Others may simply lessen their efforts, consciously or not, by resting comfortably on the thought that the rest of the team members are working very hard so it won't make a difference whether they push themselves or not (and so they don't). This is a problem that might be even more pronounced in a virtual setting, as the eyes of one's teammates and leaders are far from the work being done. Many survey participants reported that without a personal check-in on the work, accountability dropped and things just didn't get done at the pace they would have in a more traditional setting. As one person put it, "It's definitely a lot easier for people to push their own work off onto other people virtually."

- **Evaluation Apprehension.** Some people don't speak up in teams because they are afraid of having their ideas shot down. When asked, most people deny that this could happen to them, but studies have shown that psychologically, people generally feel more comfortable going with, rather than against, the ideas already in discussion (more on this later in the book). Fortunately, here we see one more advantage for the virtual teams—most people seem to be more willing to speak up, and potentially stick their necks out on new ideas, in an online setting than they are in a face-to-face one. As one person in our survey reported, "I wouldn't just walk into my CEO's office to discuss something with her, but I feel very comfortable exchanging e-mails with her."

The challenge for the virtual team, of course, is to try and maximize the synergies and minimize the losses. Understanding the effects of moving conversations and interactions away from face-to-face meetings and into the virtual realm is the first step, and then building frameworks and patterns that guide virtual teams is the next. These are the goals of the rest of the book.

NOTES

1. Cascio, W. F. (2000). Managing a virtual workplace. *Academy of Management Executive, 14(3),* 81–90.

2. Grenny, J. (2010). Virtual teams. *Leadership Excellence, 27(5),* 20.

3. Kirzinger, A. E., Weber, C., & Johnson, M. (2012). Genetic and environmental influences on media use and communication behaviors. *Human Communication Research, 38(2),* 144–171.

4. Leonard, B. (2011). Managing virtual teams. *Society for Human Resource Management HR Magazine,* June, 39–42.

5. Majchrzak, A., Malhotra, A., Stamps, J., & Lipnack, J. (2004). Can absence make a team grow stronger? *Harvard Business Review,* May, 1–9.

6. Chudoba, K. M., Wynn, E., Lu, M., & Watson-Manheim, M. B. (2005). How virtual are we? Measuring virtuality and understanding its impact in a global organization. *Journal of Information Systems, 15,* 279–306.

7. Gibson, C. B., Gibbs, J. L., Stanko, T. L., Tesluk, P., & Cohen, S. G. (2011). Including the "I" in virtuality and modern job design: Extending the job characteristics model to include the moderating effect of individual experiences of electronic dependence and copresence. *Organization Science, 6 (11–12),* 1481–1499.

8. Chudoba, K. M., Wynn, E., Lu, M., & Watson-Manheim, M. B. (2005). How virtual are we? Measuring virtuality and understanding its impact in a global organization. *Journal of Information Systems, 15,* 279–306.

9. Workman, M. (2007). The effects from technology-mediated interaction and openness in virtual team performance measures. *Behaviour & Information Technology, 26(5),* 355–365.

PART I
VIRTUAL COMMUNICATION

ONE
Understanding the Problem

It is worth noting at the outset that e-mail in particular is the focus of this (and other) sections of the book, though of course e-mail itself is far from the only choice in computer-mediated forms of communication currently in use. "E-mail" is in part used as shorthand, because in many cases, all computer-mediated text-based communication tools act alike. E-mail itself has also been the most widely studied tool to date. Therefore, the research that has been done on how communicating virtually can change both the content and the context of the message applies most directly to e-mail. And finally, most business professionals do rely on e-mail as a primary mode of virtual communication. It is certainly possible that this will change as technology evolves, but current business practices ensure that nearly every working person is no stranger to e-mail, for better and worse.

PROS AND CONS

Primarily, the advantages of using e-mail fall under three headings.

1. *Providing written records.* E-mail use allows for the creation of transcripts of all information exchanged, which is useful as a reference for what was previously discussed or decided. In spoken language, by contrast, information can sometimes be remembered differently by the various parties at best, and forgotten (conveniently or honestly) at worst. Furthermore, written text allows for the transmission of lots of information very quickly, without overwhelming the other side with a real-time need to keep up with all the details.

2. *Working at your convenience.* The convenience aspect is hard to overstate. It explains why e-mail (and other electronic text-based chat tools) has become so entrenched in our daily communications, and shows few signs of disappearing. Indeed, written text can actually be more efficient than spoken conversation. For example, one estimate reports that people can read about six times faster than they can listen.[1] Therefore, people should be able to attend to more information more quickly in this way. Moreover, electronic text has the option of being used as a "hot" (conversing in real time) or a "cold" (sending messages and replying later) communication process.[2]

3. *Ability to formulate careful replies.* Reading and then responding allows more thought to be put into replies, as opposed to real-time conversations. This is especially useful if the information received is contentious or difficult to understand in any way (whether due to a language barrier or just based on the content itself).

Put another way, the benefits of e-mailing are essentially that it allows you to read messages and think about them, respond in your own time, and refer back to the information later. However, these advantages are balanced by, or can even be outweighed by, several critical disadvantages. And to truly learn how to use e-mail most effectively, it is important to first uncover the tendencies (both large and small) that can prevent text-based communication from succeeding. Some disadvantages are more readily apparent than others. For example, people often pay less attention to e-mail messages than they should (see Chapter 3 for more about this topic), and thus may miss important details in the process. This problem is compounded by the sheer volume of e-mails that most professionals have to deal with each and every day—a problem that seems to be getting worse instead of better. Messages with action items in them become buried in an ever-expanding inbox, and each message gets less and less attention as the stack grows.

Quotes from the front lines: *"While I don't see a lot of emotion expressed in the e-mails I get at work, I certainly have a lot of emotion about my work e-mail. I have to psych myself up every morning just to get in there and tackle the enormous in-box that's always there. Everyone I've spoken to about this feels the same. It's just a huge drain on everyone's energy."*

Quotes from the front lines: *"Everyone's heard the urban myth of the companies that have 'no e-mail Fridays' and how much everyone likes the chance to unplug and get some work done. But even if we had that, it wouldn't help—the inbox would just be that much bigger the next day.*

There really isn't a question anymore of checking in from home or vacation—it is necessary just to stay on top of the deluge."

Text-based conversations also greatly increase the chances of misunderstandings. Though most people feel confident about their ability to fully understand the messages they receive, research has shown that they overestimate this ability in the majority of cases.[3] Furthermore, although people *can* read and absorb messages efficiently, it doesn't always happen in reality. Instead, people quite often skim instead of read and miss important parts of the content. And the absence of tone of voice in and of itself can lead to mistakes in understanding both information and intent, and can lead to more conflict and hurt feelings as a result. Overall, the process of coming to decisions via text-based communication can often be a frustrating one.

Quotes from the front lines: *"It drives me absolutely crazy when we end up having a long back-and-forth process for something that could have been discussed and decided in mere minutes out loud. If I want to send you an e-mail, I have to take the time to compose my thoughts and spell-check them, then send it out and wait for a response because maybe you don't read your e-mail right away. Then you finally read it and send me back an e-mail with a question. Then I have to read your e-mail and think, 'Oh, he doesn't get it,' and then have to write up another e-mail to clarify it. It has added so much complexity to our work."*

Lastly, as mentioned in the introduction, getting to know others is indisputably more difficult over e-mail than in a face-to-face meeting. In person, people tend to rely on non-verbal cues to make quick judgments about traits such as personality and abilities. Research has shown that these "zero acquaintance" (meaning the very first moments of meeting) snap judgments are fairly accurate.[4] People so deeply rely on these visual first impressions as an opportunity to "size someone up" that they may feel psychologically unsettled without that information. If they must engage in a blind relationship (for work or otherwise) without this ability to judge someone in person, they will often still try to form a first impression based solely on the text of the other person's first few e-mail messages. This type of impression is built on much weaker data, since unfortunately, the ability to judge either personalities or skills falls considerably when text is the only medium available. Instead, there is a much higher reliance on stereotypes or previously set expectancies about people met in this way.[5]

SENDING X BUT RECEIVING Y

Communication problems are often subtle and may cause complications even without people being consciously aware of them. For example, people think they are generally better than they really are at understanding the messages that they *receive*. This is also mirrored by the fact that people think they write more clearly than they actually do in the messages they *send*. Both are examples of a more general bias called the "curse of knowledge." This refers to the difficulty you face when you know something very well, since it is hard to truly remember that other people do not know the same thing. A vivid experiment demonstrates this effect. In it, one person is asked to tap out the "tune" of a well-known song to a listener, and try to get the listener to correctly identify the song. Tappers in this study estimated that about 50% of the listeners should be able to guess the song correctly, but in reality only about 2.5% were able to do so (yes, that's two-and-a-half percent, and not 25%!—as in, nearly nobody). Why? While the tune was playing alongside the taps in the mind of the tapper, the listener only heard a succession of tuneless noises and silences that don't necessarily help to identify the rest of the song.[6] This is the same reason why website designers may fail to understand how difficult it is for a layperson to find the needed clicks and the links embedded on a webpage, since they themselves know so well where to look to find them.

The curse of knowledge also applies to how well we communicate with others, especially in a more ambiguous form such as e-mail. One series of studies set out to demonstrate that people systematically overestimate the level at which their readers would understand the tone of their e-mail messages. In the first of these studies, participants were asked to write five sentences that were serious in tone, and five that were sarcastic (without labeling them in any way). Sentence-writers were then asked to guess: What percent of people will correctly identify which sentences were which? On average, writers expected the readers to be able to correctly distinguish the serious from the sarcastic in 97% of the cases. After all, when they thought about the sentences in their own heads, the tone was so crystal clear that it became very difficult to imagine anyone reading the same sentence with a different slant. In reality, most participants *did* in fact label the sentences correctly, but not 97% as predicted—only 84% were correct. Recall that these were sentences that the senders had *specifically designed* to be either serious or sarcastic, and yet still 16% of the readers missed the intended tone.

In a follow-up study of more typical sentences (selected from a list provided by the experimenters in this case), the success rate in correctly identifying serious versus sarcastic tone fell to 50%, which is no better than chance! The researchers compared this number with people listening to the same sentences out loud, and there was quite a difference: out loud, people were able to correctly identify the tone nearly 75% of the time. To make sure that the sentences themselves were not just needlessly ambiguous, a different group of people were told which sentences were sarcastic and which were serious, and were then asked to estimate how many readers would correctly identify the tone of these phrases. They guessed that nearly 90% of the sentences would be obvious to the other side, when as we saw above, the right answer was closer to 50–50 (for written text). And it's not just sarcasm or serious tones that are problematic. Similar results were found for other emotions as well, including sadness and anger.

The next follow-up question in this study related to how well the sender and receiver already knew each other. To rule out this potentially confounding variable, the authors next compared sender-receiver pairs who were friends with sender-receiver pairs who were strangers. A reasonable explanation for the findings could have been that people may be weaker than expected at picking up on the sarcastic (or other) tones from a stranger, but once someone is well known, the intended meaning of the sentence should come through more clearly. But, the findings remained the same even for the sender-receiver pairs who were friends prior to the exercise. In other words, friend pairs were *just as inaccurate* as stranger pairs at this task. This provides very strong evidence that even when people are communicating with others whom they already know and who presumably know something about their conversational style, there is a sizable gap between the assumption made about how much the reader will understand about tone and how much is actually accurately decoded.[7] Thus, even with those you know very well, your ability to correctly identify the exact meaning they had intended is probably worse than you think.

> **TIP**
> Written text is more ambiguous than you think, not only with strangers but even with those whom you know. Don't assume the reader will catch your meaning, or your tone, unless you take special care to make your messages clear.

In the next section, we discuss another one of the hidden costs associated with e-mail use: an unintentionally negative attitude.

NEGATIVITY AND DECEPTION: THE CHEATING, LYING, AND INSULTING PROBLEMS

For whatever reason, people just aren't their nicest selves online. For example, negotiators using e-mail or instant messaging instead of face-to-face or phone conversations have been shown to use more threats and demanding behavior (and offer fewer concessions), resulting in fewer deals being achieved and a lower sense of credibility overall.[8] Perhaps this is due to the lack of the instant feedback from another person's facial expressions that you would get if you were speaking face to face. Perhaps it is the fact that the person on the other side of a computer message feels less human than does someone standing in your presence. Perhaps it is the (often false) sense of anonymity people have when typing as opposed to speaking out loud. Perhaps it is all of these things and others, but regardless of why, the fact remains that interacting online can often bring out the worst in people. More specifically, people seem to give themselves permission to cheat, lie, and insult others more readily in the online environment than they do in any other realm, whether it be in face-to-face interactions or even written text on actual pieces of paper.

To help explain this, psychologists have identified a state of mind they have termed disinhibition. Disinhibition is defined as a lack of restraint. In other words, it refers to the moments when people give themselves permission to act in ways that are impulsive without regard for rules or risks. More specifically, disinhibition prompts people to:

- Act on their desires without fear of the consequences;
- Pay great attention to their own internal states and very little attention to the interests and experiences of others;
- Use others as a means to an end; and
- Engage in action, as opposed to spending time thinking.

Disinhibition is a classic hallmark of people in power. Even regular people, when put into a position of power over others in the room, can start displaying these tendencies.[9] Research has identified the reason for these feelings, and it relates to an inflated sense of control over outcomes. For example, people primed to think about a time they were in power felt that they were in more control of random events (such as the roll of a die), were more likely to assume that they could make events turn out the way they wanted them to (such as the performance of a new marketing strategy), felt higher self-esteem on the whole, and even felt more control over national issues such as the economy.[10] This potentially overblown sense of control seems to allow people to release themselves from dedicated concern for others. Unfortunately, disinhibition is also displayed by people engaging in electronic communication. As an aside, disinhibition also helps to explain many of the morally dubious behaviors we see displayed both by people in positions of power and by those communicating electronically.

In the online environment specifically, disinhibition is thought to be due to a combination of factors, beginning with the overblown sense of anonymity most feel when typing messages. In other words, if your message does not feel tied directly to you personally and thus does not necessarily represent you, it may be that much easier to take liberties with the standards of polite conversation. A sense of anonymity may also arise based on the fact that much of the time, people are physically alone when working on a computer. This feeling can also exaggerate the sense of the self as opposed to focusing on the other person(s) at all, let alone their needs and feelings. Being alone and typing can also minimize any sense of an authority figure in the situation. The lack of immediate visual feedback from one's counterpart is a contributing factor, especially since being able to see someone's facial expressions and reactions when you speak to him or her can actually change the signals your brain sends to you about the entire situation.[11] Taken together, these factors can promote disinhibition via anonymity, which in turn can help to explain some of the less-than-stellar behaviors observed in online conversations. Below, each of the problems of cheating, lying, and insulting that are unfortunately all too common in this realm are explored.

Cheating

Most people don't cheat for sport; they cheat because they believe it will get them something that they could not have (easily) attained otherwise. One version of cheating has to do with being on a team but skimping on your efforts toward the *team's* credit in favor of your efforts for your *own* credit. The tension between your goals and the team's goals makes this a mixed-motive situation, and becomes especially challenging when there are too many competing demands for your time and attention. Do you work hard in ways that benefit the group as a whole but potentially fail to highlight your own personal contributions, or do you make sure that your own work is what you spend your time on, even if that comes at the expense of the team? Ideally, team dynamics and rewards are structured in such a way as to avoid this choice, but in reality, it arises anyway. Research has investigated this type of setting and has found that team members engaged in face-to-face meetings err on the side of decisions that both help and protect the whole group. On the other hand, team members communicating through online discussions lean towards more individual-istic decisions. Trust is lower in the online setting (see Chapter 6 for more about this), and people seem to feel a stronger pull to protect their own interests in the face of a more anonymous team interaction.

To explore this further, researchers often examine groups in a setting called a *social dilemma*. This kind of task is one in which people have com-peting incentives to minimize their own efforts but simultaneously maxi-mize the value of the group product. For example, people who watch public television have these types of competing interests. A certain number of peo-ple need to donate money so that all people can continue to watch and enjoy the programming. One individual can decide to be a "free rider" and assume that others will carry the burden of financial contribution to bene-fit all, or that same individual can decide to donate a small amount, hope others will do the same, and thus help provide the benefit to both the con-tributors and the non-contributors alike. Each individual has an economic incentive to contribute as little as possible, but collectively they must reach a set amount of donated funds or else the shows will be lost for everybody.

In one particular research study,[12] participants were asked to role-play as the owners of various shark-fishing businesses, who are facing an ever-depleting population of shark in the waters. If all owners continued to fish at their current rates, the shark population would soon be non-existent and all the businesses would fold. If, on the other hand, they all cut their current rates significantly, the shark population could remain at a sustain-able level. So, each player needs to weigh the current value of their profits against the future losses if the shark population disappears. All "business owners" in this study met and made tentative decisions about their har-vesting plans, but the actual fishing decisions were not made until later, in a private setting. During their discussion time, most groups came to a consensus on the amount each would refrain from harvesting so as to ensure the safety of the shark population for the future; however, the pri-vate nature of the actual decision moment gave each player the opportu-nity to "cheat" and fish more than the agreed-upon amount without the input of their group-mates.

To assess the differences between face-to-face groups and those inter-acting virtually, half of the teams in this study had their meeting in person, and the other half had them via computer-based text chat. In the end, the half that met online were significantly *more* likely to cheat—that is, to take for themselves as opposed to cooperate with the rest of the group—than were those who met in person. A second setup in this study demonstrated the same effect but in a different setting: when offered the chance to donate money to a common pot that would pay out only if most members also donated their money, nearly 86% of the groups who interacted online were uncooperative (that is, kept the initial money for themselves instead of risking it by giving it to the group pot), whereas only 25% of the groups who interacted face to face decided to act in this more self-serving manner. It seems that people just don't trust others whom they cannot see the same way as those they meet face to face, and their willingness to cooperate with them plummets accordingly.

Lying

People have also shown themselves likely to lie more readily when interacting online. This can range from the more mundane examples of stretching the truth on a dating website to the more extreme ones such as falsifying factual information for personal gain. One study explored whether people would misreport information if it meant they stood to gain additional resources from the lie[13] (which, indeed parallels most cases of professional fibbing—like cheating, not many lie without a clear sense of individual gain to be had from the act). First, the conclusion: people in the online condition of this study, as opposed to those writing information down on paper, were indeed much more likely to lie to pad their own bottom line. Now, the details: Participants in this experiment were told that they were selected as the decision maker for a pair of people (the focal participant and an unnamed partner). The decision makers were told that a certain amount of money was available to each pair, and that they alone knew how much was in the total pot. They were then told that they needed to decide how much money went to themselves and to their partners, and that their partners would have to accept whatever decision was made without any input whatsoever, and without ever knowing the true pot size. This afforded an opportunity to seem fair while actually taking a greater share of the money for oneself without repercussion. For example, let's say you told your partner that you were given a budget of $5000 for a particular set of projects and thus you were splitting the funds 50–50 and giving $2500 for your partner's use and keeping the other $2500 for yourself. This would seem perfectly reasonable, unless anyone should discover that the actual budget you were allotted was $7500, meaning that you yourself netted $5000 out of this seemingly "fair" split of the pie, and lied to your partner to maintain an illusion of equality.

In the research study, participants reporting their decisions online lied in over 90% of the cases. Those filling out a paper form lied more like 60% of the time—still a big number but not as shocking as the nearly ubiquitous 90+% in the online group! People continued to lie online, and in greater proportions, even in situations where they learned that their partners *would definitely* be informed of the falsehood after the fact—the temptation to lie was apparently that strong. This provides more evidence for the fact that online interactions seem to allow people to take for themselves and become less concerned with the needs of others, including their teammates.

Quotes from the front lines: *"You know the old saying 'Don't believe everything that you read'? I've taken that to heart over the years. I don't believe anything I haven't heard out loud. Of course this is an exaggeration, but I have found that when something seems off in an e-mail, a phone call often unearths an entirely different slant on the conversation."*

Insulting Others

Compared with cheating and lying, insulting one another online seems to be a lesser offense, but it is still a problematic tendency. From the earliest observations of e-mail, researchers have found that people are more willing to express anger, to name-call, and even to bully other people when communicating in this way.[14] For example, in one anecdote reported in a newspaper article, a teenager noted that awkward moments came up regularly in his peer group when one person wrote something to another via text that would never have been said out loud, and then the air failed to be cleared afterwards, since when face to face, nobody was willing to comment on the inflammatory remarks.[15] Similarly, a research study paired total strangers together and initiated an e-mail conversation. The investigators were stunned to see as many as 20% of the conversations take an almost instant turn for the worse, containing both rude and lewd content.[16] Interestingly enough, people also seem more willing to label *themselves* in negative ways when they are communicating through electronic text instead of through other mechanisms.[17] Disinhibition once again arises as a common theme in the behaviors observed in online communication. Though not always consciously or intentionally, people do seem to give themselves permission to act in more self-serving and less sensitive ways when interacting online.

Since electronic interactions are not likely to go away, the right path forward is to learn how to manage them in our lives. The rest of this book is devoted to analyzing and strategizing ways to overcome these negative tendencies in electronic communication, so that virtual teams and co-located employees (using text to connect) alike can better manage both their relationships and their tasks. One simple solution seems warranted right up front, and that is to intersperse other forms of interaction with the use of electronic text. Some assume that this requires regular face-to-face contact (a practice that many virtual teams embrace, beginning with a kick-off meeting). However, regular in-person check-ins can be inefficient in terms of each time, money, and the flow of work, and are not the only viable solution to the challenges that e-mail presents. There is also always the promise of newer and better technologies to connect people from afar without the stripped-down nature of text-only interaction. Better technologies may help make sure that the communication partners are reminded of the actual person on the other end of the conversation (perhaps through improved videoconferencing? communication via avatars?—more on these ideas later in the book). In the meantime, the simple idea that no single channel should be used exclusively can be helpful. Mixing up e-mail exchanges even with just the occasional one-on-one phone call can change perceptions and connections for the better.

TIP

Recognize the greater temptation to lie, cheat, and insult others in online exchanges for yourself and for others. Reconnect using tools with greater "bandwidth" occasionally to re-inspire cooperation.

Before proceeding to other topics, the issue of emotional expression in text-based communications warrants some attention, because the problem of negativity can arise here as well.

EMOTIONS ONLINE

Most work e-mails are dull. In fact, lack of emotion might even be considered a bigger problem than too much emotion in most people's experiences of e-mail! However, emotions are important. They give us information about whether a situation is beneficial or problematic, and give us clues as to how to respond to others. For example, your reply to an angry manager would probably not be identical to your reply to a delighted one. If e-mail inhibits people from obtaining an accurate read on the emotions of others, this is yet another obstacle that must be understood and overcome to use this tool successfully. Similarly, if positive emotion is difficult to express and understand over e-mail, it can limit the ease with which we can form effective relationships to others with whom we communicate primarily online.[18] Unfortunately, both of these concerns about e-mail (harder to read others' state of mind and harder to connect with them) are well founded.

Quotes from the front lines: *"So many of the times that I've interpreted an e-mail as angry, I've been wrong. Therefore, I really try not to guess how the sender is feeling, even for messages sent with red exclamation points or in all capital letters. It is a difficult thing to do, though, since it is a human response that you cannot escape. At times, there is nothing left to do but make a phone call and make sure everyone is on the same page."*

However subtle, emotion *is* present in many online exchanges, and recognizing how it works and how it tends to be understood can be advantageous. Sometimes, text even allows for greater emotional expression than would be found in a face-to-face setting.

Quotes from the front lines: *"Emotions can come out more strongly in electronic chats than in person. In our company, in the middle of virtual meetings, it is typical for colleagues to start Instant Message conversations right alongside the meeting itself. One time, our boss's boss was presenting something about our new strategic direction, and a colleague pinged me and said 'That is SO not what he said last week!' Those kinds of side-channel comments are like whispering in a face-to-face meeting, except things can be said with much more force than would be possible in the room itself."*

It was noted above that people can tend towards being more negative in what they write online. Additionally, people also seem to *interpret* messages more negatively than they were intended—positive messages can be interpreted as neutral (called the *neutrality bias*), and neutral ones can be interpreted as actually negative (called—you guessed it—the *negativity bias*).[19] Negative messages also seem to fall prey to the negativity bias, in that they tend to be interpreted as even more negative than they were originally intended.[20] Furthermore, the presence of even slight hints of negativity seems to override other elements of the message, leading to a general sense of negativity about the whole message.[21] In short, the language used in e-mail messages seems to be something of a minefield, whereby any hint of negativity can explode in the receiver's mind and cause the entire tone of the message to change in dramatic ways. Perhaps in part for this reason, even jokes are rated as less funny when they are presented over e-mail.[22] Negative language may also be read as a sign of dominance in the sender.[23] Finally, the less well the receiver knows the sender ahead of time, the more exaggerated this negativity effect can be.

Quotes from the front lines: *"Once I got a phone call from a colleague that I didn't know very well, named Gary, asking me to please contact a mutual colleague of ours, Alex, on his behalf. Apparently, Gary had received an e-mail from Alex, and was sure that he had somehow mis-stepped and had angered him based on the tone of the message he received. I did contact Alex, who of course had no idea what I was talking about since he wasn't one bit upset with Gary."*

TIP

Remember that emotion is often interpreted more negatively than intended: positive messages are read as neutral, neutral ones as negative, and slightly negative ones as very negative. Re-read your own text before sending with this in mind.

How is emotion actually expressed online? People have always been attuned to emotional cues sent by the body language of others, and in the absence of posture, facial expressions, and tone of voice, the language itself must step in to give the impression of emotional tone. There are generally two channels through which emotion can be communicated through text. It can either be stated in the words themselves or it can be implied through the use of non-word symbols or signals. Using the words themselves to express emotion can be accomplished by using emotion-laden words directly (for example, "I am so delighted with the way this project is progressing") or through the presence or absence of greetings. The degree of formality of the language used can also signal emotion to some degree. Non-word symbols might include the use of exclamation points for emphasis, the use of emoticons ("faces" created with various punctuation marks, such as :-) for a smile or :-P for a tongue sticking out), or the use of capital letters. Signals might include particularly short or long messages, or messages that come back either quickly or after a lengthy delay. As an aside, it is interesting to note that there seems to be a generational effect at work here as well: older people seem to both use and perceive less emotion in e-mail messages than do younger people.[24]

One study explored the expression of emotion in electronic text by coding actual e-mail messages sent and received in a professional setting. What was found was that each positive and negative emotion appears differently in this environment. While positive emotion was generally expressed through the use of exclamation points (indicating friendly inter-action), the use of positive words, and the use of greetings and closures, negative emotion was expressed through negations ("I don't think . . .") and by generally being more succinct in what was said.[25]

This implies that it is easy to read negative emotion into what *isn't* said—the lack of a greeting or closing, or the timing of a reply. Messages that don't get a reply promptly (or one at all), for example, often inspire the sender to assume that the receiver was displeased with the content. Yet this seems to leave an awful lot of room for misinterpretation. Are all very short messages (or those that don't get an immediate response) meant to convey negative feelings? Surely not, but if that is one of the signals used by those in a negative mood to convey displeasure, it could make it tough to know when to assume that a short (or a late) reply is meant to be effi-cient (or is delayed for irrelevant reasons), and when it's meant to signal anger. People also seem to gravitate toward e-mail to deliver bad news,[26] since it affords them a degree of separation from the person receiving the news (see Chapter 8 for more on this topic).

Quotes from the front lines: *"When I was first introduced to e-mail, I used all capital letters because I didn't realize that it meant yelling. People receiving my e-mails probably thought I was angry at them, but really it was just my ignorance of e-mail etiquette. After somebody finally told me what it meant, I stopped doing that. I am also now wary of using features such as bold, underlining, etc., as there may be unintended nuances to the emotions that those express."*

Additionally, in the online setting, people can spontaneously interpret all kinds of seemingly neutral content-based statements as indicative of a positive or a negative mood. In a negotiation context, for example, flex-ibility in response to the proposals on the table (for example, "We could do it this way, or we can work with a different format as well") came with the assumption that the sender was in a positive mood, whereas resolute-ness ("Unfortunately, that's not something that we'll be able to accept") implied that the sender was in a negative mood.[27] Complicating this matter is the fact that different people can read the same messages and come away with very different interpretations of the intended emotional tone. In one study, some people interpreted long messages as positive in tone, while others read negative emotion into them instead![28] Even emoticons are not free from misinterpretation.[29]

Quotes from the front lines: *"I've noticed that the way I interpret e-mails is often based on my prior interactions with people. If I have had a negative experience with someone and then receive an e-mail from that individual, I might perceive that to be a negative e-mail that is attacking or condescending. If I had a positive experience with someone, my perception would probably be the opposite."*

How should you deal with this problem? One company took the issue to its extreme, and put a mandatory signature line at the bottom of all of its e-mails stating: "This e-mail may display a telegraphic style that gives the false impression of curtness or insensitivity."[30] While this might help to alleviate the problem, it is probably more heavy-handed than most companies would prefer. Instead, encouraging openness norms that permit a receiver to question the state of mind of a sender when necessary may help. One suggestion is to provide examples of text that should be permissible, such as, "It seems that X (the issue at hand) is very important to you," "This seems to have upset you," or "Has this not met your expectations thus far?" and then follow up with questions such as, "Is that an accurate interpretation of the situation?" and "How can we proceed more effectively?" Chapter 2 will provide a more detailed look at policies that can help guide effective e-mail use.

TIP

Encourage follow-up questions to seek clarity on messages with an ambiguous tone.

People tend to match features of the messages that they receive in their replies (more on this as well in Chapter 2). For instance, very short messages are usually followed by similarly short ones, etc. The emotional tone of the messages is no exception. Positive messages tend to be as "catching" as negative tones. Even more interesting is the fact that matching the emotional tone of the sender's message is not just a linguistic reflex, but it can actually cause you to *feel* these emotions personally. In other words, if you receive a note with a snippy tone, and you respond with more curtness because of it, odds are that you will walk away from the interchange feeling more negative than you did before it began. Similarly, good moods can also be spread through mirroring the tone of messages that you have received. Experiments using four-person virtual teams have demonstrated that even one individual on a team can increase the negative or positive emotion felt by all four team members.[31] For this reason, it can be important to take a step back from negative exchanges and regain your perspective before engaging in a downward spiral.

SUMMARY

Writing to others via electronic text seems to inspire an unconscious state of disinhibition in many people. This generally translates to a more self-centered view without adequate concern for other people or for broadly held moral guidelines. Make sure you remember that everything you send represents you to the world. And although emotion is not a feature of every text-based message, people still infer emotion and react accordingly to all kinds of signals, whether they be words themselves or other features, such as length or response time. Leave as little room for misinterpretation as possible, both in terms of the content and the emotional tone of the messages that you send.

NOTES

1. Williams, C. (2010). *MGMT2*. Mason, OH: South-Western Cengage.

2. Sivunen, A. & Valo, M. (2006). Team leaders' technology choice in virtual teams. *IEEE Transactions on Professional Communication, 49(1),* 57–68.

3. Kruger, J., Epley, N., Parker, J., & Ng, Z-W. (2005). Egocentrism over e-mail: Can we communicate as well as we think? *Journal of Personality and Social Psychology, 89(6),* 925–936.

4. Ambady, N., Hallahan, M., & Rosenthal, R. (1995). On judging and being judged accurately in zero acquaintance situations. *Journal of Personality and Social Psychology, 69,* 518–529.

5. Epley, N. & Kruger, J. (2005). When what you type isn't what they read: The perseverance of stereotypes and expectancies over e-mail. *Journal of Experimental Social Psychology, 41,* 414–422.

6. Ross, L. & Ward, A. (1996). Naïve realism in everyday life: Implications for social conflict and misunderstanding. In E. Reed, E. Turiel, & T. Brown (Eds.), *Social cognition: The Ontario Symposium* (pp. 305–321). Hillsdale, NJ: Erlbaum.

7. Kruger, J., Epley, N., Parker, J., & Ng, Z-W. (2005). Egocentrism over e-mail: Can we communicate as well as we think? *Journal of Personality and Social Psychology, 89(6),* 925–936.

8. For a review, see Friedman, R. & Belkin, L. (2013). The costs and benefits of e-negotiations. In M. Olekans & W. Adair (Eds.), *Handbook of*

research in negotiation (pp. 357–384). Cheltenham, UK: Edward Edgar Publishing.

9. Gruenfeld, D. H., Keltner, D., & Anderson, C. (2003). The effects of power upon those who possess it: An interpersonal perspective on social cognition. In G. Bodenhausen & A. Lambert (Eds.), *Foundations of social cognition: A festschrift in honor of Robert S. Wyer, Jr.* (pp. 237–262). Hillsdale, NJ: Erlbaum.

10. Fast, N. J, Gruenfeld, D. H., Sivanathan, N., & Galinsky, A. D. (2009). Illusory control: A generative force behind power's far-reaching effects. *Psychological Science, 20(4)*, 502–508.

11. For a review, see Goleman, D. (2007). Flame first, think later: New clues to e-mail misbehavior, http://danielgoleman.info/2007/flame-first-think-later-new-clues-to-e-mail-misbehavior/.

12. Naquin, C. E., Kurtzberg, T. R., & Belkin, L. (2008). E-mail communication and group cooperation in mixed motive contexts. *Social Justice Research, 21,* 470–489.

13. Naquin, C. E., Kurtzberg, T. R., & Belkin, L. Y. (2010). The finer points of lying online: E-mail versus pen-and-paper. *Journal of Applied Psychology, 95,* 387–394.

14. Erdur-Baker, O. (2010). Cyberbullying and its correlation to traditional bullying, gender and frequency and risky usage of Internet-mediated communication. *New Media & Society, 12(1),* 109–125.

15. Goleman, D. (2007). Flame first, think later: New clues to e-mail misbehavior. *The International Herald Tribune,* February 20.

16. As reported in Goleman, D. (2007). Flame first, think later: New clues to e-mail misbehavior. *The International Herald Tribune,* February 20.

17. Joinson, A. (1999). Social desirability, anonymity, and Internet-based questionnaires. *Behavior Research Methods, Instruments, & Computers, 31,* 433–438.

18. Barsade, S. (2002). The ripple effect: Emotional contagion and its effect on group behavior. *Administrative Science Quarterly, 47,* 644–675.

19. Williams, C. (2010). *MGMT2.* Mason, OH: South-Western Cengage.

20. Byron, K. (2008). Carrying too heavy a load? Communication and miscommunication of emotion by email. *Academy of Management Review, 33,* 309–327.

21. Walther, J. B. & Addario, K. P. (2001). The impact of emoticons on message interpretation in computer-mediated communication. *Social Science Computer Review, 19,* 324–347.

22. Kruger, J., Epley, N., Parker, J., & Ng, Z-W. (2005). Egocentrism over e-mail: Can we communicate as well as we think? *Journal of Personality and Social Psychology, 89(6),* 925–936.

23. Belkin, L. Y., Kurtzberg, T. R., & Naquin, C. E. (2013). Signaling dominance in online negotiations: The role of affective tone. *Negotiations and Conflict Management Research, 6(4),* 285–304.

24. Higa, K., Sheng, O. R. L., Shin, B., & Figueredo, A. J. (2000). Understanding relationships among teleworkers' e-mail usage, e-mail richness perceptions, and e-mail productivity perceptions under a software engineering environment. *IEEE Transactions on Engineering Management, 47,* 163–173.

25. Belkin, L. Y. & Kurtzberg, T. (2013). The role and the impact of affective displays in e-mail communication: The evidence from the lab and the field. In N. M. Ashkanasy, W. J. Zerbe, & C. E. J. Härtel (Eds.), *Research on emotions in organizations* (Vol. 9, pp. 279–308). Amsterdam, NL: Elsevier. Also Belkin, L. Y. (2007). Emotional contagion in the electronic communication context in organizations. (Unpublished doctoral dissertation). Rutgers University, Newark, NJ.

26. Markus, M. L. (1994). Finding a happy medium: Explaining the negative effects of electronic communication on social life at work. *ACM Transactions on Information Systems, 12,* 119–149.

27. Chaskin, A., Rafaeli, A., & Bos, N. (2011). Anger and happiness in virtual teams: Emotional influences of text and behavior on others' affect in the absence of non-verbal cues. *Organizational Behavior and Human Decision Processes, 116,* 2–16.

28. Byron, K. & Baldridge, D. C. (2005). Toward a model of nonverbal cues and emotion in e-mail. *Academy of Management Proceedings, B1–B6.*

29. Walther, J. B. & Addario, K. P. (2001). The impact of emoticons on message interpretation in computer-mediated communication. *Social Science Computer Review, 19,* 324–347.

30. Martin, J. (2004). Miss Manners: Apologies beforehand signal a weak effort. *Milwaukee Journal Sentinel,* January 21, http://www.json line.com/lifestyle/advice/jan04/201304.asp, as cited in Byron, K. (2008). Carrying too heavy a load? Communication and miscommunication in of emotion by email. *Academy of Management Review, 33,* 309–327.

31. Chaskin, A., Rafaeli, A., & Bos, N. (2011). Anger and happiness in virtual teams: Emotional influences of text and behavior on others' affect in the absence of non-verbal cues. *Organizational Behavior and Human Decision Processes, 116,* 2–16.

TWO
Pace and Policy

THE QUESTION OF EFFICIENCY

It is not always clear whether communicating electronically yields a more *efficient* process overall. You may save some time by not having to schedule a meeting to accomplish something, but you may also spend more time overall having multiple choppy conversations instead of one start-to-finish event. Similarly, while it is a tremendous advantage to be able to prioritize the demands on your time by controlling the flow of work, there is the potential frustration that results from an always-full inbox. E-mail is not something that most people can ever cross off their to-do list.

Quotes from the front lines: *"If I didn't have the electronic intermediary, I would be flooded with requests for immediate attention from others without a handy way to do my own prioritizing. Yet even so, I sometimes feel like I haven't actually accomplished anything even though I've spent a full day typing away at my e-mail. With e-mail, you never really finish it. There's always more!"*

So is it more efficient or not to use text instead of spoken conversations? The answer may depend on what exactly you mean by efficiency. It can certainly be thought of as efficient to be able to say exactly what you want, when you want, without the chance of interruption or a derailed thought process. In addition, e-mail can also send a signal to the other side that one's time is not being wasted.

Quotes from the front lines: "Our clients hate to pay for face-to-face conversations within our team of lawyers, since it feels like they are getting double-billed for their time. E-mail, on the other hand, gives the necessary appearance of efficiency, whereby someone is organizing information, following up where appropriate, and not getting distracted by niceties or other conversations."

Not all signals that the use of e-mail sends are positive ones, however. Some topics are not a natural fit for e-mail, and proceeding with their use can give the appearance of "un-seriousness" in more critical conversations, such as giving feedback (see Chapters 4 and 7 for more on this topic).

E-mail's efficiency can also depend on the content of the exchange. Ironically, e-mail may be the most efficient choice for either the most complicated or the simplest types of messages, but the ones in between can be a toss-up. Simple messages (confirming the time of a meeting, for instance) that are unambiguous and take little time to respond to are rarely problematic. Calling or stopping by and interrupting someone for this same information would surely be less efficient. And in theory, e-mail can also be useful for conveying complicated information: dense data, for example, or questions with many parts to them. This type of message can be effective because the receiver benefits from time to think about what's presented or asked, can review it repeatedly if necessary, and then prepare and organize a response. In reality, this only works if both (a) the sender has taken the time to clearly organize the information or requests being sent, and (b) the receiver actually takes the time to read and think about the response, which is increasingly hard to count on as professionals get busier in general and more overwhelmed with the number of messages they receive each hour. Instead, problems arise when messages of at least some depth of content are fired off without clear enough thought about either the organization in the message itself or the effect it may have on other people—which, in all likelihood, describes a great many messages sent and received each day. As examples, consider the "just my two cents" message offered by one person that causes a flurry of opinions and defenses from everyone else copied; the "cover my rear" messages that are sent only because it is easily done but cause "noise" for everyone else; and the half-explained thoughts or "quick questions" that make no sense out of context.

Quotes from the front lines: "We had an assistant once who was clearly taught to 'close the loop' on every message she received by always replying to it, no matter what it was. Sometimes this was helpful, but often it was ridiculous. I might ask to have something mailed, and she would e-mail back just to say 'okay'. So I would feel like I should then say 'thanks' and she would reply 'no problem!' It started to feel like a competition about who could get in the last word, and it was absurd how many extra minutes in a week were spent looking at these types of messages."

Clearly articulated and well-organized content on material that is critical to moving the work forward is the hallmark of efficient e-mail messages.

TIP

It is no exaggeration to say that using e-mail is simultaneously the most efficient and the least efficient thing that many professionals do with their time. Pay attention to the question of efficiency and make sure that the messages you send have each passed the quality and necessity tests.

While further on in the book the focus will shift to the idea of how to make your messages accessible to the receiver (see Chapter 3), the next topic here is on how to manage the pace of e-mail messages for best success.

"MIRROR AND MATCH"

It goes without saying that developing rapport with the other person in a conversation is one important goal. While you certainly can accomplish professional tasks and make effective decisions with others without any sense of rapport, it is both less efficient and less pleasant to do so. Speaking seems to elicit a strong sense of "connection" between some people very rapidly, but not necessarily between all people. Although there is a long list of reasons why you might be more drawn to some people than to others, one such variable relates to the similarity of your speech patterns. The famous quote "People who like each other tend to be like each other"[1] applies as strongly in the communications domain as it does in other areas of interaction.

Sometimes people are naturally similar to each other, but many other times, people use reciprocity to "mirror and match" the behaviors of others to make themselves more similar to each other. To take a simple example, while it's just considered good manners to try and do a favor back for someone who has done a favor for you, it also creates a sense of psychological comfort for people to match others in their levels of helpfulness and generosity (or their levels of aggression, competitiveness, or unkindness). In addition to one-on-one interpersonal exchanges such as matching favors, reciprocity works on both larger and smaller levels as well. For example, people can show reciprocity with whole institutions, as they seem to work harder for organizations that they feel have made efforts to take their needs into account.[2]

In terms of communications, reciprocity can also guide the unconscious choice of certain words or behaviors. Two people in conversation generally, over a short amount of time, start to display reciprocity in their conversational patterns. The matching of word style choices, speech patterns, and slang appear regularly. People having a face-to-face conversation also tend to synchronize the nonverbal parts of their interaction over time. In other words, their head-nodding, eye-blinking, or finger-tapping types of movements tend to mirror each other as the conversation progresses. This synchrony serves a purpose by making the speakers feel more comfortable with each other, based on the idea that others who are more similar to you are naturally more trustworthy.

Whether created consciously or unconsciously, synchronized communication creates a smooth flow and allows you to take advantage of the bias people feel towards others who display similar characteristics. While in day-to-day interactions this process tends to occur both spontaneously and unconsciously, it can also be used as a tactic to make someone feel more comfortable with you. Salespeople are often trained in this "mirror and match" technique to try to act and speak like the customer in front of them to make for a more comfortable interaction and thus, inspire more trust (and hopefully a sale).

When conversations move to text (such as e-mail), however, the mirror and match instinct takes a slightly different turn. People do still have the unconscious tendency to "mirror and match," but not on exactly the same things. Two very common "mirroring" tendencies in this medium are length of message and time delay before answering. Without consciously deciding to, most people dash a quick one-line answer off to someone who has asked a quick one-line question, and are more likely to provide three paragraphs of information to someone who has written a long, detailed request. To some degree, this is not only good for building rapport but can also be logical and appropriate—someone asking a quick question might well be annoyed by a pages-long answer.

The fact that people tend to mirror each other unconsciously, however, is where the potential complications lay. Let's look at the matter of pace. Some people fire off reply e-mails the minute they see the message, while others take days to send anything. What's interesting is that even those who tend to respond quickly in most situations may find themselves delaying a response to someone who typically responds more slowly. Similarly, it can be ineffective to try to squeeze important content into a one-sentence e-mail simply because that is the type that has been sent to you.

Quotes from the front lines: *"I like to answer e-mails promptly. It's efficient and gets people the information they need. Plus, I dislike leaving things undone—half the time I forget about it entirely if I don't do it right away, and then have a moment of panic later when I remember that I hadn't yet gotten back to it. Despite this, I have recently noticed that there are several people whose messages usually make me think 'well that can wait' about answering them, even though it puts me in danger of forgetting about it! Once I thought it through, I realized that the people who I delay answering are exactly those people who never respond promptly to me. I never thought of myself as a 'tit-for-tat' type of person, and once I saw the pattern, I realized it was hurting me as much as them."*

A related problem is the fact that even though a lengthy reply may feel more appropriate to a lengthy request, the extra time that it takes may make many people push that task off the immediate to-do list. As one newspaper article put it, sometimes people don't end up replying at all and seeming like they did not care about the message, when in fact they cared *too much* to send a quick reply, and thus ended up failing to respond at all (or within a reasonable timeframe).[3]

TIP

While it can create rapport to have people mirror and match each other's communication patterns and styles, this instinct should never overwhelm basic common sense about what needs to be conveyed, and when, to get work done effectively.

Lastly, it is worth noting that the pace question in e-mail response time is also linked to power. The higher up the receiver of your message, the less likely you are to get a quick reply. Most people attend to messages from their superiors first, and let the people below them wait. And the reverse is true as well, in that delayed responses from low-status people are judged more harshly than identical delays from higher-status people.[4]

Quotes from the front lines: *"The 'real life' status that different people have within an organization is perfectly reflected in e-mail. When I come to work in the morning, the first thing I do is to scan all of the e-mail that* *came in overnight, and to quickly prioritize those messages to read and respond to. Messages from my boss and his boss get responded to first! And now that I'm the boss of more things, I feel more in control and less like I have to jump for others. I mind much less than I used to if messages sit around, unanswered, for days or even a week."*

In addition to the length and the pace, even the language choice itself can fall into the pattern of mirroring what others have sent. One research study on this topic found that within any one organization, there was a very high degree of consistency about whether individuals used close or distant styles of communications, how extensively they used greetings and closings, and how friendly and familial were the language choices. Across different organizations, however, there was a great deal of variance. Thus, the common patterns found within a particular organization were likely not random, but were instead a reflection of the culture and of the customs of that workplace.[5] This can be explained in part by the mirroring instinct—when you receive a curt e-mail with no greeting, you are more likely to respond in kind. A warm greeting and closing may also inspire you to choose the same style. The importance of understanding these tendencies lies in the realization that one message may have a rippling effect on lots of other messages.

TIP

Know that your word choice and tone can inspire a chain of like-minded responses. Avoid dashing off negative messages, as the repercussions may last much longer than your original mood.

THE "CC" TRAP

It's so easy, and so tempting, to copy lots of people on messages. For one thing, it highlights to those above you what you are doing and shows that you are working hard. This, of course, often drives those in high-level positions crazy, as it places unreasonable demands on their time. The provost of a major university once lamented, "You wouldn't believe how many people copy me on their work just to show off."

Quotes from the front lines: *"In fact, the majority of the e-mails I receive are ones where I am just being 'cc'd' on something. But it still takes hours of time to go through them all and check to see if I have to do anything or* *if they are just for informational purposes. 'Cc-ing' is used mostly so that everyone knows you did something. But they don't realize that it just bogs down the system, and also makes me sometimes miss things that I was supposed to act on since it was buried in the stack."*

Clearly, this is a problem, and companies large and small are beginning to respond with policies limiting or eliminating entirely the use of "cc" and/ or "bcc" on e-mail. Furthermore, different people may each have their own "cc" personalities, in which some like to use/overuse this option and others prefer not to. So while the spirit of policies like these is sound, in practice, they can backfire. This is primarily because it is nearly impossible to dictate a generalized "line in the sand" for who needs to know what on a given topic. Companies resorting to blanket policies such as "no more than four addresses may appear on any one given message" or "only people whose name appears in the document can be copied on the message" (both real examples of existing policies) may feel like a reasonable attempt to rein in the problem of e-mail overload, but they also potentially limit the scope of what can and should be accomplished by the message in the first place.

It is important to know, as well, that using "cc" can have unintended effects on the message itself. Perhaps not surprisingly, people speak and write differently to one person than they do to a group of people. Therefore, in addition to the other concerns, getting your message through in and of itself is more complicated as you add people to the recipient list. People seem to write using more formal language and style when more people are copied. They may also need to review information that many already know, to get the "outsiders" up to speed. These changes can sometimes unintentionally hide the intended meaning of the original message. Additionally, having multiple receivers on a message creates another layer of complexity in terms of ranking their importance.

The first signal that someone is secondary to the conversation is the decision about whose address to put in the "send" field and who is in the "copy" field. Copying someone who does not need to be directly involved in the conversation can put that person into the role of side-participant, bystander, or eavesdropper. A side-participant is someone who might not voice an opinion on the topic at hand, but whose potential reaction may weigh on the original message sender nonetheless. Bystanders are those people for whom you might just say "FYI"—here is some information you might want to know about, but no reaction is expected from you at all. Eavesdroppers are those for whom their presence is not even recognized by all of the discussion participants—either by oversight or because the address is hidden from view.

The language used in the message itself can also signal the "copy" status of the participants. For example, people are more likely to speak of someone in the third person when that person is copied instead of directly addressed, such as, "Maria will get back to you to address that concern" or even "I believe Maria will take care of that (?)."[6] This kind of statement can also be included to indirectly ask for approval or collaboration from the copied party. In both of the above examples, an indirect question to Maria has been asked, but is in a format that is atypical in other types of communication. Some might say that this format is efficient and saves time; others might find it impolite because it does not directly ask for the necessary input from the focal person. Thus, "cc" has created whole new avenues for communicating, some of which may unfortunately lead to whole new avenues of misunderstanding. The more people on the list, the more you have to pay attention to make sure your message makes sense to all of them, while still accomplishing the original goal.

TIP

Keep it simple, and copy as few people as possible on any given message. This allows you to write more directly to those you are addressing.

Though thus far "cc" has been painted as nothing but trouble, here are a few reasons why "cc" should not be abolished completely (listed first and then explained in turn):

- Sometimes, a lot of people actually do need to know the information
- Being visible does make people work harder
- It can be kinder to include a "cc" than to "tattle" on someone, or make a giant issue out of a problem that may be brewing

The Need-to-Know Basis

It's a fine line between angering people by cutting them out of the loop and angering people by overwhelming them with information they don't actually need.

Quotes from the front lines: "*Recently, a group of about 10 lawyers were working together on a deal—half from my firm and half from the client company. We all used e-mail to communicate with each other, and used "cc" a lot to make sure the whole team was up to speed on what was happening. My boss then decided that it looked problematic to have that many e-mails flying around, so she made a policy eliminating "cc" options on e-mails within the team. After that, we started running into problems, as people no longer had the current information on the status of the work. We all started using "cc" again—but this time, leaving off the boss's address instead!"*

TIP

Ask first if you are unsure if someone wants to be copied on a particular e-mail conversation.

Visibility and Motivation

Nearly a hundred years ago, historic research occurred in a factory called Hawthorne Works (a Western Electric factory outside of Chicago) that set out to identify whether certain changes in conditions, such as brighter lights, would improve productivity. The primary investigators found something they weren't looking for: individuals thrived most when they worked in spontaneously derived teams—and thus the field of team management was born. However, a second investigator later returned to the original data and noticed additional trends. For instance, when the lights were brightened, employees performed better. When they were dimmed, productivity also improved. Similarly, changes such as clearing work spaces, relocating work stations, or moving obstacles from the floors all seemed to improve performance. After a time, though, productivity fell back to normal rates. The overall conclusion was centered on the power of having these workers *observed* at all. In other words, when the lights were brightened, or dimmed, or anything else was changed, workers knew that someone was paying attention to them, and they rose to the occasion with improved performance. When the change became routine, they felt the attention had diminished, and they relaxed.

If the power of a "cc" can aid that process, it might just be a useful tool after all. When used strategically for key pieces of work, perhaps this ability to highlight attention can be a motivational boost. However, this does of course have to be balanced with the natural resistance that most people experience when being micro-managed (and adds a burden on the time and in box of those involved). Perhaps it is wise to create periodic "windows" to allow for supervisors to be copied on mundane project messages, as both a check-in on the work and a chance to feel like extra attention is being paid.

> **TIP**
> When used sparingly, asking to be copied on messages on a particular topic can be an efficient way to bring your attention to the work of others, without much cost to you.

Avoiding the Tattletale

Being hassled by a colleague or an external stakeholder, having to constantly remind someone of something that needs doing and is holding you up, or reading something that strikes you as worrisome are examples of small problems that could become big problems. In the pre-text days, your choices were either unlikely to help resolve the problem (if you should choose to do nothing at all), or had the potential to escalate a conflict (if you should choose to report the problem officially to a superior). Although the decision to "cc" a superior on a problem such as this is largely the same as calling a meeting to report on the problem, it is often taken more kindly. And though you cannot resort to this action constantly without becoming thought of as a problem yourself, this generally provides the intended result: the colleague who has been ignoring your requests until now will probably answer quite rapidly once the boss has eyes on the situation.

> **TIP**
> Know that you should not copy a superior on every small situation that arises. Save that option for times when you really need it.

ONCE YOU HIT *SEND* . . .

While the discussion of "cc" covers intended exposure of e-mail messages, it is also worth commenting on the unintended exposure that can result from the ability to forward messages from person to person. For example, as part of an ongoing feud between teammates Sally and Mike, Sally decided to forward a message written by Mike to an employee in the IT group. The message stated Mike's opinion that the IT department in their company was all but useless and that they should not bother trying to go through them to solve their problem. The IT employee promptly forwarded the message to his own boss and Mike's boss, and replied to Mike, "I'm sorry you feel that way." We can all guess what kind of IT service Mike was going to get from that point forward for the duration of his time at that company! This problem can be exacerbated by the ability to fire off messages, especially on hand-held devices, without fully thinking things through.

Quotes from the front lines: "The ease and speed with which e-mails can be written sometimes leads people to 'hit send in haste and repent at leisure.' Just last week, one of my colleagues sent off a message that was harshly critical of a suggestion made by another colleague; within an hour, he wrote to apologize and back down from his criticism when he realized that he had gone too far."

Quotes from the front lines: "Everyone has a story about hitting 'reply all' by accident, or something similar. Mine has to do with mistakenly hitting 'reply' instead of 'forward'—by accident, instead of asking our PR person how to deal with a crazy reporter, I asked the reporter herself for this advice."

Other examples of misfired e-mails are:

- An employee learning of his termination when he was accidentally copied on an e-mail sent to the company's IT department to disable his account
- An e-mail accidentally sent to a customer with complete pricing information on a service, because the customer and a team member shared a first name (so the wrong name and address auto-filled in the "to" field)
- Full salary information on all employees in a company was sent to several employees by accident from HR

TIP
Once you hit "send" on a message, it leaves your control entirely. Don't write anything that you aren't prepared to defend if seen by each and every member of your company. And check the address field specifically before sending!

This advice goes double for those working in the public sector. But for anyone working anywhere, public or private, it is critical to understand that at this point in time, there is still a lot of uncertainty about whether e-mails belong, in a legal sense, to the sender, the recipient, or the organization that provides the e-mail account. The classic advice that nothing should be typed in an e-mail that you wouldn't want to see on the front page of the newspaper tomorrow has some merit.

Quotes from the front lines: *"Since I work in the public sector, we have the added level of complexity: all of our electronic communication can be subject to Freedom of Information Act/Public Records Requests from any member of the public or press. This requires us to archive our emails and to be prepared to make them public at any time. Given that, we should have clearer policies and guidelines than we do currently for the use of electronic communication."*

POLICIES

The lack of clear understanding about what is expected of people in the e-mail realm frustrates many. Though these can be difficult to pin down, this next section explores some ideas on what might make a useful start to an e-mail policy. Note that expectations can be codified using two different types of statements: actual specific policy rules, and more general guidelines. Specific policies would be rules like the above-mentioned example—"no more than four addresses may appear on any one e-mail." They can also include decisions about when employees are expected to be available and if messages are expected to be answered on the weekends or after hours. General guidelines tend to be statements that essentially just ask people to use their own judgment on various issues (whom to copy, what to say, when to expect a response, etc.).

Though it may seem like no guidance at all to just say "use your judgment," vast amounts of research in psychology demonstrate that merely raising awareness and asking for compliance results in much better decision making than would occur without such discussion. For example, many students are asked to sign "honor code" statements in which they promise not to give or receive unfair help on graded assignments. In theory, those willing to cheat should also be willing to sign and then go back on their word, but in reality, a great many people feel quite differently once they have been asked to think about and commit to these actions in the abstract, and cheating decreases as a result.

Similarly, people are much more likely to be patient and understanding about difficulties if they have been warned ahead of time that such problems may be likely. Consider, for example, the problem that a business school had when first-year students were shocked and angry that their first semester contained classes that many of them found to be tedious and uninspiring, such as basic statistics. A suggested change was to address this problem with all incoming students in their orientation week, and essentially give them a "bear with me" message. By doing so, the school could send a message that said *yes, you may find that the program gets off to a slow start and we recognize that this can be frustrating, but these skills are absolutely necessary for truly understanding effective decision making, and the courses will take off into richer topics by the spring semester.* "Bear with me" messages put you all back on the same team.

A classic exercise done with MBA students can deliver the same point. In the exercise, a CEO has died unexpectedly of a heart attack, and the students are asked to step into his role and deal with everything in his inbox. While the primary goal of the task is to get students to think about how to prioritize work, a second valuable lesson can be slipped in about the value of the "bear with me" message. Rare is the student who thinks of this spontaneously, but in truth the first action that should be taken by this new CEO has nothing to do with the content of the issues contained in the inbox (despite the high-priority nature of many of them), but everything to do with asking the staff to understand the circumstances and to pitch in to help. A message along these lines can go a long way to garnering support instead of resentment for requests that might otherwise feel unreasonable, such as: "We find ourselves in difficult circumstances. I'm asking for your extra effort and support over the coming weeks as we sort out the change in leadership and deal with a backlog of tasks, some of them quite urgent." If the message indicates that the leader appreciated your understanding and your willingness to pitch in during the challenging times, it would feel more like an honor to help out, instead of a burden.

Returning to the context of e-mail policies and the like, asking for people's understanding ahead of time about some of the commonly encountered problems can sometimes head them off. For instance, one typical issue is that of mistaken tone and intention. Sending a very clear "bear with me" message on this topic can be so much easier than dealing with the conflict and hurt feelings that might result otherwise. A reminder to the team at its outset that intentions are often mistaken in a "lean" communication medium such as e-mail, followed by a "let's all give each other the benefit of the doubt" statement, may be all it takes.

While specific policies may well be needed and appropriate for your work setting, they need to be decided in and for your situation alone. As a place to begin, read the e-mail guidelines below from one organization, and note that although there is not a single item on the entire list that is a hard-and-fast rule, the overall spirit of consideration comes through very clearly. This list may be longer than you feel is necessary for your own situation, but it is offered in its entirety to give an example of the breadth of topics that may warrant preemptive attention.

1. Be cautious. Consider words carefully and read over text before sending.
   a. Think twice about how your words will be interpreted. Research has shown that people interpret ambiguous e-mail messages as negative even when that was not the intention.
   b. Think twice about what you mean. People do tend to be more negative over e-mail than when communicating in other ways, perhaps even without meaning to.
   c. Think twice about your feelings and motives. People may act in less cooperative and less trusting ways over e-mail. They even lie and cheat more.
   d. Remember that e-mail is not private: it is often forwarded. It is the property of this employer and can be retrieved, examined, and used in a court of law.
2. Avoid trying to use e-mail to resolve disagreements or address sensitive matters. These topics come with emotion, and emotions are often misinterpreted over e-mail.
   a. Do not use e-mail as an excuse to avoid personal contact. Don't forget the value of face-to-face or even voice-to-voice communication.
   b. Do not put any kind of sensitive or personal information in an e-mail. This includes complaints and even suggestions for improved performance. Don't complain to someone about his or her actions or statements in an e-mail, don't copy him or her on such an e-mail, and don't forward such an e-mail to him or her.
   c. Do not forward any e-mail that contains sensitive or personal information. In general, do not forward an e-mail unless you are sure this is okay with the sender. Do not forward a string of e-mails if you have not read them all.

    d. When explaining a problem, be informative rather than defensive. When you emphasize that a problem is not your fault, others feel that they are being faulted.

    e. Do not respond to an e-mail without reading it all. You may be jumping to a conclusion.

3. Avoid wasting the time of others. They are busy too.

    a. Try to send information only to those who need it. The time you save by using an e-mail list may be dwarfed by the time of others you waste.

    b. If you need only one person to act, do not address your request for action to more than one person. If you are unsure who can take the action, ask the person to whom you address your request to pass it on as needed. Include someone in the "cc" line only if the person really needs to know what you are doing.

    c. Think twice before launching an e-mail discussion. If you need three people's advice, you may learn more (and more quickly) by contacting each of them separately.

    d. If you must write to several people, be clear about what you need from each person. Break your message into bullets, and say who needs to respond or act on each one.

    e. Avoid "reply to all" whenever possible. Often only the person asking for your advice needs it. In any case, take the time to omit any recipient who has asked to be left out of an e-mail discussion.

4. Be charitable. Do unto others as you would have them do unto you.

    a. Do not expect a quick response. Give people time to think. That being said, the "one-day rule" should be your guideline for answering messages that you receive.

    b. Do not interpret lack of response as dereliction of duty or disrespect. It is humanly impossible to respond to all one's e-mail or to avoid mistakes in the triage.

    c. If you need the person you address to act, make this clear. It may help to add "Action Required" to the subject line.

    d. Do send e-mails of praise. Everyone has time to be praised.

Lastly, one of the most beneficial features of e-mail messages is that they are searchable after the fact. To maximize the usefulness of the information contained in e-mails, some companies and teams have implemented a "one topic" policy for e-mails. Just as it sounds, these policies state that each e-mail should cover only one topic, and importantly, should be labeled appropriately in the subject heading. This allows for easier retrieval of messages after the fact, and while it may feel cumbersome initially, once it becomes a habit, it is not a difficult rule to follow.

> **TIP**
>
> Consider every e-mail as a deposit into a knowledge repository. Label e-mails with the correct subject, and do not include multiple topics in the same message. Perhaps, among team members, there should even be agreement as to what keywords belong in the subject heading, to get and keep everyone on the same page about where to find the information that they need.

SUMMARY

E-mail inefficiencies clog up everyone's workday. Make sure all messages contain useful information, are sent to the appropriate people (and nobody else), and comply with the spirit of best practices.

NOTES

1. Anthony Robbins, www.quotationsbook.com.

2. Rhoades, L. & Eisenberger, R. (2002). Perceived organizational support: A review of the literature. *Journal of Applied Psychology, 87,* 698–714.

3. Tugend, A. (2013). The anxiety of the unanswered e-mail. *The New York Times, Personal Business Section*, April 20.

4. Sheldon, O. J., Thomas-Hunt, M. C., & Proell, C. A. (2006). When timeliness matters: The effect of status on reactions to time delay within distributed collaboration. *Journal of Applied Psychology, 91,* 1385–1395.

5. Waldvogel, J. (2007). Greetings and closings in workplace email. *Journal of Computer-Mediated Communication, 12(2),* 122–143.

6. Skovholt, K. & Svennevig, J. (2006). Email copies in workplace interaction. *Journal of Computer-Mediated Communication, 12(1),* 42–65.

THREE
The Multitasking Effect

DISTRACTION'S CONSEQUENCES

People don't seem to do just one thing at a time anymore. Maybe busy people never did, but the proliferation of computers and hand-held devices have made it that much more tempting, if not actually necessary, to keep at least partial attention on multiple streams of thought simultaneously. While some argue that this can be an opportunity for real-time problem solving and efficiency,[1] a wealth of research shows that the costs of this behavior are actually quite high, and both attention to immediate tasks and interpersonal relationships can suffer as a result. This temptation affects people differently and to a greater or lesser degree; we all know people for whom having a face-to-face conversation involves not meeting the other person's eyes but watching that person watch a screen instead. The resulting frustration you may feel in this situation can wreak havoc on both the conversation you were trying to have and your opinion of the distracted person. This chapter is a review of the facts on multitasking, and its effects not just on you, but on those around you.

MULTITASKING: MORE PROBLEMATIC THAN YOU THOUGHT

The sad truth (based on numerous research studies) is simple to summarize: multitasking does not work as well as most people think it does. Warnings abound cautioning against trying to carry on a cell-phone conversation while driving, for instance. Even when using a hands-free arrangement, the focus of your attention on something not physically present in your environment effectively "turns off" your brain from processing critical information coming at you from the road.[2] What you are doing when you simultane-ously engage in multiple lines of thought is not really multitasking, but is more accurately described, on a cognitive level, as rapidly switching your attention from task to task. Simply put, our brains *cannot* think about two different things at the exact same moment. If you think of your attention during multitasking as a lever, then, what you are actually doing when try-ing to attend to two things at once (like a meeting and an e-mail message) is pulling the lever back and forth many times quickly. This action does not occur without cost in terms of your ability to function cognitively, or in layman's terms, to think clearly. Your brain gets tired doing this, and will do everything more slowly and less completely than it would if you were only focused on a single element at a time.

The single most convincing piece of evidence for this effect is the sur-prising fact that people who consider themselves to be "expert" multitask-ers (those who engage in this behavior regularly and fully defend their ability to "handle" and even thrive on the cognitive overload that results), are actually *worse* than average at absorbing and retaining the informa-tion presented to them during this practice. Instead, they simply get accus-tomed to treating ideas on a more superficial level and so the process feels more successful to them, when in fact it is less effective.[3] Many of these self-proclaimed experts also try to hide behind the idea that when they want to, they can apply "laser focus" to one idea and return to high levels of concentration and effective thinking. In fact, they are wrong about this too—the brain, now wired for multitasking, seeks out forms of distraction and can no longer focus as it once could.[4]

Now that you understand the problems associated with multitasking, let's switch and look at the effects on the other side of the conversation. There are two elements inherent in the act of someone interrupting your conversation to focus on something else, such as checking or responding to a message on a hand-held device. The first is the time-delay that results, and the second is the reaction that people have to being put "on hold" while someone focuses else-where. First, delays are costly, as they ruin the rhythm and thought processes of all parties in the conversation.[5] Second, evidence exists showing that peo-ple not only notice, but react emotionally, to the multitasking behaviors of others. Though you may (unconsciously) expect people to be "paused" while you attend to a momentary interruption from our mobile phone, much in the way a DVD can be paused during viewing to answer a phone call, people are instead likely to be actively annoyed by the interruption.

Quotes from the front lines: *"A team leader I once worked with, Rob-ert, was routinely texting on his cell phone instead of listening to the* *ideas that the team was discussing in a meeting. After several meetings in which Robert followed up his texting activity by asking us to go over something that we had in fact just recently stated out loud, the whole team decided to stop talking entirely when Robert took out his cell phone. Team meetings from that point forward regularly contained moments of total silence as Robert attended to his phone and we all just rolled our eyes at each other."*

When you do not pay attention, not only might you miss content, but the emotional tone of the interaction may change as well. A study of negotiations,[6] for example, showed that when one person repeatedly picked up a cell phone to attend to an incoming message, even if just for a brief moment, the other party reacted strongly. Let's call the two parties in this negotiation the "message-checker" and the "insulted party" (the partner who watches while the other side pauses the negotiation at hand to read a message). After the negotiation ended, insulted parties reported lower levels of trust in their message-checker partners, as well as rating them as less professional in general and someone with whom one should not work again, if given a choice. Insulted parties were also less satisfied with the overall experience, which can have lasting effects for how the interaction unfolds going forward.[7] Finally and most dramatically, these feelings translated into more mercenary tendencies by the insulted party during the negotiation, leading that person to claim more value in the deal than was received by the distracted message-checker. Quite simply put, this means that the message-checker earned *less* money in the deal than did (a) their partners, or (b) other non-distracted parties negotiating the same case. Message-checkers thus lose out in two ways:

1. By being too distracted to keep track of the complicated conversation, and thus missing out on opportunities to claim more value, and
2. By losing the goodwill of the other side, and thus being "taken" for all they have. Overall, a very consistent pattern emerges whereby the message-checker ends up with a raw deal simply because the other person does not wait without reaction while the phone task is being attended to.

Distractions are a particularly strong problem during conference calls. Here, the temptation can be overwhelming to work on secondary tasks when the other team members can't see you. Even an early solution to add a video component to the interaction seems to have backfired in many cases, as meetings with more than two people can lead to a screen full of small pictures of too many people doing too many different things,

---

Sidebar 3.1.   Creating Effective Conference Calls

Rare is the job that doesn't entail conference calls, and rarer still are the individuals who actually *enjoy* this process. Conference calls can be thought of as a necessary evil: they are generally nobody's favorite way to have a conversation, but they are much more efficient than trying to wait until everyone can meet in person. Here are 10 tips for keeping conference calls on track and getting the most value out of the time people spend on the phone with each other.

1. Don't use speaker phones. In fact, you've probably experienced this exact phenomenon: you are on a phone call with someone (let's call him Sam), and after a minute Sam says, "I'm going to put you on speaker so that Jody can also participate." Admit it, your heart sinks when you hear those words. You know that what is likely to follow is a scratchy, distant-sounding set of voices from which you will only catch about half of the words, and to which you will have to now spend your time shouting to make sure they can hear you. Unless you have *excellent* technology at your fingertips, make sure everyone picks up an actual phone.

2. Set an agenda and materials/visuals ahead of time, and stick to them. Focusing is hard enough when you aren't in the same room. Don't make it harder by wandering off topic.

3. Know that some types of conversations may be less well suited to conference calls (like brainstorming or idea-building) while others are easier in this format (like updates or creating a shared understanding of next steps).

4. Be as succinct as possible. Half-hour calls are ideal; 90 minutes is a good guideline for the maximum length.

5. Make rules clear. For example, everyone should introduce themselves at the beginning of the meeting; late entrants are expected to announce their presence when they join; and all participants should respect set time limits for each agenda item.

6. Make goals clear. What is expected by the end of the call—is it input? Is it agreement or consensus? Is it just to know what others are up to?

7. Specify how participation is expected. Is a round robin format to be used, where each person speaks in turn? Or is input required only when requested? While "cold calling"—asking for someone's comment without warning—is probably a source of unnecessary anxiety, you can certainly announce ahead of time that you will want to hear from certain people. An extra kindness is to use first names at the beginning of the statement or question instead of at the end, to alert the focal person that input will be required. For example, "Joe, what are your thoughts about whether XYZ or ABC makes more sense as our next step?" rather than, "We can either go with XYZ or ABC. Joe, what do you think?" In the latter construction, there's a good chance that upon hearing his name, Joe's first reaction will be, "Wait, what was the question again?"

8. Always have a facilitator, and have that person be very active in running the meeting. If reasonable, rotate the role among all teammates to get each person involved.

9. Recap often, not just at the end of the call. This is a chance for those whose attention has waned to jump back into the process. (While 90 minutes is a good guess on attention span overall, attention actually zooms in and out every few minutes for most people.)

10. Having some people in the same room and others on the phone *just doesn't work*. The people who are "virtual" never catch the entire conversation going on in the room, and so they often feel like the call is a waste of time. Instead, the "virtuals" start doing other work simultaneously, while thinking, "I'll just catch up on this content later in a one-on-one conversation with someone." Those in the room often forget that the rest cannot see their facial expressions, or see their notes on the flip chart, or hear their little quips (and they invariably speak more quickly to each other than when addressing those on the phone). Those present nearly always dominate the conversation. If you *must* have this half-and-half format, make these problems explicit at the beginning and make sure all participants know their responsibilities to each other and to the agenda at hand. If you can avoid it, though, moving all participants to equal footing (all on the phone, for example) is a much better idea.

See http://blog.gcsagents.com/2011/02/15/6-tips-conference-call/ for more on this topic.

---

creating a distraction of its own. See Sidebar 3.1 on creating effective conference calls for tips about how to make these meetings and conversations clear and useful.

E-MAIL ADDICTION: WHEN "CHECKING IN" BECOMES THE END AND NOT THE MEANS

It is a nearly universal phenomenon by now: the itch you feel when you have a free moment and you immediately want to use it to check your work e-mail, even when you're at home and supposedly off the clock. What does "off the clock" even mean anymore in today's fast-paced and super-connected world? Even while at work, the overblown instinct to check your inbox can prevent you from fully immersing yourself in other tasks, and can block you from thinking as deeply as you should about your work.

Why do so many people do this? The easy answer is that people can become addicted to online activity in the same way that they become addicted to other activities, such as gambling or shopping.[8] Research in cognitive neuroscience has shown that these forms of addiction are no different, physiologically, from drug addiction. All of them light up the pleasure center in the brain.[9] And once addicted to the speed of electronic communicating and the excitement of multitasking, it can be frustrating for people to engage in the slower back-and-forth process of a real-time, face-to-face conversation (with its greater tendencies towards social niceties in addition to actual content).[10] The deeper question, though, is why checking your e-mail can register in your brain as a reward, when much of the time the news you find there is full of demands, pressure, or inefficiencies.

Quotes from the front lines: *"My work is 100% virtual, and my typical day finds me in eight straight hours of meetings via VOIP—in other words, I'm connected to a conference call on my computer, with a headset on for sound and the ability to share documents on my screen, all day long. Mostly, my own screen is not visible to the crowd, and I admit that during slower moments in the meetings I nearly always switch to my e-mail to check on other issues, including ones concerning my children's schedules. During the few moments when my screen is visible to others, I have to literally remind myself every minute—don't check the e-mail, don't check the e-mail, or else I do it automatically without even thinking about it, and everyone else could see it. Once or twice I've actually done this when others could see!"*

CHECKING IN FROM HOME

There are two schools of thought on why people become addicted to checking in from home. The first has to do with stimulation, and the second has to do with escape. Starting with the latter, it is easy to understand how a home life that is either too busy or too slow can sometimes create its own stresses, and having the release of focusing on work instead can feel like an advantage. The stimulation argument, on the other hand, purports that there is a kind of "high" that comes from dealing with lots of information in a very rapid fashion, and it can be difficult to allow your mind to slow down enough to return to regular-paced interaction.[11] Either route can lead to the same two outcomes:

1. Strain on your home life and relationships
2. Resentment of your work life

Ironically, checking your e-mail more heavily from home makes people feel *more* overloaded at work, not less, and thus your satisfaction with your job goes down.[12] As a result, instead of remaining on top of all the details as they arise and thus smoothing out your professional demands, checking in too frequently can have the reverse effect. It can cause, in and of itself, a greater burden on your mind and thus tarnish your feelings about your work in general.

CHECKING IN FROM WORK: THE URGENT VERSUS THE IMPORTANT

Thinking hard is, well, hard work. It takes concerted effort to fully immerse oneself in a problem or project. The "easy" way out is to find something quick to do and simple to think about, thereby checking something off your to-do list and making you feel like you have accomplished something real, when in fact you are actually avoiding the true work that requires your full attention. The snippets of time that reading e-mails consume more readily fit our ever-shortening attention spans. Plus, the messages can feel like the introduction to a conversation, and can inspire a wish to answer immediately, the same as you would feel in a face-to-face exchange.

In general, busy people often make the mistake of attending to the things that feel "urgent" instead of the ones that are truly important. This short-term focus causes people to spend their days in reaction mode instead of action mode. In Chapter 2, a classroom exercise was discussed where business school students were asked to step into the role of a busy executive with a long to-do list. In this task, people routinely prioritize the nearer-term and simpler task of organizing a talk at a local event over dealing with the possibility of getting sued by some of the employees, which could potentially shut down operations entirely. People have a general preference for dealing with things that are (a) easier, (b) able to reach completion, and (c) have nearer-term timelines than they do for things that are distant in time, are complicated, or are ongoing in process. Checking e-mail instead of completing other work tasks falls into the former categories much of the time, hence its attraction as a "first order of business" event throughout the day.

Decades ago (in the pre-e-mail era), when referring to the interruption of thought that resulted from a ringing telephone, some management experts lamented the fact that it could take a full 15 minutes after the interruption to truly settle back into deep thought processes. These same experts yearned for a system whereby we could all leave each other silent messages to be attended to *in our own timeframes* without the need for constant interruption.[13] How ironic it has become that most people take this very silent system (e-mail) and feel the need to check messages *constantly*, instead of conveniently scheduled around the times protected for thinking and working as originally envisioned.

When you become so lost in thought on something that you no longer notice time passing, psychologists say you have entered a state they call *flow*. Like an athlete wholly engaged in the game or the race, intellectual work also has the ability to completely take over as you focus fully on the problem or work at hand. That, the psychologists argue, is when truly good work gets done.[14] Working with constant interruptions, such as checking messages all day long, results in a fragmented thought process and reduced work quality. The age-old observation that people sometimes needed to come in early or stay late (or worse, even take a vacation or sick day) just to get work done without interruption demonstrates a version of this problem. Today, the constant ability to check in can prevent even those formerly quiet times from being productive. In fact, research has shown that while feeling a greater connection to your colleagues at a distance is important for developing trust and working well together, it comes with the negative by-product of increasing the number of stressful interruptions of your work.[15]

Checking in with some regularity is, of course, required for most jobs; however, workers today tend to overdo it. Give yourself this test at work tomorrow: How many of the messages that you get in a day actually *require* your immediate attention? Could the issue at hand wait until the end of the day, or at least until the next hour? Breaking yourself of the habit of continual availability to respond to the needs of others can free up your time and your mind to do the work that you were actually hired to do. At the beginning, before you are used to *not* checking your e-mail all the time, set a schedule for yourself for when you will check and respond to messages. Over time, if this system does prove to lighten your burden, it will become second nature. And the best part of using a system like this is the fact that others will come to know what to expect from you as well, and will not be surprised if your answers come slightly later in time than they used to.

Even better, manage the expectations of your message-senders by updating them on when they can expect to hear back from you. This is another concept that falls under the famous phrase "an ounce of prevention is worth a pound of cure." Just as people commonly create a "vacation notice" that auto-replies to all sent messages, you could also consider sending an auto-reply out on days that you are either busy with meetings or are trying to protect time for thinking. One example is a standard reply note (to the first message sent per person) such as, "Please note that I routinely check my e-mail at noon and 5pm. If you need my attention sooner, please call or text." In this way, you avoid giving others the impression that you just didn't care enough to answer. Similarly, within a team, it can head off a lot of misunderstandings to have a norm whereby each person updates the others if there are days when messages will go unanswered.

A more extreme example of this principle comes by way of a classic exercise in the classroom as teams of people work on a decision-making task entirely via e-mail over the course of a week. Invariably, numerous teams are unable to complete the assignment because one or more members are unavailable or unresponsive to the messages of others, without pre-informing the team of when they would be focused on the task. By the time these people resurface, several members are typically so disgusted with them that the potential for cooperation is lost.

TIP
Unplug yourself to allow your mind to do other work. It may take some getting used to, but doing only one thing at a time and perhaps using a set schedule for attending to e-mail is better for you, and those around you, in the end.

Of course, some of the need to check in constantly may be due to the expectations of those above you. There are numerous stories from employees whose bosses send e-mails at all hours of the day and night, even when on vacation themselves, and expect the same behavior from everyone else.

Quotes from the front lines: "I had a boss who would send e-mails at all hours and the whole team was expected to be available to answer them. So, what would happen is that the boss would send out something late at night, and then one person would send a reply, and everyone else would add a useless comment each, just to show that they were also responding. It was absurd and I eventually quit."

Some degree of this problem can be managed by setting expectations appropriately for when you are and are not available. Additionally, it may help to cite the findings to such a person about the value of "unplugged" time on the quality of your work. Or, unfortunately, one small subset of demanding bosses can only be avoided by changing your current position.

It is worthy of one final note on this topic from the other side of the table: the person who checks/responds to messages too *in*frequently. This, of course, is the motivation for telling people when they can expect a response from you.

Quotes from the front lines: *"Over the course of my career, I've worked with a small number of people who either don't respond to e-mails at all, or reply only after a long delay and usually after I've sent several requests. Simply put, I hated working with each of these people. I liked them when I saw them face to face, but it was just too frustrating to throw a question or request into the 'black hole' of their inboxes, only to leave the item unchecked on my own to-do list for ages afterwards."*

> **TIP**
> People are annoyed by delays, or worse, may interpret them as being ignored on purpose. Manage their expectations ahead of time by letting people know when you will and will not be available.

THE ACCESSIBILITY SOLUTION

"Out loud" conversations are often considered the gold standard when it comes to understanding another person's message. Yet, one estimate places actual retention of spoken language as low as a mere 25%.[16] The acts of interrupting, finishing another person's sentence, hurrying someone along, or simply not paying attention as the mind moves ahead in the conversation or onto wholly unrelated topics can all get in the way of true comprehension.[17] In spoken language, even though people can sometimes go back into their short-term memory and "replay" what's been said most recently, it is impossible to go back and truly re-listen to the entire conversation. In theory, then, having information come in text form should have the edge because the content is more permanent and doesn't have the same "hear it now or lose it forever" aspect to it. However, this advantage only materializes if sufficient attention is given to the written text, which is not always the case.

The "overload culture" of e-mail thus has yet another consequence, which can be called the *skim effect*. Because most people get a double-digit (or even triple-digit) number of electronic messages each and every day, instead of reading them all, many messages get skimmed instead. As a result, there is a notable tendency for people to only notice, and subsequently respond to, only *one* element of a given message. Indeed, despite the fact that it is possible to review the exact content later, people are *more* likely in this medium to skim, miss things, and only respond to one idea.[18]

Quotes from the front lines: *"Twice recently I've had the experience where someone only read the first line of my e-mail, and missed important information (in one case) and a request (in the other) that were presented further down. The new e-mail systems that display the beginning of the message right in the inbox itself seem to imply that that's all there is to the message. I've started putting more information in the subject line itself such as "Two Things" to make sure that people know to keep reading!"*

This problem is compounded by the increasing use of hand-held devices for receiving and reading messages. Hand-held devices limit attention in two ways:

1. The size of the screen being used to see the message is much smaller than that of a full-scale computer, making it physically more challenging to see the message and absorb its intent.
2. Hand-held devices mean that people are very likely to be reading the messages you send while somewhere other than at a desk, and while simultaneously doing something else entirely.

Remember Robert, the team leader from the above example, whose team waited impatiently while he ignored them to look at his phone and tap in quick answers to the incoming messages? Now imagine that you're the sender of that message. How much of Robert's attention are you really getting, while he actively attempts to keep at least some of his attention (or at the very least, the appearance of his attention) on the meeting going on around him? Needless to say, it won't be all of it, and it might not be as much as you really need.

Quotes from the front lines: *"I admit that I'm a 'dinosaur' when it comes to technology, and have resisted using a hand-held device for anything other than the occasional phone call. As a result, all of my e-mails are done from my desk, which makes me forget sometimes that everyone else is getting and sending e-mails as if they were text messages on their cell phones. So even though they would probably prefer shorter snippets of information instead of long explanations, it's hard for me to remember to get right to the point in an e-mail and not explain all my thinking. As people keep misunderstanding what I'm trying to say, though, I'm getting the sense that I'm working against myself, so I'm trying to change this pattern."*

> **TIP**
>
> As much as possible, keep e-mails to one main point only, and get right to that point as quickly as possible. Remember that as a rule, readers give far less attention to what's being said than do writers. If an e-mail requires multiple items, number them and ask for responses on each item.

SUMMARY

People spend more time looking at electronic messages than ever before, but use less attention when they do so. Multitasking is tempting and addicting, but in the end can lead to burnout not only in yourself but in terms of what others think of you. Make a conscious effort to do each task in a given day to the best of your ability and with your full attention. This will result in both better thinking on your tasks and better connections with your colleagues. Remember this quote: "Attention is the rarest and purest form of generosity."[19]

NOTES

1. Reinsch, Jr., N. L., Turner, J. W., & Tinsley, C. H. (2008). Multicommunicating: A practice whose time has come? *Academy of Management Review, 33(2),* 391–403.

2. Strayer, D. L. & Johnston, W. A. (2001). Driven to distraction: Dual-task studies of simulated driving and conversing on a cellular telephone. *Psychological Science, 12(6),* 462–466.

3. PBS Frontline. (2010). Digital nation: Life on the virtual frontier. Original air date February 2, 2010. Available at http://www.pbs.org/wgbh/pages/frontline/digitalnation.

4. Nass, C. (2013). From *The myth of multitasking,* interview on science friday.com, May 10. Available at http://sciencefriday.com/topics/body-brain/segment/05/10/2013/the-myth-of-multitasking.html.

5. Ghosh, D. (1996). Nonstrategic delay in bargaining: An experimental investigation. *Organizational Behavior and Human Decision Processes, 67(3),* 312–325.

6. Kurtzberg, T. R., Naquin, C. E., & Krishnan, A. (2014). The curse of the smartphone: Electronic multitasking in negotiations. To appear in *Negotiation Journal, 30(2)* (April 2014).

7. Curhan, J. R., Elfbein, H. A., & Kilduff, G. J. (2009). Getting off on the right foot: Subjective value versus economic value in predicting longitudinal job outcomes from job offer negotiations. *Journal of Applied Psychology, 94(2)*, 524–534.

8. Brenner, V. (1997). Psychology of computer use: Parameters of Internet use, abuse and addiction: The first 90 days of the Internet Usage Survey. *Psychological Reports, 80(3, Pt 1)*, 879–882.

9. Holden, C. (2001). "Behavioral" addictions: Do they exist? *Science 2, 294(5544)*, 980–982.

10. Nelson, D. L. & Quick, J. C. (2009). *Organizational behavior: Science, the real world, and you.* Mason, OH: South-Western Cengage Learning.

11. Armstrong, L., Phillips, J. G., & Saling, L. L. (2000). Potential determinants of heavier Internet usage. *International Journal of Human-Computer Studies, 53(4)*, 537–550.

12. Turel, O., Serenko, A., & Bontis, N. (2011). Family and work-related consequences of addiction to organizational pervasive technologies. *Information & Management, 48(2/3)*, 88–95.

13. DeMarco, T. & Lister, T. (1987). *Peopleware: Productive projects and teams.* New York, NY: Dorset House Publishing.

14. Csikszentmihalyi, M. (2003). *Good business: Flow, leadership and the making of meaning.* New York, NY: Viking.

15. Fonner, K. & Roloff, M. E. (2012). Testing the connectivity paradox: Linking teleworkers' communication media use to social presence, stress from interruptions, and organizational identification. *Communication Monographs, 79(2)*, 205–23.

16. Nichols, R. G. (1971). Do we know how to listen? Practical helps in a modern age. In J. DeVitor (Ed.), *Communication concepts and processes.* Englewood Cliffs, NJ: Prentice Hall.

17. Williams, C. (2010). *MGMT2.* Mason, OH: South-Western Cengage.

18. Hattersley, M. E. & McJannet, L. (2008). Management communication: Principles and practices (3rd ed.). New York, NY: McGraw-Hill.

19. Simone Weil, http://www.searchquotes.com/quotation/Attention_is_the_rarest_and_purest_form_of_generosity./312583/.

FOUR
Crafting Effective Messages

CONTENT AND STYLE

Effective business communication contains two elements: content (knowing *what* to say) and style (knowing *how* to say it). The content of what you need to say is driven by your task and needs at hand. It is obviously not only necessary but also critical to be clear in your meaning. However, many an important message is lost in translation because the speaker/writer fails in the delivery, or the *how*. This problem is magnified for two reasons when speakers are not face to face. First, the loss of nuances (tone of voice and gestures) makes information more difficult to decode. Second, people are less likely to express confusion and ask follow-up questions if not face to face. In the virtual realm, it is therefore much more important to understand the art of effective message creation.

For instance, take a look at the two messages below.

MESSAGE 1:
To: Senior Staff on Project X
From: Manager ABC
Re: Concerns about Inefficiencies in Our Process

In our meetings with the SC, we have been discussing some of the inefficiencies that have come to our attention with the way that we are dealing with our vendors. Some of the time things seem to progress very smoothly, particularly in cases where we have been working with the same vendors for years, but in other cases, things seem to get muddled and we might even be losing business over it, or at the very least wasting time. Based on this, we have been looking into new approaches, and have been trying to compare notes with other firms who are about our size in the industry. We've come up with some proposals, and have met with some folks over at the SDC who sell software that may help us to get organized. We will be holding a meeting next Wednesday morning around 10 to go over all of this. In the meantime, if you have any of your own observations about how this process is failing us and what needs to be changed going forward, go ahead and shoot me a line before the meeting, or grab me for a quick chat on the phone. Thanks to everyone and I *know* we'll get this all sorted out before long.

MESSAGE 2:
To: Senior Staff on Project X
From: Manager ABC
Re: Meeting on New Vendor Process

The Steering Committee welcomes your input/observations on where you find our process for dealing with vendors to be inefficient. Please contribute via e-mail or in person before next Wednesday at 10 a.m., when we will meet on this topic. At that time, we will:

—Discuss findings from a recent benchmarking study of other firms in our industry.
—Review proposals from several software vendors with products aimed at solving this type of problem.
—Set a date for a final decision.

We hope that the revision of this process will make your jobs easier by improving your interactions with vendors. We look forward to hearing your ideas and value your input.

Message 1 is (probably) an exaggeration of a style of writing that is overly informal. This "stream of consciousness" type of writing is often easier to compose than is a carefully crafted message. But, like being angry and sending off a harsh message, it is satisfying to the sender only at the expense of the receiver. Furthermore, when people write these messages based on their thoughts at one particular moment, they are also more likely to forget important information, leading to the need for additional messages.

Quotes from the front lines: *"I had a boss once who would send a general message on a topic, and then send a whole bunch of follow-up messages* *every time he thought of something else related to that topic. It was so inefficient and annoying."*

While Message 1 may feel warmer (and is certainly more "chatty" in tone) than Message 2, it runs several risks when it comes to comprehension. The first is the risk of losing the attention of the reader partway through the single long paragraph. Remember, nobody reads with the same attention with which they write. Message 2, through the use of lists, breaks up the text more effectively, allowing more information to be captured at a quick glance. Even the two subject lines demonstrate this same problem. Although both messages introduce the topic to be discussed in the subject line, Message 1 has more words, and less clarity, than Message 2.

The next (though perhaps less obvious) risk is the different ordering of information in the two messages. Message 1 essentially says, "We're having this problem, we've been looking into it, and you are invited to share your thoughts and come to a meeting on it." Note that this message launches first into an explanation of the problem and then ends with the request. This order may reflect the way people think about things, but it is much less likely to make a clear impression on the reader. Message 2 instead begins with the request for action. The rule of thumb is that it is better to start with your conclusions and then follow up with your rationale than it is to walk the other person through all your logic before stating the overall objective. In other words, the more you can emphasize your purpose at the beginning, the more likely you are to help your reader absorb the major message you are trying to convey.[1]

TIP

Since you need to assume that the reader will *skim* instead of read your message, put your main point (your conclusions) *first*, and fill in details afterwards in organized lists.

Another difference between the messages is the connection made between the content and the receiver's interests. Message 2 directly highlights the potential value to the reader for being interested in/becoming involved in the process (which can be a useful motivator), while Message 1 lacks this entirely. In fact, one of the most common themes in the communications literature is to make sure you sell the audience on the positive impact of your idea for *them*. However, a note of caution is in order on this approach. While there is reasonable logic behind this—people should be more willing to do what's in their own best interest—this can be overstepped. If the benefit does not feel genuine, it can lead to resistance instead of compliance. In other words, if you need to stretch too hard to finish the sentence, "This will be good for you because . . . ," then you might be best off skipping this step.

Quotes from the front lines: "I used to have a colleague who always presented requests in ways that tried to make it seem completely for my benefit. Once, for instance, this person asked me to switch roles on a project, when I had more expertise in my original assignment and had already even started the work! Instead of asking me to switch as a favor for his convenience, he tried to sell it as a great opportunity for me to learn something new. I completely resented that, and I became wary of any kind of request from this individual."

> **TIP**
> Sell the benefits of the idea instead of its features, but be honest about your intentions. Don't push off requests for favors as advantageous to the other side.

Lastly, Message 1 also contains formatting that might not translate into the user's system and acronyms that may not be obvious to all readers. Excess formatting is easy to avoid if you stay away from:

- Italics
- Bullet points (note that Message 2 uses dashes instead of actual bullets since they are text proper and thus more likely to retain their shape in any system)
- Drag-and-drop characters such as animated smiles (which might not arrive intact)

When it comes to using jargon and acronyms, the simple and easy to remember rule is: *Don't do it.* If you cannot be 100% positive that the readers/listeners know what you mean, you are likely to lose their attention while they try to figure it out. This is harder than you think. As described in Chapter 1, once you know something well, it is extremely difficult to appreciate that others may be in the dark on it. This "curse of knowledge" refers to the tendency to over-assume information of listeners simply because the sender has said it or heard it so many times personally. The use of acronyms in electronic text has exploded, but it is incredibly frustrating for the receiver to figure out what is meant by the letters if it is not immediately obvious. For example, though most people know that BTW means by the way, how many can decode FWIW (for what it's worth), TIA (thanks in advance), FBM (fine by me), TYT (take your time) and TC (take care)? Though it may be tempting to use these shortcuts, you can't count on getting through to your audience.

Quotes from the front lines: "I'm a scientist with a PhD in chemistry. I was once giving a presentation to a group that included one of the directors of our parent lab, who was visiting for the day. I knew this man also held a PhD, so I used some technical acronyms and jargon in my talk. About three slides in, the director interrupted me to ask me what some of those terms meant. I later realized that although the man did indeed hold a PhD degree, it was in physics and not chemistry, and so he was completely lost in my talk!"

In this case, the mistake was rectified when the director asked for clarification. But people often hesitate to admit that they don't understand something that's being said to them, and the meaning of your message gets lost in the process.

Quotes from the front lines: "In a virtual team meeting, I could see the computer screens of the other participants. A number of times, I noticed other people using search engines to look up words and phrases used during the conversation. Most of the time, it was because non-native English speakers weren't following some of the words chosen by the native English speakers, but some of them were also technical terms. Without this window, literally, into their minds, I would have had no way of knowing that they weren't following the conversation."

TIP

The burden is always on you, as the message sender, to make sure that the information that you are presenting is accessible to the audience. With this in mind, it is best to decide not use jargon, ever.

RULES FOR CLARITY

Some rules of thumb for clear communication are based on common sense, but they are often forgotten in business-writing, especially when the

Table 4.1.   Keep It Simple

Don't Say	Do Say
Endeavor	Try
Initiate	Begin
Ascertain	Find out
Discontinue	Stop
Incontrovertible evidence	Proof
In the event that	If
In spite of the fact that	Although
In view of the fact that	Since
At the present time	Now

messages are crafted electronically. Start by keeping the overall message as short as possible. Some say that messages should rarely take the reader more than 10 seconds to read. Remember to also use common words instead of complicated ones, and choose familiar words over unfamiliar ones. Furthermore, always opt for shorter words instead of longer ones, and use concise sentences as well (taking care to remove meaningless phrases).[2] See Table 4.1 for some examples.

In addition, be concrete instead of general; provide real examples for any idea that is not immediately vivid to the reader. For example, instead of saying, "Compliance rates for user feedback were quite low," you could choose to say, "Only 15% of our customers filled out the survey." It is also best to remove negative words whenever possible (such as mistake, loss, or failure). Moreover, aim for courtesy and personal connection in all messages. Be as personal as possible, and avoid generic phrases that don't add to the content. For instance, instead of saying either, "Thank you for your time and consideration" or, "A prompt reply will be appreciated," it would be much more meaningful to say, "Your answers by Oct 15th will help us to move forward with the hiring decision." Also make a point to notice the phrases and expressions that you use all the time, and try to limit them.

Quotes from the front lines: *"This is embarrassing to admit, but it's a true story. Once, we had a manager who used certain phrases so often (out loud and in writing) that my colleagues and I created Bingo game cards for those phrases, and would mark them off every time we saw or heard them. For instance, every time we heard "outside the box" or "push the envelope" or "last but not least" someone got to mark* *off a square. It kept us focused on his messages, but not for the right reasons!"*

Additionally, organizing questions and providing options for the reader greatly increase your chances for a successful exchange. Numbering your questions gives the reader a clear directive, and also highlights the problem if answers to only some items get attention instead of all of them. In this age of over-scheduled everyone, it can also be a courtesy to cut problems down to size by providing a list of choices. For example, instead of asking the general question, "What should we get Anne for a retirement gift?" you might think to offer three (numbered) choices, making the response that much easier on the reader.

TIP

The aim in every message is to be as short and as direct as possible. Short refers not just to total message length but also to word choices and sentence length. Increase the odds of getting your points across by numbering or listing them, and providing options for replies where appropriate.

One last suggestion about clarity needs to be made, although it will most likely be met with dread. There is just no way to skip the revision process if you want to be a truly effective writer. Look your message over with specific objectives in mind. First, look to make sure it achieves the goals you had for writing in the first place. Next, look to see that it is coherent and direct. Finally, make sure that requests for action from the reader are easily spotted.

TIP

Never send out a message that you haven't read over entirely.

It is worth noting that the categories *direct* and *indirect* communication are not a black-and-white distinction, but are instead an infinite scale from one extreme to another, both of which can be problematic. Indeed, though direct communication is often hailed as the gold standard (even in this chapter!), in truth a more nuanced approach is important. The most direct way of asking someone to do something, for instance, is to order it in a command format, but this is not likely to win any goodwill from the recipient. On the other hand, a truly indirect way of presenting a request may be so ambiguous as to leave recipients unclear on what, if anything, is being asked of them. Look at the following five sentences that proceed from direct to indirect:[3]

1. I need the report by 5pm.
2. Can you please send me the report by 5pm?
3. If possible, I'd like to have the report by 5pm.
4. I'm interested in your input on the report. If you have ideas to share, how about sending them across this afternoon?
5. Is today a possibility for hearing from you on those issues?

The first might seem a bit rude; the last might not accurately convey your needs. Where you fall in the middle should depend on both the relationship you have with the receiver and the history of the conversation to that point. Topics already discussed at great length can survive an overly direct style, whereas new topics typically need a few more words to get the ideas across.

As this example illustrates, e-mail messages can be used not only to convey information, but also for requests. Some requests are simple and straightforward affairs, while others will require a more delicate touch—explaining the situation, justifying the request, and persuading the reader that compliance is warranted. Messages that must include a persuasive element need even more thought and planning than do other types of communication. The next section looks at persuasion more closely in this context.

PERSUASION

Workers no longer ask merely what they need to do. They also focus on *why* they need to do it. When most people think of the word "persuasion," the images that come to mind typically involve either sales or deception, or both. At best, many feel that to persuade another person, they would need to "win the debate" by using a combination of logic, persistence, and personal enthusiasm. While these tools have their place, true persuasion spans far beyond those first impressions. Instead, persuasion involves the act of getting people to open their minds to a new idea or a new way of doing or thinking about something, but not by begging or cajoling. And in the realm of electronic messages, it is critical to create solidly crafted communication since noticing and adjusting to subtle resistance from the other side is much more difficult.

According to experts, effective persuasion starts with careful preparation.[4] Planning involves knowing the audience members and their positions, as well as the details and alternative views of their own proposals. You can start by asking yourself preparation questions such as, "What level of information needs to be laid out at the beginning? To what degree are the readers experts in the topic at hand? To what degree are they potentially supportive of the ideas? If not, why not?"

Effective planning and proper argument framing almost always require one-on-one interactions ahead of time with each of the individuals who will be involved with the final decision. Not only will this allow you to gauge where the other side is coming from and which areas of concern you may face (and thus, help in answering the questions listed above), but it also allows you to introduce ideas slowly over time. People rarely latch on to new ideas in an instant, but instead need to get used to ideas and blend them with their current thinking. Just remember to be clear about your intent when you have these one-on-one conversations, either before or during the persuasion process.

Quotes from the front lines: *"Recently we had a meeting that a VP was not able to attend, and he was disappointed at our decision. About a week later, I got a follow-up e-mail from him asking me to justify the team's decision. I felt so out of place being asked to represent the team in this way, until I found out that he had approached all members of the team in a one-on-one fashion like this, to make sure he could address each and every one of our concerns. Once I knew this, I had no problem communicating with him."*

Individual communications can additionally serve the purpose of reminding yourself to keep an open mind about the ideas at hand and think through possible compromises. Remember, it might be the other person who comes up with the best idea for proceeding, but that's still your "win" in the grand scheme of getting a problem solved.[5] Again, this is based on the idea that effective persuasion is about getting things done and is not about forcing a fait accompli onto other people.

Persuaders also need to establish credibility, and unfortunately, most managers overestimate their own credibility with their employees. This is a problem that is magnified in the virtual team setting, where the distant connection between people makes it that much harder to rely on the perceptions of high credibility that people might ordinarily take for granted. Go out of your way to refer to your experience and expertise.

TIP

Persuasion is based on long-term investments in an ongoing conversation, and not just a sales pitch based on dry facts. Forming connections in the virtual setting can also require establishing credibility for the topic at hand.

Choosing an approach for your message may also be based on the combination of your relationship to the material and to the audience members themselves. One model categorizes four different approaches as the Tell, Sell, Consult, and Join methods.[6] *Tell* involves simply issuing non-negotiable statements. This may be appropriate if you need to assign tasks, or if you are sharing knowledge about which you are the expert. The *Sell* approach steps into the realm of persuasion, and is typically used when the receiver retains at least some of the final decision-making power. *Consulting* translates into trying to build consensus for an idea, while *Joining* means that your idea is just one among many, and you may want to fold in your own views with those of the others in the group. As you may notice, the level of authority decreases as you move from Tell through to Join. Note that this doesn't automatically mean that you don't *have* the authority; instead, you may choose to change the tone of your message depending on how important it is to you to get buy-in from others. Similarly, as you move through this chain, the communication itself will likely move from direct to more indirect, as you shift from announcing your own thoughts to asking others for their thoughts.

The next questions you need to consider cover whether and how you expect the receivers to react to your message.[7] If you expect them to generally be on board with what you're trying to say, your work is easy. In this case, the message can be direct and should be coupled with a reminder of the importance of the receiver(s) in accomplishing the idea/task. Negative receivers, on the other hand, are probably hostile and not especially likely to change their minds regardless of what you say. In this case, your best foot forward may be to explicitly recognize that you understand *their* point of view and then go on to explain why you have elected to endorse a different position. This can, at best, move negative receivers to be more neutral. The hardest work comes with people who start out neutral (or, as is common, those who are mixed in their initial opinions, seeing both some positive and some negative elements in the ideas). These are the ones for whom the exact crafting of your message can make or break an opinion change and the potential garnering of support for your views. One very successful tool is to explain the reasoning that convinced *you* to support this position in the first place; another suggestion is to reiterate the overall goal that all of you have for solving a common problem.

> **TIP**
>
> To create a persuasively written message, try using these four steps (in order): (1) Recognize the points of the opposition explicitly to disarm their need to state and restate them; (2) State the overall goal you have of moving forward; (3) Explain what convinced you to endorse a particular viewpoint; and (4) Restate the importance of the message receivers in accomplishing the tasks you are proposing.

DELIVERING BAD NEWS

Sometimes, bad news is unavoidable. How should it be broached? The guiding principles are that messages should be prompt, honest, direct (as much as is reasonable), and kind. Chapter 7 will discuss the potential complications involved in delivering certain kinds of bad news (such as negative feedback) via e-mail, but here the focus is on what the message itself should contain to have the necessary impact without some of the unnecessary emotional fallout. Here's a Top-Ten list for softening the blow of bad news in a virtual setting.[8]

1. Tell people news as soon as you have it, even if it needs to come in parts. Nobody likes being surprised by bad news. Even if you don't have any more to say than "I don't know much about this yet, but in the coming weeks it should become more definite," people will respect your honest and forthright inclusion of them in the process.
2. Recognize the negative aspects of the situation up front, and get right to the point. As one famous quote put it, "I've never known bad news to improve with keeping." Long introductions will merely serve as stress-builders. But also, balance this need for directness with the need for kindness. Though it is very direct, it seems harsh to answer a request with a one word "no" as a reply.
3. Include specific and concrete reasons for the state of events. As noted earlier, people generally want to know *why*. Research shows that bad news is accepted more readily if it is coupled with

an explanation. These types of "cushioning the blow" statements can indeed help make the news itself more palatable.[9] Nevertheless, always brace yourself for "blame the messenger" and briefly explain how this situation is the result of a larger context of events.

4. If possible, frame the situation in terms of "it could have been worse." This plays in on the innate psychological tendency to feel better with comparison to a worse possible outcome. Without crossing the line into disingenuousness, try to explain any silver linings in the events.

5. Think through whether the receivers would be in a bad position with or without the position you are announcing, and describe this.

6. Offer alternatives and solutions if you possibly can, and invite suggestions for proceeding.

7. Follow up and follow through. Bad news messages are not single-instance events. Updates on what's happening, check-ins on how people are reacting, and continuing dialogue about what could or should happen next are not only appropriate, they are much appreciated.

8. Think through the specific receiver(s) that you are addressing. The same message will mean very different things to different stakeholders, and should be tailored accordingly.

9. Put it in writing, either initially or as a follow-up to a spoken conversation.

10. Remember that you are dealing with real people with real emotions, and treat them as kindly as you can. Think through how you yourself would like to hear news such as this before proceeding.

There is also an unexpected benefit to delivering bad news in the virtual setting. Research has shown that as compared to face-to-face or telephone conversations, people tend to distort negative information *less* when they communicate via computers. Positive information seems to remain the same in any channel, but apparently the pressure of having to face someone's reaction in real time can cause some verbal "hedging" that may muddy the message itself.[10] Freed from the imposing thoughts of the other person, message-senders seem better able to get to the point of their bad news.

A last point related to bad news is not about delivering it, but receiving it. Especially if you are in a position of power over others, people may be reluctant to share bad news with you. Be explicit about your willingness to hear problematic messages, and by what means you prefer to be contacted with such news (e-mail, phone, etc.). Breaking the ice in this way promotes more effective and timely communication, and will likely help you to avoid complications down the road.

> **TIP**
> Share bad news as early as possible, and make it clear that others should not shy away from telling you bad news as soon as they are aware of it.

GENDER AND E-COMMUNICATION

Several decades of research have noted that men and women use language differently in many situations. Though not all agree, many find that men tend to be more competitive, proactive, opinionated, dominant, and task-oriented in their speech and writing than are women. They also use "strong" words more readily (like "damn" or "hell"). In contrast, women tend to ask more questions, to write longer and more expressive statements, and to choose dominant speech patterns only when in the presence of men of equal status. They also tend to be more emotionally connected, reactive, and focused on the non-verbal communication than are men. Women tend to use more question tags ("is that right?"), more disclaimers ("this may be right, but"), and more qualifiers (like "probably," "kind of," or "actually"),[11] leading to less direct communication on the whole. Other research notes that power or status—and not gender—guides appropriate language choices.[12] Summarizing these differences, typically male speech has been dubbed "report talk" while typically female speech has been dubbed "rapport talk."[13]

The next question is whether these types of differences persist in online communication. One study of over 700 online postings on various topics (newsgroups) showed that although men tended to post content more often, men and women offered opinions at about the same rate.[14] In another study, the mere expectation that one was communicating with a man versus a woman seemed to change the language chosen by a message sender.[15] A third study showed that even when typing under anonymous pseudonyms, women tended to use language more to establish connections between themselves and others.[16] A final pair of very convincing studies showed that (1) even when given anonymously, the gender of a message's writer was correctly identified in more than 90% of the cases,[17] and (2) even when specifically told to mask their gender in their written messages, the writer's gender was still easily identifiable.[18] In sum, it does seem to be the case that men and women predictably use language in different ways, even when interacting virtually.

But does this matter, and if so, what should you do about it? It matters only to the extent that noticing and identifying gender differences serves to hold people back. One study showed that task assignments are even more gender stereotypical when group members expected to meet virtually than when they planned to meet face to face. Thus, even the mere suggestion that one was working with a woman in the virtual setting, for instance, may make the team more naturally (if unconsciously) likely to ask her to act in the role of "recording secretary" for the group, regardless of her qualifications for other work.[19] Additionally, if gender is made more salient by writing style, it can (in teams of both men and women) potentially serve as a source of natural alliances or divisions among the team members (see Chapter 6 for more on this topic).

One gender researcher has identified four schools of thought on what can be done about these inequalities: (1) Fix the Women, (2) Celebrate Differences, (3) Create Equal Opportunities, and (4) Revise the Work Culture.[20] The Fix the Women approach suggests that women should learn to communicate more like men, but this of course assumes that the male types of communication are automatically superior, which is not always the case. The Celebrate Differences perspective aims to teach people that there is value in each approach, and all should be tolerant of each other. This approach, however, has the potential to reinforce stereotypes and doesn't seek to understand what elements of each style are actually the most effective in various situations. The Create Equal Opportunities and Revise Work Culture approaches say that if different styles are a result of both conscious and unconscious power differences, then equalizing the power roles of men and women will serve to reduce the communication gaps. This model may have a point, but it is not a simple fix to be sure. So what can you do? Take a random sampling of e-mails from your "sent" box and look them over to see if you fall into any of the categories listed above that make the messages jump out as distinctly male or female in style. Then work on removing those elements. You want your messages heard for what they need to convey, and not be clouded by the characteristics of your writing style.

One last point of interest about how gender plays out in the virtual realm comes by way of a study of avatars. Avatars are computer "cartoon" representations of an actual person (of you, in most cases) that can move around the screen and interact with others in the situation (games or meetings alike). Avatars have been shown to create great feelings of closeness between the real people behind them. Many who have used them report that avatars are more effective in creating a sense of closeness than are actual pictures of the real people in real time used in some videoconferencing tools. The interesting twist about avatars is that they don't necessarily *have* to physically represent the actual person using them. One study found that when people were randomly assigned to an avatar of either male or female gender, and were then asked to work with another random avatar (again either female or male), the pairs with *matching avatars* (that is, two male or two female characters on the screen) exhibited stronger team affiliation than did others, regardless of the actual gender of the person behind the avatar![21] This depicts the similarity effect in the digital age. It doesn't seem to matter if you're *actually* alike, just that you seem alike on the screen. While this research may not be imminently practical as a virtual teamwork tool, it is fascinating nonetheless and possibly an area where developments will continue as technologies change.

TIP

Make note of the characteristics of typical male and female types of speech, and then ensure that you don't only use one type exclusively.

Fittingly, the end of this chapter covers a topic found only at the end of e-mail messages—the use of signatures or disclaimer messages. Though they are generally thought to be harmless additions, this is not universally true.

E-MAIL SIGNATURES AND DISCLAIMERS

It is fairly common to include a standard signature at the bottom of every e-mail message sent. Generally these are fine—it is a shortcut for the sender to not have to sign each e-mail, and it can be a help to the receiver to have your contact information readily at hand if your signature includes these details. Thus, unless your signature veers off into the area of long quotes (even if the quote contains no off-putting content, it is still a distraction for the reader, especially if people get multiple messages from you with the same quote attached), signatures are generally not a problem.

A second type of signature contains some form of disclaimer message within it. For example, a recent trend is to attach a disclaimer (specifically in regards to messages sent from hand-held devices) to the effect of *"Sent from my mobile device, typos are inevitable."* This approach falls under the heading of what psychologists call *self-handicapping behavior*.

Self-handicapping is any statement that explains ahead of time why some-thing or someone might not be performing at the expected level. Imagine someone beginning a speech with the sentence, "Forgive me if I don't make perfect sense, I was up all night with my teething baby." Self-handicapping behaviors are ways of managing the impressions that others form of you. In essence, you are asking people to lower the bar of what they expect from you and you have given them reasonable cause for doing so. This practice makes some sense, but it contains one danger. Once you have used self-handicapping statements to pre-emptively release yourself from some of the responsibility for high levels of performance, you may slack off as a result. Research has shown that self-handicapping behavior has been associated with a drop in levels of performance, learning, and moti-vation.[22] Applied to the virtual context, then, don't forget that the messages you send represent you, and you don't want to come across as sloppy or inarticulate under any circumstances.

Many companies have also started putting formal disclaimer messages as a standard signature at the end of all of their employees' outgoing messages. To explore the effects of these messages, one study compared three types of messages, sent to three different groups of people. The first had a full legal disclaimer that stated something like, "This e-mail message and any attachments are the opinion of the sender and not nec-essarily that of ABC Company." The second contained a signature (but not the legal jargon) that said, "This e-mail message and any attachments may contain confidential information from the sender. Do not distribute without sender's explicit permission." The third group of e-mails had no signature whatsoever. Surprisingly, even though the first two signature statements read very similarly, the receivers of each type had strongly different reactions. Receivers of the first type of legal disclaimer sig-nature showed less trust in and discussed issues less thoroughly with counterparts than did those receiving either of the other two types of messages (which contained either a non-legal disclaimer or no signature at all).[23]

Several important points can be drawn from this study. The first conclu-sion is that people *do* in fact notice and react to these disclaimer messages, even if they just seem like harmless "noise" at the bottom of the message. Second, you should not assume that signatures and disclaimers will do no damage to the relationship with the receiver. Still worse, it seems that it is not easy to predict which types of messages will have negative effects and which will have no effects whatsoever. As stated above, the two example disclaimer signatures may feel alike, but they elicited different reactions from the receiver. The second signature ("e-mail may contain confidential information") acted virtually identically to the message having *no* signature at all, while the legal signature ("opinion of the sender and not necessarily the company") had a strong negative effect. The difference in wording is subtle, but the effect was quite sizable.

In our litigious society, it may seem like a wise move to protect the company's interest by disclaiming liability from any statements contained within, but the above results show that there are risks that need to be weighed before using such statements. Perhaps it is because messages like this give the subtle yet real impression that a big, intimidating company is behind the scenes, ready to step in with legal muscle if need be. Perhaps it is because these signatures give the impression that the sender is not fully trustworthy—even this person's *company* seems to want to distance itself from this person's statements! In other words, the comment may be interpreted as the company stating, "We're not sure what this person is going to say, so we don't necessarily want to be associated with it, since it may or may not be what we wanted." Whatever the reason, the effects are worth noting, and caution is warranted when adding *anything* to the bottom of your messages.

> **TIP**
> Don't attach anything in an electronic signature that isn't absolutely necessary. You cannot be certain of the effects that even a seemingly harmless statement may have on the recipient.

SUMMARY

Communicating well is hard, and when you remove face-to-face connections, the challenge of getting your message understood increases. Being clear in your presentation of information, requests, attempts to persuade others to align with your viewpoint, and/or bad news is paramount. Be aware of gender-stereotypical writing styles and seek balance in your own messages. Don't let needless signatures and disclaimers derail your message. Finally, use the following summary list to make sure you have done the best job possible with your outgoing messages.

Tips for Writing E-Mail[24]

- Send a separate e-mail for each topic. This makes it easier for recipients to acknowledge and respond to or read and delete the message.

- To make your message stand out in a recipient's crowded inbox, use the subject line to write a clear statement or specific request.
- Put the most important content at the beginning; recipients don't always scroll down to the end.
- Make it brief, focused, and specific. Deliver the most information in the amount of least space.
- Keep paragraphs short (three or four lines). Attach files if you need to send something longer or you need to use headings, bullets, tables, graphics, and other formats to make your message easier to read and understand.
- When replying, use your software's quoting feature to include a copy of the original text. This is a handy reminder for recipients who might not recall what they wrote previously.
- Never write e-mail when your emotions are raging. Anger and sarcasm often come across stronger in text than they would in person. An e-mail is a permanent record that can come back to haunt you.
- DON'T USE ALL CAPS because it looks like you're shouting.
- Watch out for inappropriate humor.
- Proofread! Always review your message before pressing *Send*. Think "AAAA" to double-check that your message contains: correct *Address*, correct *Attached* files, suitable *Attitude* and tone, and a statement of the *Action* you want the recipient to take.

NOTES

1. Hattersley, M. E. & McJannet, L. (2008). *Management communication: Principles and practice.* New York, NY: McGraw-Hill.

2. Rentz, K., Flatley, M. E., & Lentz, P. (2011). *Lesikar's business communication: Connecting in a digital world* (12th ed.). New York, NY: McGraw-Hill Irwin.

3. For a review of this issue, see Thompson, L. (2000). *Making the team: A guide for managers.* Upper Saddle River, NJ: Prentice-Hall.

4. Conger, J. A. (1998). The necessary art of persuasion. *Harvard Business Review,* May–June, Article #98304.

5. Warshaw, M. (1998). Open mouth—Close career. *Fast Company,* December, 241–249.

6. Munter, M. (1992). *Guide to managerial communication.* Englewood Cliffs, NJ: Prentice-Hall.

7. Hattersley, M. E. & McJannet, L. (2008). *Management communication: Principles and practice.* New York, NY: McGraw-Hill.

8. Bies, R. (2012). The 10 commandments for delivering bad news. *Forbes Leadership Forum*, May 30. http://www.forbes.com/sites/forbesleadership forum/2012/05/30/10-commandments-for-delivering-bad-news/, and Sun, C. (2011). 10 tips for delivering bad news. *TechRepublic*, April 6. http://www.techrepublic.com/blog/10things/10-tips-for-delivering-bad-news/2396.

9. Rentz, K., Flatley, M, & Lentz, P. (2011). *Lesikar's business communication: Connecting in a digital world* (12th ed.). New York, NY: McGraw-Hill.

10. Sussman, S. W. & Sproull, L. (1999). Straight talk: Delivering bad news through electronic communication. *Information Systems Research, 10(2),* 150–166.

11. Borisoff, D. & Merill, L. (1985). *The power to communicate: Gender differences as barriers.* Prospect Heights, IL: Waveland Press.

12. For a review, see Sussman, N. M. & Tyson, D. H. (2000). Sex and power: Gender differences in computer-mediated interactions. *Computers in Human Behavior, 16(4),* 381–394.

13. Tannen, D. (1990). *You just don't understand: Women and men in conversation.* New York, NY: William Morrow.

14. Sussman, N. M. & Tyson, D. H. (2000). Sex and power: Gender differences in computer-mediated interactions. *Computers in Human Behavior, 16(4),* 381–394.

15. Matheson, K. (1991). Social cues in computer-mediated negotiations: Gender makes a difference. *Computer in Human Behavior, 7,* 137–145.

16. Jaffe, J. M., Lee, Y-E., Huang, L-N., & Oshagan, H. (1999). Gender identification, interdependence, and pseudonyms in CMC: Language patterns in an electronic conference. *The Information Society: An International Journal, 15(4),* 221–235.

17. Thompson, R. & Murachver, T. (2001). Predicting gender from electronic discourse. *British Journal of Social Psychology, 40,* 193–208.

18. Herring. S. C. & Martinson, A. (2004). Assessing gender authenticity in computer mediated language use: Evidence from an identity game. *Journal of Language and Social Psychology, 23,* 424–446.

19. Heilman, M. E., Caleo, S., & Halim, M. L. (2010). Just the thought of it!: Effects of anticipating compute-mediated communication on gender stereotyping. *Journal of Experimental Social Psychology, 46(4),* 672–675.

20. Ely, R., Foldy, E., & Scully, M. (2003). *Reader in gender, work and organization.* Oxford, UK: Blackwell Publishers.

21. Lee, E-J. (2007). Character-based team identification and referent informational influence in computer-mediated communication. *Media Psychology, 9(1),* 135–155.

22. Elliot, A. J. & Church, M. A. (2003). A motivational analysis of defensive pessimism and self-handicapping. *Journal of Personality, 71*, 369–396.

23. Naquin, C. E. & Kurtzberg, T. R. (2010). Electronic signatures and interpersonal trustworthiness in online negotiations. *Negotiations and Conflict Management Research, 3(1),* 49–63.

24. Swaab, R. I. & Meyer, E. (2012). *Managing global virtual teams.* Managing Global Virtual Teams Programme, INSEAD. Fontainebleau Cedex, France.

PART II
VIRTUAL TEAMS

FIVE
Teambuilding and Networking

WHAT MAKES A TEAM?

Before addressing some of the specific hot points of a team's potential, including how to get started and how to maximize the effectiveness of networking (both inside and outside of the team itself), it is important to establish some general guidelines on what makes a team successful overall. Much has been written on this topic, and a consensus among many experts indicates a few common themes. A very condensed summary is offered below, to give some scope to what seem to be essential components of professional teamwork.

- *Membership must be both concrete and appropriate.* Too often, team membership is decided by who thinks they ought to have a say about the team's work, or who wants to keep an eye on it, and not based on who is best suited to actually do the work required. Experts caution that though the majority of teams all *think* that they have set unambiguous boundaries, as many as 90% of team members actually have disagreeing lists when asked to identify who is and who is not on the team![1]
- *Teams need both big picture and specific goals.* Goals serve a number of purposes, not the least of which is making sure team members don't end up pursuing different agendas. Goals must also specify why and how the team needs to collaborate in order to justify and explain the reason for the team's existence. Goals also help to motivate people, and can focus both discussions and conflict towards productive

ends. Finally, teams need to know whether their main objective is to: (a) recommend or decide something, (b) make or do something, or (c) oversee others.[2]

- *Teams need support from the outside and the inside.* This includes appropriate coaching, a clearly defined task, norms of openness and constructive interaction, and an organization that both values and rewards the work being done.[3] Too much insulation can lead to the common problem of a team that is in love with its ideas, only to be shocked to learn that the outside world doesn't respond in the same way.[4]

- *Teams work better when they enjoy each other.* It is intuitive that people would rather spend time with others whom they enjoy. The interesting thing from a psychological perspective is that enjoyment can be built via a number of different channels, only one of which is to have a meaningful social connection to the other people. Virtual teams in particular are often sensitive to the idea that team members need time to get to know each other (and hopefully even eat and drink together) to form friendships and to further each person's loyalty towards, and understanding of, the others. Few would argue that this is not time well spent, but physically getting together is not always practical and so a further understanding of the various routes to enjoyment is worthwhile.

   a. Both satisfaction and trust are built from successes, even more so than the other way around. Making sure that team members achieve some simple successes early on can inspire a more closely connected relationship among the members.

   b. Humor is a valuable tool. While truly funny people walk among us here and there, many others feel ill-equipped to introduce humor and light-hearted fun into the workplace. However, they should know that even when attempts at humor come across as contrived or forced, *they still have much of the same the intended effect.* Like flattery, even if you know someone is using humor specifically to "butter you up," it still serves to change our impressions of the sender in a positive way, releases tension, and promotes collaboration. The good mood inspired by humor (as long as it steers clear of anything inappropriate, of course) can also open up team members to be more tolerant of others, more optimistic, more creative, and more accurate in subsequent discussions.[5]

   c. People are generally inspired by honesty. Leaders who explicitly and positively acknowledge the expected difficulties that lay ahead for a team, for instance, are more likely to have driven team members who enjoy the challenge of the task and rise to the occasion to work at it together.

d. People like the team more when they are able to contribute to it, but sometimes need to be invited and encouraged to do so. Leaders who announce to, and then regularly remind, their members that they were chosen specifically for the input they are able to provide create better atmospheres and better outcomes for their teams.[6]

GETTING STARTED: CRITICAL FIRST MOMENTS

The incredible importance of the first message sent between virtual team members has the potential to set the tone for the entire relationship (see Chapter 6 for more on this topic). Just as first impressions can have a lasting impact in face-to-face meetings, both the first communications and the first processes used in the virtual team can leave their mark on how people expect the rest of their time together to unfold. Therefore, during the team's early interactions, managing what happens and how it happens is one of the most important jobs of a manager.

Consider this example of expectation and tone setting in the classroom. In a particular type of class, student participation in the discussion is very important. It not only ensures that the time is spent in an engaged and lively way, it also greatly increases the actual learning that goes on. However, encouraging students to participate can sometimes be an uphill battle—many students, even at the graduate level, prefer the lazy way out in which they sit back passively and let the conversation or lecture wash over them, undoubtedly absorbing some elements and missing others in the process.

There are, of course, many ways to change the dynamic in the classroom. Many professors choose to add a "class participation grade" to the evaluation of students, and thus threaten/promise to recognize and both positively and negatively reinforce the behaviors that they want by exchanging them for grades. Some take the immediacy of the feedback one step further and keep a bag of candy at the podium: students offering good comments and insights get instantly rewarded with a piece of candy lobbed into their hands. Sleeping students beware—you might get pelted with a piece!

Both of these solutions provide a reason that's *external* to the work itself—they provide an incentive for participation that has nothing to do with the learning or the interaction. Instead, it's driven by the wish for the reward (which is either the grade, the candy itself, the honor of being singled out by the professor, or all of the above), independent of the value of participating. Psychologists warn that motivating people entirely with external rewards can be less effective than motivating based on true engagement with the task itself. Of course, there is certainly a time and a place for this rationale (how many people would still show up for work the next day without the promise of a paycheck, for instance?). While the issue of motivating people will be addressed in more detail later in Chapter 7, here the focus is on the related topic of *expectation setting*.

Other professors swear by a different procedure instead: get it right on the first day of class and the rest of the semester is easy. The process begins on the very first day with an easy brainstorming exercise, called a "softball question," in which the students are asked to respond to a simple question or idea about which they each could have something to say. For example, one professor often starts by asking students: "Think about a great class you have taken and a terrible one. Think about what made them different. Then, when you're ready, raise your hand and volunteer one reason why either a good class was good, or why a bad class was bad. I'll start two different lists here on the board and we'll discuss it all afterwards." One of the important features of this first question, besides being something that all students are likely to be able to speak about, is that the list is just for the sake of collecting experiences, not answering a question with a right or a wrong answer. In other words, there should be as little fear of evaluation or criticism as possible. Note that asking team members to reflect on their previous team experiences is a direct analogy, and a potentially useful first activity.

In some classes, students jump in instantly and start volunteering answers. In this case, it's easy and the tone of participation is set seamlessly. If there is silence in the room, there are two follow-up options. The first is harder than it sounds: do absolutely nothing, and just wait it out in silence. Let the quiet stretch for seconds upon seconds (which can feel like an eternity), and usually someone will break the silence and say something, even if it's just to crack a joke. If even one person jumps in and voices something, others are sure to follow. The first voice is the hardest one to find, and once the ice has been broken, others become eager to join. The norm then has been established: it is the class's job to provide input when asked, or nothing else will happen. Imagine a professor who, at this critical early juncture in the class, asks a question, waits a beat or two, and then jumps in and starts answering it himself out loud. What message has *that* professor sent? In this scenario, the message would be that all questions asked are rhetorical in nature, and participation is entirely voluntary and not expected or demanded.

The second option is only for dire circumstances when the class simply refuses to participate at all; no one brave soul will take the plunge and break the ice. As stated above, the worst thing the professor could do would be to gloss over the problem, move on, or state answers herself. Instead, these students might need a practice round before being put on the spot to volunteer answers to the whole class. In this case, the professor next announces the start of a "two-minute buzz," during which the students have two minutes to speak to the person sitting next to them regarding the question at hand. After two minutes, people are generally more willing to raise their hands and share something they have already spoken about with a peer. If not, it is easy, and perfectly reasonable, to call on someone to share what they have just discussed, since all have now rehearsed for this moment already. Another version of this is called a "write, pair, share," in which students first write their own thoughts down, then pair up with another classmate, and then share their ideas with each other.

You have an opportunity at the outset of a team's life together to set the tone for the kind of participation and communication that you expect. How do you get a real team, let alone one that's virtual to boot, started in conversing with each other? By immediately demonstrating and setting up the kind of communications you're after. One version of this, particularly for teams with cross-functional membership, is called a "voicing fragments" exercise.[7] In it, the team begins with a phone call (although this could be adapted to use a chat-function as well). On this call, team members are asked to voice their brief thoughts, phrases, concerns, and experiences as they relate to the upcoming team project. One team coordinator is asked to compile the spoken words into a list, which is later circulated to all members. Like the first-day-of-class activity above, this exercise asks people to share ideas and first impressions that should be easily formed for each person, and to do so in a context in which they will not be evaluated for what they offer.

Engaging in this activity has two purposes, one driven by content and the other by structure. In terms of content, the idea is to start getting team members to know where the others are coming from in terms of their thoughts on the project and its challenges, their previous experiences, and perhaps even some hint as to their ideas for how to proceed. The intention is to avoid a long, awkward, and probably boring discussion in which each person delivers a mini-speech to the group by trying to describe their thoughts on this in an organized fashion. As discussed more below, people don't tend to be that good at delivering (or listening to) these mini-speeches about themselves or their thoughts. On the other hand, through this activity, the team has a starting point; the members can review the captured list, address what they feel the challenges may be for the task, and suggest approaches to work most successfully.

Setting the tone for future group conversations is the main structural advantage of this activity. For one thing, it allows all members to hear each other's voices and ideas. Once people open up, they are more likely to do so again. A second (similar) meeting, later down the line, would be easy on everyone. Additionally, the exercise gives people an introduction to each other in a relevant way. People should be encouraged to follow up with each other to continue the conversation if thoughts from one person trigger ideas or responses in another. Unfortunately, the issue of ice-breaking is a big one. "Never spoken, never will speak" is a rule of thumb that is often accurate. Getting first conversations and contributions out of the way is an absolutely critical part of running a successful team.

TIP
First conversations set the tone for the interaction of the team. Make sure you schedule a discussion early on in which all people feel comfortable voicing their thoughts, such as through a "voicing fragments" exercise, or a frank discussion of the good and problematic areas of teamwork that members have experienced. This will pave the way for easier connections throughout the life of the project.

INTRODUCTIONS AND ICE-BREAKERS

A whole industry has sprung up to address the need that new team members have for getting to know each other and becoming more comfortable working together. There are books sold, consultants available, even a plethora of off-site training programs designed to help a team through these "ice-breakers" and, hopefully, help them to build the trust necessary to carry them through their work together. Depending on the particular circumstances, virtual teams may experience even greater difficulty getting through the getting-to-know-you stage, especially if the team members have not met in person before, or if they are not able to meet face to face often (or at all). Yet this obstacle certainly can be overcome, even without a tremendous influx of money and time (as it might cost to fly everyone to the same place to meet, for instance). As with many of the concepts for effective virtual team management, what the virtual team needs is not necessarily different from what a face-to-face team might, but it needs to be done with more explicit attention to the directions and the execution. What follows here is a description of how basic introductions can and should work to connect people in effective ways, by understanding and applying three basic rules of human behavior.

Rule #1: People hate, and are generally terrible at, public speaking. Of course, this cannot be universally true. But, based on having taught thousands of students (most of whom were already adult professionals seeking MBA degrees), the conclusion that the vast majority of people are indeed terrible at, and typically strongly dislike, formal speaking in front of a group of people is well founded. As an example, take the common practice of everyone in the room introducing themselves before a meeting or a class begins. This seems like a reasonable and a useful way to start, right? Next time you find yourself asked to do just this, however, pay close attention to both your own reactions and those of others while the activity is going on. Here's what tends to happen: Person #1 begins to speak, saying something like, "My name is Josh Baker, I'm in QA for XYZ Pharmaceuticals, I have a background in engineering, and I'm looking forward to learning about ABC." During this mini-speech, the other people in the room are trying to simultaneously think about three different things (and you already know, from the discussion in Chapter 3, how problematic it is to assume that they can actually successfully think about multiple things at once):

- First and foremost (and taking up the most brain space), they are trying to psych themselves up for when it is their turn in the spotlight. In fact, as the speaker position moves closer and closer to each individual person, the adrenaline of that person spikes and any attention paid to what the current speaker is saying is greatly diminished, if not totally lost. Extroverts get excited, introverts get nervous, but all are experiencing a rush of emotions which are not conducive to effective listening.
- Second, they listen to what Josh Baker is saying, but mostly to think about *how it relates to what they themselves want to say*. In other words, they might be thinking something along the lines of, "Oh, name, job, what I want to learn, that's the protocol. OK, I know my name and job, as for what I want to learn . . . let's see . . . I guess I could just say the same thing that he said . . . or should I try to come up with something more unique . . . ?"
- Third relates to listening to others *after* one has spoken already. If all of the stress and divided attention is due to the need to prepare for one's own turn to speak, then it stands to reason that listening should be easier and more fruitful after this point. This is somewhat true, but not as much as you might imagine. After speaking, the body is still

"high" from the adrenaline rush of having spoken out loud in front of people. The mind is reviewing the performance, while also listening to the next speakers; the words often tumble over the busy mind and wash away.

Add to this the problem that many people speak too softly, or perhaps with an accent that is difficult to understand at first, and we get the final answer. Shockingly little information gets retained by anyone in this type of activity or introduction. To hammer one final nail into this coffin, people are actually quite poor at describing themselves in any useful way. Think of people writing their personal introductions for a dating website (take a look at one at random if you've never seen any, to see if you agree!): they tend to be either boring or come across as if they are trying too hard, and they rarely accurately represent the person in either case. In short, self-introductions generally just don't work.

People do a *much* better job introducing someone else they know as opposed to introducing themselves. This removes the need to carefully step around the issues of bragging, for example. One can easily say: "This is Eleanor. She's an absolute whiz at making models predicting the economic impact of our decisions, and she's reliable and easy to approach." Those are all terrific things to know about a new teammate, but they are unlikely to arise out of a self-introduction. However, when the entire team is new to each other, as so often happens, this process is not as easy, but it is not impossible even then. For example, having teammates interview each other, even in front of the rest of the team, is one way around this obstacle. See below for more on this idea.

Solution #1: Pair off as early and as often as possible for more intimate, and less stressful, connections. Especially in relatively small groups, it is well worth the time to first have pairs of people connect directly, one on one. It will be much easier to build these solid pairs into a larger interaction later than it would be to do the reverse (which is to try and get the whole team to connect and then later expect each pair to automatically feel comfortable with each other). The difference should be notable. How people talk when they are interacting with just one other person is an entirely different experience from how they talk to more than one person.

Rule #2: People feel silly being asked to do silly things. A common theme among options for ice-breaker activities is asking people to do things that take them outside of their comfort zone, or to talk about things they wouldn't ordinarily bring up, in order to create a bonding moment with the other people present. For example, you might be asked to "tell everyone something that nobody in the group already knows about you" or "describe the best day of your life." While these might create memorable answers, we still have the two-fold problem of (1) people spending most of their time worrying about what they themselves will say, and (2) people getting information about each other that's not likely to advance their professional connection to each other. There are more relevant ways to get people introduced and ultimately create that shortcut to having people feel close to each other.

Solution #2: Stay task-focused, even with ice-breakers. Building connections among team members has two overarching goals, both of which relate to creating effective pathways for teammates to work together and to helping one another in productive ways: (1) make sure each member knows what the skill sets are of the other members, so that they know where to turn when they need help, and (2) build enough trust so that members feel comfortable approaching each other for assistance or collaboration when needed. Instead of asking out-of-the-box questions about each other, then, consider staying in the box and having team members interview each other for more task-helpful information. Example questions include:

- Aside from what I could learn on your résumé, what made you decide to follow this career path, including any random (i.e., non-professional) events or people who may have influenced you?
- What problem are you currently working on? What is the most challenging thing about it?
- What does a typical day at the office look like for you, start to finish?
- When you're stuck on something, what do you do and/or who do you approach?

This kind of information gets right at the heart of how these people work and will help them to connect going forward in relevant ways.

Rule #3: People generally spend more time trying to be liked than trying to like someone else. This is ironic, because the thing that makes people like you the most is the feeling that you really like them. This problem is related to the one described above whereby people spend more time mentally rehearsing for their own turn to talk than they do listening to the other person speaking. Most of us are charmed by someone who is extroverted and charismatic, and many people try to emulate these traits when interacting with others. But unfortunately, spending time enacting these exact traits actively *interferes* with good listening. So ultimately this is only a short-term fix for the problem of connecting with others.

Solution #3: Search for similarities. Connections don't come from being admired, but they can come from having something in common with the other person. Teach all the team members to actively search for ways that they are similar to each other when they are in the "getting to know you" phase.

Spending time early on in a team's life developing trust will pay rewards in lots of very intuitive ways. One additional benefit to this trust-building process may not be as obvious, yet it relates to the reaction people have to the discussion of rules and procedures. An interesting study had pairs of people engage in a problem-solving task (a type of negotiation, but one in which parties could work together to earn a more valuable solution for both) entirely using e-mail. Some pairs were given the opportunity to spend the first few e-mail exchanges getting to know each other, some pairs were told to use these first exchanges to develop rules to guide their subsequent inter-actions, and some were told to do both. Interestingly, those who developed rules and procedures with each other *without* also spending time develop-ing rapport ended up trusting each other *less* than did any other type of pair. Rules and procedures can certainly help guide a smooth process, but given without a context of goodwill toward the others on the team, it seems that they could also be interpreted as signaling a lack of trust.[8]

TIP

Group introductions can be challenging. To make this process easier, first break the group into pairs and let them interview each other to determine points of similarity (do several rounds if possible to expose people to multiple teammates). The trust that is built during this initial time will help pave the way for success.

BUILDING CONNECTIONS: DEVELOPING AND USING YOUR INTERNAL AND EXTERNAL NETWORKS

Virtual teams are created to allow for access to a diverse set of expertise. In addition to unique skill sets, bringing together people from different locations also expands each team member's network of contacts through their own connections. For instance, imagine a team of seven people all drawn from a single location of 50 employees. In all likelihood, all seven team members will each know most (if not all) of the other 43 employees in the larger group. If needed, any one of the members might volunteer to approach one of these external (to the team) colleagues for information, input, or advice. In the networks literature, these are what are known as *redundant ties*, because the connection to any one external individual can be made by multiple internal team members.

However, imagine now that the seven team members in this focal team reside in seven different locations, each of which has about 50 employees. In this case, should the need for external expertise arise, each member will probably have a much larger pool of *non-redundant ties* to draw from. In other words, each person has access to more unique individuals. In order to capitalize on this advantage, members of virtual teams need to be especially adept at creating and maintaining their professional networks both within and outside of their immediate job. And while this idea feels intuitive to many, the actual science behind managing your network connections may not be as obvious as it seems. The rest of this section is devoted to understanding the ins and outs of how networks work, and how they can best serve you, to help both your virtual team and your career.

Based on formal organizational charts, everyone knows who is supposed to be in contact with whom. Reality, though, often looks quite different as the informal network connects people in sometimes very different ways. This is not necessarily a problem, but it is worth knowing what kinds of networks work the best for helping to promote access to the most useful information. Early research on networks identified that there may be entirely different people whom you would approach based on what it is you wanted to know or discuss. Friendship networks, trust networks, and advice networks have all been shown to be distinct from each other. This probably rings true for you as well, as the people whom you consider your friends at work might not be the same ones you would go to for career counseling advice, for example.

Part of what a network analysis does is figure out where the "bridges" are between various networks.[9] In other words, do you know two people who don't also know each other? Of course you do. Now imagine that your first colleague has some information that the second colleague has been looking for, and you are the only one who might be in a position to connect the two of them. Should you do that? Some say no. By keeping them apart, you maintain a position of power whereby they both need you to find out new information. While this does have some logic to it, newer studies maintain that those who go out of their way to make these kinds of connections help the entire group to innovate.[10] As one connection blossoms into others, the resulting knowledge flow can help everyone.

One of the most interesting things to come out of the networks research is the idea of "the strength of weak ties," which means that having a broad network of people whom you don't know very well (friends of friends, for instance), can actually provide you with access to better information than can those in your close networks.[11] This makes sense—if you're looking to find out about new job openings, for instance, you may instead already know about the things that your close friends and colleagues know about, but someone tapped into an entirely different network can let you know about opportunities you wouldn't otherwise have heard about.

Some people spend lots of time actively trying to build their external networks with strangers. Others spend lots of time trying to maintain ties with people whom they've met or used to work with but don't see regularly. Both can be useful pursuits; however, both also take an awful lot of time and energy. Good news surfaced from some recent research in this area, though, that can lessen the burden of that task. Researchers set out to find out about what they called *dormant* ties, or those that have "gone quiet" for quite some time.[12] They asked executives to contact two people with whom they used to work (one close, one more distant) who might be able to help with a current work problem. What they found is that trust fades little, if at all, across the years. Even someone whom you haven't spoken to for ages (decades even!) is likely to (a) remember you, (b) be happy to hear from you if you should choose to reconnect, and (c) be willing to help you, if possible, with information, with expertise, or with introductions to others. In fact, the study participants were generally shocked at how efficient it was to reconnect with people, as opposed to trying to build brand-new ties. Remember, the thing that connects people together the most readily and the most strongly is similarity, and by nature of the fact that you and this person have a shared past of some sort, you are likely to feel similar to each other, at least in this one regard. In fact, this research found that on average, the reconnected ties helped people *more* with their current work problems than did their current colleagues. This may be due to the fact that someone not already closely connected to the work may have an unexpected approach or insight. Finally, these researchers found that the pool of dormant ties was surprisingly deep. Even when asked to list and contact 10 people with whom they had lost touch, the tenth was as useful, on average, as the first. Given all of the drawbacks discussed so far about the electronic age we live in, this is one of the advantages. It's easier than ever to find contact information for old connections, and it's not nearly as daunting to drop someone an "out of the blue" e-mail as it would be to call or arrange a visit.

> **TIP**
> Don't hesitate to reach out to people you used to know. They can be very useful to you and you to them.

The last piece of the network puzzle is reciprocity (as introduced in Chapter 2), or the incredibly strong instinct people have to help out others who have helped them in the past. What's even better is that reciprocity does not need to work in directly equal quantities—in other words, someone else is likely to say yes to a big request from you, even if you have only helped this person with something small in the past. In part, because of this, some suggest that the way to think about building and maintaining your networks is by valuing them as an opportunity to help others, not as a chance to get help yourself. Being helped yourself (when you need it) will come naturally as a by-product of having helped others in the past and built trust with them (by connecting them to information or ideas, to other people, or by offering personal support). In fact, the psychological need to repay others who have helped us or gifted us in the past is so strong that people will actively *seek out* opportunities to help you in return.

"Networking" is sometimes used as a verb, but when used this way, it can lead to some incorrect assumptions. Sometimes called the "coin-operated network" approach,[13] this vision implies that one should be able to enter a room full of strangers, spend 15 minutes getting to know someone new, and then expect a direct return on that time, perhaps by way of making a sale or by following up with a request for help. This is the wrong assumption and doesn't take advantage of how powerful networks can be. Looking for the direct bottom line, or thinking of it in terms of a one-for-one exchange, can work in the short term. But this approach may also "use up" the power of the new relationship in mere minutes instead of creating ties that can help you across your entire career.

Quotes from the front lines: "I was a consultant for a short time early in my career. I clearly remember a colleague I met at my first job in that industry. After I moved on from the job where we briefly worked together, for a while he would call me faithfully every six months, just to 'check in' and say hello. It was so transparent that he had been schooled in the art of networking and went through his Rolodex twice a year to maintain this tie in case I might be useful to him someday. It was really off-putting."

Instead, and perhaps ironically, reciprocity works best when you don't try for it, but just know in the big-picture sense that having a personal policy to help others as often as possible can and will result in more valuable and useful connections for you than will any other approach.

TIP

Try to freely help others, without regard for what they might do for you. You will be repaid with a solid and generous network of ties throughout your career. The question "How can I help you?" can be the most important one you ask.

And how do you help people? Often people assume that they know what others want and need, when in truth, all relationships, even the closest ones, contain a cognitive gap whereby you probably don't know other people as well as you think you do. Starting from this assumption can help you engage in conversation, and active listening, with the sole purpose of understanding what the other person is trying to say. Nevertheless, stripped of body language and eye contact, this process is much more difficult when you are virtual, and may well require more back-and-forth exchanges to make sure true clarity is reached. Similarly, investing in others takes different forms when you are not face to face and cannot so easily share a "human moment" with each other. You can certainly do more than nothing, though. For instance, forwarding a relevant article to a colleague with a note along the lines of "I thought this might interest you—hope you find it useful" maintains the idea that you have that person's interests on your mind. Some even find it easier to connect in the online environment—and online dating is a testament to this idea as well!

Quotes from the front lines: "I may be in the minority on this, but I actually think that electronic communication makes me feel closer to my colleagues. We can be in touch at all times (if we want), and it actually promotes the conversion of professional relationships into friendships. If I notice something on a weekend that I think may interest a colleague, I'll e-mail or text it to her, and that opens up new avenues in our relationship. If I run an evening meeting that goes poorly, I can text my colleagues and bosses for immediate moral support (as my colleagues have texted or called me after tough meetings). I try to be sensitive with after-hours communications—as I expect others to be sensitive to me—but I think my colleagues and I (most of them) have a pretty good sense of our boundaries and what works for each of us."

SUMMARY

Teams need very concrete definitions of who they are, what they need to do, and what support they will have to do it. Getting team members comfortable with each other and having meetings run smoothly takes an active hand in the first few encounters. Tone and norms, set in the very first interaction, can pervade the rest of the team's work together. Start with relevant questions but ones easy enough that all members can respond. Also allow people to get to know each other in pairs instead of assuming they will approach each other later as the need arises. Make sure all team members know that good networking skills are built around freely *giving* help away to others.

NOTES

1. Hackman, J. R., Wageman, R., Nunes, D. A., & Burruss, J. A. (2008). *Senior leadership teams: What it takes to make them great.* Cambridge, MA: Harvard Business School Press.

2. Katzenbach, J. R. & Smith, D. K. (2005). The discipline of teams (HBR Classic). *Harvard Business Review,* July–August, 1–11.

3. Hackman, J. R. & Coutu, D. (2009). The HBR interview: Why teams don't work. *Harvard Business Review,* May, 2–9.

4. Druskat, V. U. & Wolff, S. B. (2001). Building the emotional intelligence of groups. *Harvard Business Review,* March, 80–90.

5. Eisenhardt, K. M., Kahwajy, J. L., & Bourgeois III, L. J. (1997). How management teams can have a good fight. *Harvard Business Review,* July–August, 2–10.

6. Edmonson, A., Bohmer, R., & Pisano, G. (2001). Speeding up team learning. *Harvard Business Review,* October, 5–11.

7. Majchrzak, A., More, P. H. B., & Faraj, S. (2012). Transcending knowledge differences in cross-functional teams. *Organization Science, 23(4),* 951–970.

8. Paulsen, G. D. & Naquin, C. E. (2004). Establishing trust via technology: Long distance practices and pitfalls. *International Negotiation, 9,* 229–244.

9. Burt, R. S. (1992) *Structural holes: The social structure of competition.* Cambridge, MA: Harvard University Press.

10. Obstfeld, D. (2005). Social networks, the tertius iungens orientation, and involvement in innovation. *Administrative Science Quarterly, 50,* 100–130.

11. Granovetter, M. S. (1973). The strength of weak ties. *American Journal of Sociology, 78(6),* 1360–1380.

12. Levin, D. Z., Walter, J., & Murnighan, J. K. (2011). The power of reconnection: How dormant ties can surprise you. *MIT Sloan Management Review, 52(3),* 44–50.

13. Baker, W. (2000). *Achieving success through social capital.* New York, NY: Jossey-Bass.

SIX
Building Trust
and Cooperation Online

THE TIMING OF TRUST

What does it mean to trust someone? According to experts in this area, to truly trust another person, you must be able to answer "yes" to all three of the following questions:[1]

1. Will this person make a good faith effort to uphold any commitment made?
2. Is this person honest?
3. Can I feel sure that this person will not take advantage of me, even if the situation presented itself?

Building trust in virtual teams is the brass ring—elusive but a high predictor of overall success on a number of dimensions. Teams with higher trust do better at joint goal-setting, are better at allocating and rotating power among the group members (depending on the project stage and the level of expertise of each person), and more readily share information with each other.[2] When virtual teams first arose, some people thought that "trust needs touch" and that it would be nearly impossible to ever trust someone without face-to-face interaction.[3] There was even good science behind this idea. In one study, face-to-face team members judged their fellow teammates as more competent, reliable, trustful, and dependable than did those who worked in a dispersed setting via electronic means.[4] While it may be true that trust develops more easily in face-to-face encounters, it is clearly not a deal-breaker. So the question becomes, what does it take to build trust in virtual teams?

Research on this question shows us that there are several key elements to team trust-building. The first is the most intuitive, relating to team size. The smaller the team, generally speaking, the easier it is to form trust in, to communicate with, and to cooperate with the other members. On the other hand, large teams are overwhelming, both logistically and psychologically, for their members. So the first and most simple rule of thumb is to keep the team as small as possible for the best chance at team cohesion.[5] The more complicated drivers of trust can be reviewed in turn based on *when* they influence the team in terms of its lifespan. They are addressed below under the labels of the fast, middle, and slow routes to building trust.

The fast route, not surprisingly, refers to the things that happen right at the beginning of the team's life together. It seems that the implications of the first impression that team members make about each other can run quite deep. In a case study of newly formed virtual teams, it was shown that the first messages sent by team members set the tone for how the team interrelated long after the moment itself has passed. This mirrors observations of face-to-face teams, in which behaviors demonstrated as early as the first few seconds of a group's life have a tendency to persist far beyond that first meeting.[6] Indeed, in the first message, enthusiasm for both the project and the team nearly always set the team on a course toward trusting one another. Part of the reason for this is what's called the "swift trust" response, which means that in the absence of better information (that would build by getting to know people over time), early decisions about trust are extrapolated from whatever information you can get your hands on.[7] In face-to-face teams, it often means snap judgments based on how people look and sound.[8] In virtual teams, it means an over-reliance on the tone of those first few messages exchanged. Positive, can-do messages seem to be the key to early trust development.

TIP
First-ever messages have an outsized impact on others. Make sure this opportunity is used wisely to demonstrate your skill and enthusiasm for the project.

The middle route refers to the actual behaviors that the virtual team members engage in to inspire trust in each other. In other words, actions generate trust as confidence is built that the team can and will be able to perform well together. Some say that in the absence of having any physical interaction to draw from, trust within virtual teams is determined almost exclusively in terms of reliability. This can take the form of task reliability and communication reliability. In terms of task reliability, it can be of great use to have the team start early with simple tasks and interactions that give them a chance to develop this reliability-based form of trust. Once they see that they can count on input from the others, team members will be ahead of the game when the work becomes more complicated. Leaders can help by establishing clear definitions on task procedures and interactions, and by making sure that these kinds of early collaborations happen, even if the team members won't integrate their work until later down the line.

The second important element to reliability-based trust development is the reliability of communication patterns among members. Note that reliability is the key facet here, not frequency. It does not seem to be necessary to have everyone communicate with each other daily, for example, but it is absolutely necessary for team members to be able to count on the times when they do expect to hear from one another. In a very literal sense, team members need to be able to trust that they will remain connected for the duration of the project.

TIP

Not surprisingly, trustworthy behaviors build trust. If possible, start off with simple interactive tasks that allow team members to know they can count on each other.

Finally, there is the good old-fashioned slow route to building trust in teams based on the idea that teams should stay together as long as possible once they are formed. There are two complementary reasons why long-standing teams are better off than newly formed ones, and they both relate to members knowing each other better. For one thing, people who know each other well are more likely to feel socially comfortable with each other, and this in and of itself can build trust. Social engagement (that is, getting to know something about each other's lives outside of the work setting) can certainly inspire trust. While this can sometimes feel awkward at first, it can make the difference between having team members who seek out interaction with each other and those who avoid each other except when absolutely necessary. However, successful teams need to know how to balance this with the actual work content that needs their attention.[9]

Quotes from the front lines: *"Simply put, you are willing to call your friends for help, but not people who are just your 'associates.' When I feel like I've crossed the line into knowing someone as a person, I know I can ask for help without feeling like a burden."*

There are three kinds of knowledge that a team needs in order to function effectively:[10]

- Who knows what
- What needs to be done
- How to work together

People who know each other well also know what the other people know about (that is, what they are experts in) and thus, where to find certain types of knowledge. They also tend to have a sense of how to work together, giving them a leg up on two of these three types of knowledge.

All three types of knowledge increase over time within a team. In seminal work studying cockpit crews in airplanes, it was found that 73% of serious mistakes were made on the very first day that a new team flew together. Of those mistakes, 44% occurred on their very first flight together that day. Even when fatigued, cockpit flight teams with longer group histories made fewer mistakes than did well-rested newer teams.[11] The very same expertly trained pilots were thus performing their own work very differently depending on how well they knew the others on their team.

Why would this be? The answer relates primarily to what's known as *tacit knowledge*, which means the things people know how to do without necessarily being able to explain it in words. For example, if we asked a hobby-level tennis player to describe the way that he knows how to hit the ball to one side of the court or the other when returning a shot, it might be difficult for him to do. Indeed, he might have to go out on the court and hit the shot, while trying to pay conscious attention to the angles at which he turns his body, feet, shoulder, and racket before he could describe the process in words to someone else. This indicates that he is using tacit knowledge—things he knows how to do by rote—to accomplish this process.

Teams have a similar effect, and they learn *together* over time. In addition to feeling more comfortable with each other over time, teams also come to rely on each other for specific skills and jobs without necessarily intending to divide work in such clear ways. Just as married couples learn, over the years, to finish each other's sentences and count on each other to take on certain tasks in their daily lives, so teammates learn to lean on each other. Tacit knowledge may build more slowly in virtual teams, since members have the added constraint of not being able to observe each other at work. The information they learn about each other must be transmitted in much more explicit forms to be communicated and understood by others.[12]

Quotes from the front lines: *"In my experience, a team that's working well together can easily survive the added complication of communicating electronically. What being virtual does is show the cracks—if you don't understand and trust each other and have systems in place for effectively handing off work, trying to work together over e-mail will be a total disaster."*

To get a jump start on the type of team connections that create the benefits seen by long-standing teams, one option is to have teams train together to practice their tasks if possible. Research shows that teams that train together perform better afterwards. This phenomenon is attributed to a *transactive memory* system, which means that teammates learn, from the get-go, what they can count on someone else to remember and what they should focus their own attention on. In this way, they have access to more and better knowledge than they would have on their own. In addition, they have less trouble coordinating their actions, and count on the information that they get from each other as more credible than from other sources.[13]

Recently, cognitive psychologists have observed that having access to near-limitless information through search engines has caused individual people to remember *less* about the world.[14] To be more specific, these researchers found that if people knew that the information they were being taught was contained in a search engine (and thus easily accessed through that means at a later point), they were less likely to recall it later. Instead, they were more likely to think of a computer when asked to provide the information. The Internet seems to be acting as a giant external hard drive for our brains. While this seems like it could be problematic, in truth it is evidence of the same type of effect. As people come to rely on someone (or in this case, something) else to provide certain pieces of information, they are released from the burden of holding on to such knowledge personally, just as you allow yourself to forget phone numbers that are stored on your phone (when a few decades ago, most people could probably have recited dozens of phone numbers at will). Team members who have trained together have an easier time relying on each other to store information or possess skills, and thus tend to trust each other more.

To demonstrate this effect in teams specifically, one study had participants trained either individually or in groups of three to assemble a transistor radio. The individually trained participants were then assembled into newly formed groups. Afterwards, groups were tested on their ability to recall the instructions and then actually assemble the radios. Groups that had trained together outperformed those that were trained individually, both in the memory test and in the quality of the production function.[15]

TIP

The efficiencies gained by having teams together for longer periods of time are significant. From training onwards, the more time teams spend together, the fewer errors they make and the more efficient (and higher quality) their work becomes. Lesson learned: keep teams together for the long haul.

So while building transactive memory systems is a worthy goal, it may not always be practical to have teams present for common training sessions. Indeed, oftentimes, far-flung virtual teams are created specifically to take advantage of a breadth of expertise that has already been learned by the team members. Fortunately, some research on this exact topic has discovered that to a decent degree, transactive memory can be artificially created by distributing lists of who is good at what. This may include evaluations of the member's levels of performance (for instance, Person A is *proficient* in these two areas, and *expert* in this one), or can be a more generalized list of experiences and expertise.[16] This is a delicate task for a virtual team leader. It is critical to find the right level of detail to provide on each teammate. Too little and the information may read like a boring list of buzzwords or topic headings; too much and you may lose the attention of the readers.

TIP

Interview each team member at the beginning of the project and create and distribute a chart identifying the expertise of each. Pay attention to finding the right level of detail. Provide examples if possible, and stay away from just listing topic areas.

CULTURES OF TRUST

The general culture of the team is something else that can trigger a sense of trust (or distrust). Organizational scholars have identified four basic types of cultures that exist: the clan, the entrepreneurial, the bureaucratic, and the market.[17] Trust develops differently in each of the four types.

1. Bureaucratic culture is one in which the hierarchy is strictly enforced and team members typically have very little say in what they do or how they do it. Overall, trust may be lower in these teams, in no small part because individuals may feel that they are not trusted enough to take responsibility for their own work. But, there is some trust that can potentially be generated in the sense that members can count on their managers (and the entire system) to provide reliable direction and oversee the details of the project.

2. Market culture values and rewards the achievement of specific goals. Managers tend to shoulder the responsibility for establishing the goals, but team members generally have the freedom to set the course for how they accomplish them. Competition (sometimes friendly and sometimes not) is common in these types of teams. The trust challenge here comes from the "winner takes all" mentality that can ensue when goal achievement is the only rewarded element. This can be adjusted, however, by recognizing and rewarding the ways that interaction among teammates helps the overall goal process.

3. Entrepreneurial cultures are the ones in which group members are given the most freedom, and risk-taking tends to be the most acceptable. Some people thrive in this kind of environment, while others do not. Trust can suffer in this type of team if people find themselves at a loss for what to do. However, as long as people are inspired by their work and their own sense of how to accomplish it (both alone and collectively), trust can exist.

4. Clan culture is the one in which the team is thought of as a family. Relationships between the members are highly valued, and long-term commitment and traditions within the group are respected. These groups go out of their way to make sure that trust is one of the fundamental elements of the group.

In managing your own team (or even in being a team member), some features of the group's culture may be outside of your control, but some may be open to your influence. Especially in the virtual environment, the signals you send, the types of interactions you initiate and facilitate, and the expectations that you have for the team can all slant the team's experience toward one or another of these categories. In reality, the type of culture that is optimal may be a combination of the ones listed above. As mentioned, however, the initial meetings and conversations among the members can have a very long-lasting effect on how the team interacts for the duration of its time together. Give some forethought to the type of culture that best suits both your style and the work that needs to be accomplished. Then, think about what is needed to encourage trust within that model, and describe this out loud to the people on the team. Especially in the virtual environment, people are actively looking for clues about what's expected of them and what tone and behaviors are appropriate. Do your best to both tell them and show them—it will make them feel more comfortable with you and with the team. It will also help generate trust.

> **TIP**
> Think about what kind of team culture best matches your own style and the work that needs to be done. Explicitly explain this culture to your team members at the outset of your group's work.

In Chapter 4, the use of avatars (graphical representations of the self on a computer screen) was mentioned. Avatars seem to have an impressive impact on how people think of themselves and others. For example, in a research study, participants assigned to more attractive avatars tended to be friendlier with others and engage in more self-disclosure, while participants assigned to taller avatars behaved more confidently.[18] Avatars have also been identified as a potential trust-builder, because interacting in this way increases what psychologists call *social presence*. This refers to the degree to which people feel connected to the others with whom they are communicating.[19] Face-to-face conversations naturally have the highest degree of social presence, and text-only communications tend to have the least. Interestingly, avatars seem to amplify social presence (even more than seeing someone's actual face on a screen in a video conference) even though the representation is not of the actual self. Though they are not commonly used for virtual meetings at this point in time, there may well be an increase in the use of this type of tool to facilitate trust-building as the technology develops.

THE BLAME GAME

In the introduction to this book, the idea of social loafing was introduced, which is the tendency for people who work on teams to exert less effort than they would if they were working alone. This is due in part to the sense that others will "pick up the slack" in the work, reducing the need for them to work as hard as possible. This problem is exacerbated in larger teams, as members feel that their unique contributions are both less identifiable and less important to the finished product. Teams with dispersed members are even more likely to see less-than-stellar efforts made by its members.

To add to the troubling nature of large and dispersed teams, not only do some individuals tend to work less hard themselves, they also *blame each other* more readily for the failures that the team encounters. This is thought to be due primarily to the fact that when a team is small and physically present with each other, the whole team is thought of as one unit, and as an extension of the self for each team member. Thus, shortcomings are absorbed as part of the whole team's failures, not any one individual. However, when individuals are parts of large dispersed teams, the self re-emerges as the primary unit of consideration instead of the whole team. When problems arise, they can be more easily thought of as someone else's fault. As mentioned before, people tend to feel less of a human connection to those whom they can't see, thus allowing them to blame each other more easily.[20]

CONFLICT AND SHATTERED TRUST

Thus far this chapter has primarily described the ways that trust can form over time. The next question deals with what happens if something specific has broken the trust between team members. Unfortunately, trust is much more easily broken than built. For example, years of honest business dealings with an individual or company can be lost in a moment if you discover that they had tried to cheat you even once. Deception of any kind, it turns out, is the strongest trust destroyer out there. Of course, while major acts such as deception and cheating are possible on a professional work team, much more likely are the run-of-the-mill reasons for trust to be called into question: ineffective collaboration, shirking responsibilities, or over-claiming credit for accomplishments. Virtual teams may be particularly susceptible to these types of breaches, since the absence of the general good will that comes with having a face-to-face relationship may lead people to jump more quickly to sinister conclusions.

Repairing trust is a slow road and comes generally through repeated trustworthy acts, but there are some more explicit ways that you can try to help with the process. One set of ideas involves a 10-step process.[21] Imagine that you are managing a team in which one member has violated the trust of another, and you are attempting to help them repair the damage. This list may offer some guidance on how to approach the job of repairing the breach.

1. Make sure the two people make personal contact and have a one-on-one discussion free from interruptions (or a one-on-one discussion with you additionally included as a guide).
2. Have the parties re-emphasize the value of the relationship and the commitment each party has to the ultimate goal.
3. Let the wronged party vent. People get a tremendous amount of closure from being able to say things and feel heard.
4. Make sure that apologies are offered when appropriate, once all the issues have been put on the table. Apologies mean a lot to people, and research shows that apologies given at this stage (that is, once the wronged party has made clear what the actual offense consisted of) are much more effective than ones that are given too early in the conversation.[22] Apologies can range from full acceptance of blame ("I'm sorry that I did the wrong thing; I made a mistake") to acknowledgement of the actions ("I'm sorry that I didn't consult you") to simply acknowledgement of the difficulty faced by all parties involved ("I'm sorry that this has gotten so out of hand" or "I'm sorry that this happened"). Given this range of options, most people can find an apology that they feel they can give in full sincerity.
5. Have both parties state their original intentions and the motivations that drove their behaviors.
6. Ask for clarifying information from both parties.
7. Have each party re-state the position of the other side, to make sure that both recognize that the other understands their point of view and can empathize with why they felt/reacted the way they did.
8. Formulate a plan for moving forward. What can each party do to make this right?
9. Articulate ways to prevent this from happening again.
10. At the close of this meeting, plan an interaction for the near future to check in with the parties. This not only allows for a check-up on the relationship, but reminds them that they are still interacting team members.

MANAGING TEAM CONFLICT

Unfortunately for virtual teams, conflict may escalate more quickly when communication happens over e-mail than when the team members are able to meet in person.[23] This is thought to be due to a number of factors relating to the particulars of e-mail exchanges. For one, e-mail often strips away non-essential exchanges of pleasantries. Without these moments of chit-chat or greetings in their relationships, people may lose the buffer that comes with giving the other side the benefit of the doubt. Combined with the lack of quick back-and-forth exchanges as found in real-time conversations, misunderstandings (including comments perceived as overly negative in tone) can go uncorrected and can spiral into larger issues and conflicts. It doesn't take very much for one person to assume that the other is speaking harshly, and to respond in kind. In fact, it can take a lot of conscious thought to avoid these negative reactions. Finally, e-mail affords the opportunity to sit and re-read and re-write long e-mails alone, which can serve to further entrench people in their own point of view, without the chance for the other side to influence their opinions.

Quotes from the front lines: *"In my experience, conflict definitely happens differently in virtual interactions. Over e-mail, disagreement makes some people just keep saying (sending) the same thing over and over again, and completely ignoring the other people's input. Other people just keep cc-ing extra people on the exchange until someone agrees with them. On the phone, conflict can be seen when people who normally speak up just go silent instead. In all these cases, the conflict tends to be really indirect. In face-to-face meetings, conflict tends to be much more interactive."*

Not all conflict in teams is the same, however, and not all conflict in teams is automatically bad. When conflict does arise in teams, it tends to focus on one of three distinct areas, known as *task conflict, process conflict*, and *relationship conflict*.[24] Task conflict is based on diverging views about what should be done in the team. Process conflict centers on disagreements on *how* work should be accomplished. Relationship conflict is just what it sounds like—interpersonal strife.

The usefulness in separating conflict into these three types comes from understanding the different effects that each type can have. In moderate amounts and in settings where the tasks are complex and non-routine, task conflict can sometimes actually *help* a team.[25] Picture a team actively engaged in debate about aspects of its work, versus a team that just accepts the first idea on the table. Having differences of opinion can help all team members to stretch their thinking and more rigorously evaluate all of the ideas on the table. Process conflict, on the other hand, can be deadly for teams. People confused in any way about what they are supposed to be doing, or who is supposed to be doing what, often just resort to doing nothing at all until the conflict is resolved. Finally, and not surprisingly, relationship conflict is quite detrimental for teams as well. Open hostility does not encourage anyone to work up to his or her highest potential.

TIP

People need to know *exactly* what's expected of them. Ambiguity stops virtual teams dead in their tracks, as can anger and hostilities. However, civil disagreement on work topics can promote better thinking all around.

This typology is a good place to get started, but real conflict in real work teams does not stay put neatly in separate columns. Instead, one kind of conflict can easily bleed into others. For example, people who just don't like each other often find themselves choosing opposite sides of a task debate, whether consciously or not. This is an example of relationship conflict crossing over into task conflict. And the reverse can be true as well, with task conflict bleeding into relationship issues. Thus, even though it was noted that task conflict can be good for teams in certain settings, there is a clear threshold effect whereby too much task conflict can cause negative outcomes for the team (instead of positive ones). Why? At some point, even a healthy debate starts to get taken personally, and people will start to feel attacked and defensive. Before long the discussion has taken on an emotional weight, and no one is happy. Nobody enjoys working with people they don't like, and many people tend to disengage from the hard work required of the team when they find themselves in this situation.

TIP

Keep this guiding principle in mind when overseeing discussions among the group members: Healthy debate is useful and important, but it can easily spill over into personal-feeling attacks. Step in to keep conversations focused.

Another school of thought divides strategies for dealing with conflict into five categories: avoidance, accommodation, competition, collaboration, and compromise.[26] Selecting among the strategies may naturally give more weight to either protecting the relationship or pushing for a particular decision.

- **Avoidance:** Ignoring the conflict entirely and hoping it will just go away on its own

- **Accommodation:** Conceding to the other side simply to maintain harmony (often occurs when people value the relationship over the issue at hand)
- **Competition:** Placing your own needs above the other person's, and driving hard to get your own way
- **Collaboration:** Attempting to work with the other person to find some solution that fully satisfies the concerns of both people
- **Compromise:** Looking for an expedient solution that at least partially satisfies both sides, but typically wholly satisfies neither

These categories can be thought of as individual differences—that is, some people are just more comfortable using an avoidance strategy, while others are inclined toward collaboration as their first attempt. Most people tend to have one or two dominant responses, which they use in most situations, regardless of the problem at hand. Needless to say, it is much more effective to gauge the situation to determine the best response. All people *can* understand and even use the various approaches, and can work toward being flexible and choosing among the strategies in a case-by-case manner (overriding the natural tendencies towards accommodation, for example, when collaboration might be more effective). Different situations clearly call for different approaches, and savvy communicators know how to read the situation and know when to switch among the various approaches.

The traditional logic of conflict style effectiveness in teams says that collaboration and compromise are a group's best defenses in times of conflict. Accommodation and avoidance strategies may be detrimental to team decisions, as they prevent rigorous debate in decision processes. Additionally, competition can escalate conflict by having one party ignore the input of another. However, moving from traditional teams to virtual teams has changed the ways some strategies are interpreted. One set of researchers decided to ask two questions of conflict-handling strategies in virtual teams in particular:

1. What are the (potentially different) effects of each style of conflict handling in virtual teams?
2. Does anything change if the team has a set and rigorous process delineating exactly what they should do and when and how?[27]

Some elements of the research results mirror traditional wisdom. Avoidance was found to be detrimental, and collaboration was helpful. Others were in direct contrast. Compromising did *not* seem to help team outcomes in this setting, perhaps because in virtual work, compromising was accomplished by merely "cutting and pasting" to use some ideas from each member without working to fully integrate the ideas. Additionally and surprisingly, competing behavior actually seemed to *help*. This may be because while the sender is attempting to make a power play and drive decisions based on personal motives, in the text-only virtual realm, the receivers may only see, and may indeed welcome, the use of direct statements and increased participation. This does not mean that a competitive tone is universally recommended based on this one study, but it is yet one more bit of support for the idea that direct, effective communication is a key driver to success in the virtual team setting. Finally, accommodation did not have an effect either way on the teams studied. As for the pre-set rigorous process, it did seem to help particularly in one sense: the two strategies that worked *least* well (avoidance and compromise) were less severely problematic when the team used a prescribed method.

TIP

Conflict can be addressed in many ways, depending on whether protecting the relationship or successfully accomplishing the work at hand is prioritized. In the virtual setting, the best approaches seem to stem from direct focus on the problem at hand by either advocating for a particular solution (which in a face-to-face setting might be interpreted as competitive behavior but online can be a helpful approach) or by using a consensus-building collaborative focus.

SUB-GROUPS

Until now, the team has mostly been discussed as one complete unit, with one culture, and it has even been implied that the entire team would either feel trust or distrust universally. Of course, this is an oversimplification. Not only is the team made up of individual members each with unique experiences, insights, and reactions to each other, but oftentimes a group will break up into alliances along what are sometimes called "fault lines."[28] Fault lines are natural divisions within the team across perceived boundaries. For example, picture a face-to-face team with five men who are all engineers and two women who both come from marketing. It would not be a tremendous surprise to find out that the two women speak with each other more often outside of the team meetings, feel more comfortable with each other, and perhaps even end up in an alliance of sorts on the work content itself. Multiple overlapping similarities (such as in the example above with the gender and the department variables combining) make fault lines all the more stable.

In the literature on diversity, characteristics are divided into those that are visible and those that are invisible. Race, gender, nationality, and age are examples of the visible types—readily apparent upon a first meeting. Invisible types might be things such as educational level, department or area of expertise, or even risk-taking propensity. Regardless of its source, people feel more comfortable with others who seem similar to them, even in terms of superficial variables such as style of dress.

In the virtual team, sub-groups can be a tremendous problem. Given the more ambiguous interactions coupled with the desire to feel connected to some of the team members, fault lines are not only possible but probable in this environment. Somewhat ironically, in a virtual team where distance is not supposed to matter at all, one of the most common types of fault lines is based on geography—three team members in America and four in India, for instance, or even two in the New York office and three in Chicago. Who you are sitting nearest, literally, is the most natural cue for who you will likely feel is your ally. Of course, though this division is the one that virtual team members bring up again and again, it is by no means the only variable on which members can divide themselves.

People have a strong natural tendency to create "us versus them" distinctions, even within a team. This can happen almost instantly. It is a predictable problem, and one that can have severe consequences. Research shows that teams with fault lines can have more conflict and less trust. In fact, the tendency towards sub-groups is so strong that one study found that teams that were *entirely* mixed on the dimension of nationality performed better than those that were only *somewhat* mixed, because the formation and strength of sub-groups was so intractable in the groups with, say, only two types of team members in terms of nationality. On the other hand, groups where each person uniquely represented a country had no easy sub-group to retreat to, and so members were forced to find a common identity within the team itself. These groups seemed to perform as well as entirely homogeneous teams in this study.[29]

Yet it is worth noting that people often feel secure nestled in their sub-group, and this can help with the ever-present problem in virtual teams of people not feeling connected enough. The trick is to allow the formation of these sub-groups for the benefits they may provide without falling prey to the risk of real rifts between teammates.

> **Tip**
> Recognize that natural fault lines, especially based on geographic divisions, are likely to occur. Try to mitigate the effect by creating cross-boundary interactions between specific team members.

SUMMARY

Team members don't have to trust each other, but everything goes more smoothly if they do. Trust formation starts as early as the first message exchanged between virtual team members (and/or first face-to-face meeting), and continues through the observation of one another's reliability. Teams take quite some time to truly hit their stride, so longer-running teams tend to be more effective than newly formed teams. Trust is fragile, however, and is easily broken if the wrong kinds of conflict or other untrustworthy acts surface. Repairing trust is a slow but necessary process that needs to be addressed very explicitly. Finally, groups do not always act as a whole unit but instead can break into sub-groups that can increase trust within the sub-group and decrease trust across the dividing lines. In sum, trust needs to be noticed, cultivated, managed, and repaired when necessary for a virtual team to thrive.

NOTES

1. Cummings, L. L. & Bromily, P. (1996). The organizational trust inventory (OTI): Development and validation. In R. M. Kramer & T. R. Tyler (Eds.), *Trust in organizations: Frontiers of theory and research* (pp. 302–330). Thousand Oaks, CA: Sage Publications.

2. Panteli, N. & Tucker, R. (2009). Power and trust in global virtual teams. *Communications of the ACM, 52(12),* 113–115.

3. Handy, C. (1995). Trust in the virtual organization. *Harvard Business Review, 73(3)*, 40–50.

4. Burgoon, J. K., Bonito, J. A., Ramirez, A., Dunbar, N. E., Kam, K., & Fischer, J. (2002). Testing the interactivity principle: Effects of mediation, propinquity, and verbal and nonverbal modalities in interpersonal interaction. *Journal of Communication, 52(3)*, 657–677.

5. Sato, K. (1988). Trust and group size in a social dilemma. *Japanese Psychological Research, 30(2)*, 88–93.

6. Gersick, C. J. G. (1988). Time and transition in work teams: Toward a new model of group development. *Academy of Management Journal, 31(1)*, 9–41.

7. Meyerson, D., Weick, K. E., & Kramer, R. M. (1996). Swift trust and temporary groups. In R. M. Kramer & T. R. Tyler (Eds.), *Trust in organizations: Frontiers of theory and research* (pp. 166–195). Thousand Oaks, CA: Sage Publications.

8. Levin, D. Z., Whitener, E. M., & Cross, R. (2006). Perceived trustworthiness of knowledge sources: The moderating impact of relationship length. *Journal of Applied Psychology, 91(5)*, 1163–1171.

9. Jarpenvaa, S. L. & Leidner, D. E. (1999). Communication and trust in global virtual teams. *Organization Science, 10(6)*, 791–815.

10. Levine, J. M. & Moreland, R. L. (1991). Culture and socialization in work groups. In L. B. Resnick, J. M. Levine, & S. D. Teasdale (Eds.), *Perspectives on socially shared cognition* (pp. 257–279). Washington, DC: American Psychological Association.

11. Hackman, J. (2002). New rules for team building—The times are changing—And so are the guidelines for maximizing team performance. *Optimize,* July 1, 50.

12. Griffith, T. L., Sawyer, J. E., & Neale, M. A. (2003). Virtualness and knowledge in teams: Managing the love triangle of organizations, individuals, and information technology. *MIS Quarterly, 27(2)*, 265–287.

13. Moreland, R. L. (1999). Transactive memory: Learning who knows what in work groups and organizations. In L. Thompson, D. Messick, & J. Levine (Eds.), *Shared cognition in organizations: The management of knowledge* (pp. 3–31). Mahwah, NJ: Erlbaum.

14. Sparrow, B., Liu, J., & Wegner, D. M. (2011). Google effects on memory: Cognitive consequences of having information at our fingertips. ScienceXpress, July 14. http://www.sciencemag.org/content/333/6043/776.abstract.

15. Liang, D. W., Moreland, M., & Argote, L. (1995). Group versus individual training and group performance: The mediating role of transactive memory. *Personality and Social Psychology Bulletin 21(4)*, 384–393.

16. Moreland, R. L. & Myaskovsky, L. (2000). Explaining the performance benefits of group training: Transactive memory or improved communication? *Organizational Behavior and Human Decision Processes, 82(1)*, 117–133.

17. Hellriegel, D., Slocum, Jr., J. W., & Woodman, R. W. (2001). *Organizational behavior* (9th ed.). Mason, OH: South-Western College Publishing.

18. Yee, N. & Bailenson, J. (2007). The Proteus effect: The effect of transformed self-representation on behavior. *Human Communication Research, 33(3)*, 271–290.

19. Short, J., Williams, E., & Christie, B. (1976). *The social psychology of telecommunications.* London, UK: Wiley.

20. Alnuaimi, O. A., Robret, Jr., L. P., & Maruping, L. M. (2010). Team size, dispersion, and social loafing in technology-supported teams: A perspective on the theory of moral disengagement. *Journal of Management Information Systems, 27(1),* 203–230.

21. Adapted from Thompson, L. L. (2009). *The mind and heart of the negotiator* (4th ed.). Upper Saddle River, NJ: Pearson Higher Education, Inc.

22. Frantz, C. M. & Bennigson, C. (2005). Better late than early: The influence of timing on apology effectiveness. *Journal of Experimental Social Psychology, 41(2),* 201–207.

23. Friedman, R. A. & Currall, S. C. (2003). Conflict escalation: Dispute exacerbating elements of e-mail communication. *Human Relations, 56,* 1325–1347.

24. Jehn, K. A. (1997). A qualitative analysis of conflict types and dimensions in organizational groups. *Administrative Science Quarterly, 42,* 530–557.

25. Kurtzberg, T. R. & Mueller, J. S. (2005). The influence of daily conflict on perceptions of creativity: A longitudinal study. *International Journal of Conflict Management, 16,* 335–353.

26. Thomas, K. W. & Kilmann, R. H. (1974). *Thomas-Kilmann conflict mode instrument.* Tuxedo, NY: XICOM.

27. Montoya-Weiss, M. M., Massey, A. P., & Song, M. (2001). Getting it together: Temporal coordination and conflict management in global virtual teams. *Academy of Management Journal, 44(6),* 1251–1262.

28. Lau, D. C. & Murnighan, J. K. (2005). Interactions within groups and subgroups: The effects of demographic faultlines. *Academy of Management Journal, 48,* 645–659.

29. Earley, P. C. & Mosakowski, E. (2000). Creating hybrid team cultures: An empirical test of transnational team functioning. *Academy of Management Journal, 43,* 26–49.

SEVEN
Mastering Motivation

INSPIRING ACTION

Most managers struggle with how to effectively motivate the people who work for them. Managers of virtual teams face an even bigger challenge, since virtual work comes with more uncertainty, and in some cases more resistance, than work in a physically co-located environment. Simply put, virtual workers seem to give up more easily than do physically present employees when challenges are faced. Understanding the basic psychology of motivation, and learning from the lessons of many decades of research in this area, can help build insight into how to get people to want to do the things that need to be done. This section will start with a general overview of several theories of workplace motivation and then focus more specifically on how to use them in this setting.

Motivation is defined as a willingness to exert effort to accomplish work. When asked the question "What motivates people to do their jobs?" the first answer to arise is usually *money*. While it is true that money can motivate people to some degree and in some situations, the reality of what motivates people at work is actually much more complex. Think of all the people you know. Do the ones who are paid more uniformly work harder and better than those who are paid less? That's unlikely, so while it's true that very few people would continue to work in their present jobs if they were to win a mega-millions jackpot in a lottery, it is also true that money can't tell us the whole story behind what motivates people at work.

Instead of asking "What motivates you?" directly, it is more fruitful to change the question to "What makes a job a good one, as opposed to one you dislike?" Thinking back on their experiences, most people can now produce a much broader and richer list of answers. Typical responses include: interesting work, the opportunity to challenge oneself and learn new things, not being micro-managed, and the chance for growth and promotion. Note that these answers are all about the *work itself*, as opposed to the paycheck associated with it, which is an entirely separate matter.

MOTIVATION THEORIES

One school of thought on motivation makes a distinction between being actively *satisfied* and being simply *not dissatisfied*. According to this theory, an entirely different set of variables has the potential to create satisfaction compared to those that cause dissatisfaction. Employees will only be satisfied, this theory explains, if the work itself is challenging and they can achieve recognition and advancement. On the other hand, a second set of factors (external to the work itself) exist in the job environment that have the potential to make people dissatisfied. These include: relationship with the supervisor, working conditions, company policies, interpersonal relations among peers, and even things like the benefits available. The insight realized by this theory is that even perfect scores on this second set of variables will never, on their own, lead to job satisfaction without true engagement with the work itself. Wonderful medical benefits, a kind boss, good colleagues, and a pleasant workplace are definitely nice things to have, but boring dead-end work will not lead to satisfied and motivated employees.[1] In the virtual setting, the potential for dissatisfaction could additionally stem from things like frustrations with the technology or poor communication among team members. But like other work situations, in virtual teams as well, true satisfaction will only come with engagement with challenging work that is both recognized and valued, along with a supportive environment.

Next, the *needs fulfillment* theory is one that starts to take into account the personalities of the people involved, and notes that people may differ from each other in terms of what motivates each one. This theory is based on the idea that people apply extra effort only when it can fulfill a psychological need that they have, but while each person may be driven in part by many different needs, individuals may be stronger or weaker in any one given area. One researcher stated that most people have three main needs:

1. The need for *achievement*
2. The need for *power*
3. The need for *affiliation*[2]

For example, one person may love the feeling of accomplishment that comes from solving problems (achievement). Another may thrive on the ability to organize and influence what other people do (power), and still a third may be driven to maintain close connections with teammates and colleagues (affiliation). Understanding each employee's need style can help match the person to the right job task.

Keep in mind that although not on the list above, the need for *autonomy* is one universal need that most people feel (at least to some degree). Nobody seems to like being watched and controlled every step of the way.

> **TIP**
> Pay attention to whether people seem most engaged with tasks, organization, or other people, and use that tendency to your best advantage. But also remember that everyone needs some independence.

In the virtual context, however, autonomy is a double-edged sword. The most pressing danger in this type of work can be described as "drifting," and occurs when people disengage from the task and/or each other. Creating a concrete schedule to define how (and how often) people need to engage and to determine specific job roles will help to avoid this kind of drifting. Some of the worst-performing virtual teams have members who are entirely enthusiastic and eager to help, but don't know what to do. This problem is exacerbated when a clear leader is not defined at the outset. Think of the post-funeral problem as a metaphor. After someone dies, friends and relatives typically offer, "Please let me know if I can do anything to help." Eager, enthusiastic volunteers willing to engage in any manner of heavy lifting abound, but structure and assignments are missing. Thus, rarely do these offers actually result in any help being given. Now imagine instead a scenario where a leader emerges and creates a list of helpful activities (cooking, cleaning, shuttling children around or taking them in for play dates, helping with house repairs, etc.), and then assigns them out systematically to those willing to help. Clearly, more is going to get done in the second case than in the first.

> **TIP**
> While people do like the freedom to choose how to accomplish a task, very few people thrive on the freedom to choose what they should be doing.

A third motivation theory, called *expectancy* theory, has to do with the perceived link between efforts and outcomes.[3] This model says that for people to become and remain motivated, they have to perceive an unbroken chain among three elements:

$$\text{Effort} \rightarrow \text{Performance} \rightarrow \text{Reward}$$

In other words, people need to believe that *if* they put in their effort, *then* they will attain a certain level of performance, AND *if* that level is achieved, *then* they will be rewarded in a certain way. It sounds obvious, but this chain is commonly broken in real organizational settings, leading to many motivational problems.

The first link is between effort and performance. If an employee does not feel able to achieve the performance goal, then the motivation to try will decrease. Let's take the example of a fictitious salesman named Dave. If Dave is given a product to sell for which he believes there is no market, and no amount of effort will make the sales happen, in all likelihood he will just stop trying altogether. Note that it is the *perceived* link between effort and performance that matters to the employee, which may be more pessimistic than is necessary. If someone believes that something cannot be done, effort drops to zero. But demonstrating a course towards success can open the doors for improved motivation—showing the salesman that sales can in fact be made on the product, for example. It also helps to define the goals for performance in very precise ways, including by making them each:[4]

1. Specific
2. Challenging
3. Measurable
4. Time-Bound
5. Prioritized

TIP

People need to believe that they have it in their power to attain a well-defined goal.

The second link is between performance and rewards. Here, the employee needs to believe that if a certain level of performance is attained, then a reliable reward will follow. Back to the example of Dave the salesman, he now needs to understand that if he sells 1,000 units of his product, he will receive a bonus of $5,000. There are two critical elements to this link. The first is that the employee believes the reward will actually materialize and the second is that the reward needs to be something the employee cares about. If a promised reward fails to happen, even for just one person in a team or organization, it can have disastrous effects across the whole team. If, for example, Dave is told that he will receive a promotion if he meets his sales goals for six months, but he knows that previous promotions have been awarded on the basis of seniority instead of performance, he may fail to be motivated by the goal. Additionally, if the reward is a promotion, Dave also has to *want* to be promoted. If he thinks, "Why would I want to get promoted? It's a little more money for a lot more aggravation and time spent on the job, and I would hate that," then the resulting effort to try harder for that level of performance should drop accordingly.

Making sure that the performance element (or goal) is clearly defined and focused on exactly what needs to be accomplished is one difficulty in making this theory come alive in a real organizational setting. Dave the salesman is a vivid case of a job where performance can easily be measured: number of units sold. Though some jobs have this highly quantitative aspect to it, most others do not. In many jobs, especially those where employees could be considered "knowledge workers," it can be difficult to know exactly when the expected level of performance has been reached at all, let alone accomplished well.

Virtual work can also hide the day-to-day activities of employees, making it that much harder to know what people are doing. For that reason, it is even more important to make sure that the goals are clearly articulated and that everyone knows what needs to be done by when.

Quotes from the front lines*: "Sometimes the volume of work that's being done, and the obstacles faced, is not recognized on virtual teams. It's helpful to have direct contact with all employees and have guidelines for monitoring work and volumes. It makes the whole system feel fairer to everyone to be recognized."*

Defining goals is part of the solution, but so is making sure that rewards are only given for what it is you want to have happen, and not for what you don't.[5] People learn to "game the system" when the rewarded goal is not perfectly aligned with the actual desired behaviors. What do you think happened when a frozen food manufacturer started rewarding employees for the number of bugs that they collected from the line of vegetables moving past them? Some employees began bringing in bugs from home, adding them to the line, and then removing them, collecting handsome rewards in the process! We can see evidence of a disconnect between goals and rewards across a number of domains. Examples include athletes on professional teams who are rewarded for individual statistics instead of team performance, elected officials endorsing decisions that look good as opposed to those that do good, or doctors who order many expensive and worrisome tests to prevent the possibility of missing a diagnosis, which can be much more costly to them personally.

TIP

Make sure that (1) employees know ahead of time exactly what rewards will be based on, and (2) rewards are based on the things that actually need to be accomplished.

Another vivid example of this problem comes in the area of corporate governance. In the wake of many of the ethics scandals that came to light in the last decade, several companies decided that one safeguard against this was to have their board members elected to shorter terms. The logic was simple: if someone doesn't seem to be headed in the right direction, the company and the shareholders have less time to wait before ousting that person and moving on to a new path with someone else. However, the change unleashed some unexpected behaviors. Now, instead of focusing on the long-term health of the organization, board members had a personal incentive to boost the bottom line in a shorter-term timeframe. As a result, major investments into things like new equipment or switching to more environmentally sound practices, which could have had immense benefits in the long term, were deemed too expensive, since they would have a negative impact on the more immediate balance sheet upon which these board members felt judged when up for re-election.[6]

One last interesting study on the nature of rewards is worth noting. In a paper called "I'll Have One of Each," researchers reported finding that people were *more* motivated to keep working towards rewards if the rewards were separated into different categories (even meaningless ones) than if they were all presented on the same list.[7] The explanation is based on the thought that people felt like they might be missing out on something good if they were not able to earn a reward from each of the categories presented, which in turn kept their motivation high. This concept won't necessarily be enough to sustain high motivation forever, but if you find your team in a rut and feel that you need to jump-start motivation with some external incentives, this might be a trick worth keeping up your sleeve!

EFFECTIVE PRAISE

Now let's drill down a little further and look at one area of specific interaction between managers and employees that can greatly influence day-to-day motivation, and that is praise. Praising people seems simple enough. After all, most managers tend to understand that people thrive on praise, and need it both to feel successful in their jobs and to keep motivation high for future tasks. And most people understand the demoralizing effects of negative feedback. Even on a neuro-scientific level, there is evidence that negative feedback inhibits future learning. Students exposed to the words "clever" and "smart" before taking a test not only performed better than those exposed to the words "ignorant" or "stupid," but brain scans also showed differences in how they responded to mistakes. Essentially, those who went into the test with thoughts of being competent had heightened brain activity (indicating surprise or conflict) after making a mistake, while those who felt less competent had no reaction at all. This indicates that brains that expect to perform well take note when they do not, and are more likely to learn from their mistakes going forward.[8] But unfortunately not all praise is equal. Choosing the right words can make a tremendous difference in both the short and the long haul.

To illustrate this, look at a common management situation outside the employee-boss dynamic: parenting. Like managers, parents want to encourage high levels of motivation in their children, as well as a strong sense of self-confidence. They also understand that praise can be an effective tool for achieving these goals. Unfortunately, many parents have fallen prey to a common mistake by issuing the *wrong types of praise*. In essence, parents tend to over-praise *abilities* and under-praise *effort*. Groundbreaking work in the area of child psychology has demonstrated this effect in no uncertain terms. In an experiment, young students were given a complicated set of tasks to complete. Afterwards, they were all told that they had accomplished a certain (standard) amount on the tasks. Half of the kids were told that their performance was because they were so smart, and the other half were told that it was because they had worked so hard on the task. Then, the students were offered the chance to complete a second set of challenging tasks. Surprisingly, those who were told they were smart generally refused the chance to continue with the hard task, and those who were told they were hard workers generally elected to continue on with the challenge. Why? Psychologist Carol Dweck asserts that it is because people have one of two different mindsets, which can be activated through different triggers. These mindsets are either *fixed* or *growth oriented*. If your mindset is fixed, you feel that your capabilities are relatively set, and all performance feedback reflects on those capabilities. If your mindset is oriented towards growth, you are always seeking to improve and change your current capabilities.[9]

If you are told that you have accomplished something impressive because you are smart, the fixed mindset is activated. The high level of performance is an indication that your capabilities have shone through. A new challenge now poses a risk: What if the outcome isn't as good as it was the first time? In that case, the fixed mind worries, it might indicate that the term "smart" was misapplied, and will I now be branded as "average" or even "unimpressive"? Thus, if people feel that others' overall judgment of them is at risk every time they embark on a new task, the fixed mindset will put pressure on them to rest on their laurels instead and avoid risking their accolades. On the other hand, if praise comes in the form of highlighting the process—the extraordinary effort, the hard work, or the willingness to try out new ideas—the growth mindset is activated, and the process itself becomes the source of inspiration. In that mindset, the mind becomes eager to keep at work, always seeking more chances to demonstrate these abilities. Growth mindsets push you to continually increase the level of challenge you face.

The differences between fixed and growth mindsets have far-reaching implications. The practical application to management hinges on the idea that whether people think of their mindsets as fixed or growth oriented can *change* from one situation to the next. Thus, based on the idea that growth orientation can lead to improvement while fixed mindsets don't, managers are now given the task of trying to encourage that particular viewpoint. This can indeed be done, in no small part by the type of praise that is offered.

TIP

Praise the effort, not the result. State the value of learning and meeting challenges as opposed to impressive outcomes.

The mindset of the manager also changes the way he or she treats subordinates. Managers in a fixed mindset don't tend to take criticism well, tend not to mentor their subordinates, and don't recognize enough improvements or signs of growth. This is based on the fixed mindset mentality that says that people are what they are, and little can or will change about them (so why try?). Instead, these types of managers overvalue raw talent as the single best predictor of an effective worker, which can send the wrong signals to employees about the need for hard work.

Needless to say, placing emphasis on outcomes over processes also (unwittingly) encourages unethical behaviors. For instance, in one experiment, those primed to be in a fixed mindset (by being told they were *intelligent* after a difficult test) were more likely to lie and cheat about reporting their performance afterwards. In fact, as many as 40% of them exaggerated their accomplishments; such is the pressure to stay on top when the way you feel your value is through your accomplishments.[10] The message is clear—when people value their intelligence, the theme is "look smart or talented at any cost." And even worse, when in the fixed mindset, people seem to assume that they *shouldn't need* to work very hard, and indeed hard work makes them feel less smart! Clearly, this is not the motivational tool that will help people stretch for the job. Instead, when one values *effort* and the chance to learn, new opportunities are considered challenges instead of threats.

> **TIP**
> Make it clear that you value good old-fashioned hard work, that skills are acquirable, that mistakes are learning opportunities, and that passion, effort, and teamwork are what make for a successful enterprise.

ACCOUNTABILITY AND COMPETITION

These ideas are short and sweet. Accountability works because generally, people like to preserve their reputations. If they know they will be "on display" about what they have accomplished, it can be a very strong motivator to work hard and be impressive.

Quotes from the front lines: *"We have weekly check-in meetings, and nobody wants to be the one to have nothing to show for themselves on what they have accomplished that week."*

On competition, the key is to make the point of comparison *external* to the team and never pit one person against another inside the team. Good benchmarks for competition could be current versus past performance, and focus on an external competitor in the market or even another division within the company. This question also ties in to the reward system used—as much as possible, you don't want people within one team competing for the same reward pool.

TIP
Make accountability as visible as possible. Keep competition external to the team.

GO BIG: BIG PICTURE AND BIG COMMITMENT

People like to feel part of something bigger than themselves. In any job, the sense of greater purpose (as opposed to just the daily nitty-gritty) can make the difference between a "just get it done" attitude and being inspired to work above and beyond the call. This factor is especially important for virtual workers, who are at the greatest risk for feeling disconnected from both the work itself and a sense of belonging on a team. The value of specific and challenging goal-setting was presented earlier, but here the topic is more about the impact that the work will have in some bigger picture sense. Yes, it is motivating to try and create software in X amount of time with as few bugs as possible, but it is that much more motivating if you can explain *why* this particular software is important to the company, and to the end users, in a very vivid way.

Quotes from the front lines: *"Every other week, during our weekly check-in meeting, I bring in someone from our company who works outside the immediate team. These people are given 10 minutes of our time to describe how what we're doing relates to their job, and to tell us ways that we could help them even more. It's very useful to see how what we're doing relates to other areas in the company and has an impact on the work of others."*

In addition to the larger goals and vision that can be so important to motivation, there is also the question of commitment. Here, companies in general and many managers specifically fall short. We live in an age of high turnover—rare is the employee who works an entire career in one industry, let alone at one company, anymore. The reasons people give for jumping around typically range from the more career based (I wanted the chance to develop new skills) to the more people based (I wasn't being treated well under that boss). Contrary to popular belief, rarely does someone leave solely for the sake of more money. In fact, in the headhunting industry, it is well known that it is nearly impossible to move a happy employee, regardless of the new offer. One small change in management values can have a very big impact on retaining employees, and that is a change in attitude regarding commitment.

Contrast these two managers. Manager A believes that talent comes and goes, and you do the best you can with what you have at the time but always keep your eye out for newer and better talent. Manager B believes in hiring for the long haul, and that employees should be given every chance for growth, development, and advancement, even in cases where early evidence seems to indicate a poor fit between employee and job. Most managers fall somewhere in between these two extremes, but with a stronger tendency toward Manager A's attitude. It is much harder to truly make a commitment to your employees and follow through on that. However, avoiding this commitment entirely is akin to asking someone on a date by saying, "You're beautiful, come be with me until I no longer find you attractive (or find someone else more attractive), and then you're out!"[11] While there is certainly the possibility of going too far and throwing away time and resources on the wrong person, a healthy dose of Manager B's perspective will improve the team.

Manager A's and Manager B's approaches are based on different assumptions about what humans are and how they work. Called Theory X and Theory Y,[12] they identify sets of traits that lead to very different experiences in the workplace. Theory X describes a view of people as essentially "effort averse" and always looking for a way to do the least amount possible. In this view, people are considered to be opportunistic, and will lie to get what they want. They need constant monitoring, and a manager's job under this view is to set up surveillance and incentive systems to keep people in line. In keeping with Manager A's perspective above, employees in this viewpoint are merely thought of as a means to an end, and are thus more interchangeable (especially since they would leave you at the drop of a hat if given an even slightly better offer).

By contrast, Theory Y assumes that people are fundamentally interested in participating in the work if given the opportunity to engage with it and make decisions. In this view, people generally like to be challenged. They enjoy the chance to learn new things, and they want to make a positive contribution to their work environment. They are essentially responsible. In keeping with Manager B's view above, these people are more likely to be in it for the long haul. What you (as a manager) believe can fundamentally change the way the team reacts to you and to the work. While of course there will always be a few bad apples who are entirely out for themselves, there exists ample evidence that believing in and committing to the growth and advancement of employees will make them rise to the challenge. This idea parallels the work done on the growth mindset described above.

> **TIP**
>
> People respond to challenging environments and to working towards a larger goal.

The next topic explores the feedback process for insights into how this can influence motivation. This is done in two parts, with the first focused on how evaluations can get derailed, and the second on the feedback delivery itself. In both cases, special attention will be given to the virtual team and electronic communication contexts.

FEEDBACK PART 1: BIASED EVALUATIONS

Evaluation processes are the bane of many a manager's job. They are unpleasant at best and wholly dreaded activities at worst. For many people, the process is mandated by the company as a yearly exercise in which performance feedback is given to subordinates, along with ratings that tie the results to a tangible outcome such as a bonus or raise percentage. Though this process has enough problems and complexities to warrant a book of its own, here the focus is on the issues that result when parts, or all, of the evaluation and feedback processes are taken online.

There are two players in performance evaluations: the rater and the one being evaluated. The rater's job is to engage in a decision-making process to establish what evaluation is appropriate for the target employee. The rater must then communicate the feedback in such a way as to (a) make it clear what was decided, (b) encourage positive growth and change in the target based on the feedback given, and (c) make sure that what happens feels fair to all. Unfortunately, all three elements are changed for the worse when the process is moved to an online format from a traditional paper-based evaluation form with a face-to-face feedback element.

First comes the evaluation itself. As you can imagine, evaluating others is a tough thing to do completely objectively. Instead, many people find themselves overly swayed by a single event that was particularly vivid, or by what has happened most recently. People can even be permanently biased by their first impressions of another, even if that proved to be an inaccurate representation of that person in the long run. And beyond the immediate behaviors, some people are even unconsciously biased by generalized assumptions about fairness, such as "more senior employees deserve better ratings since they have put in so much more time." Some universities are starting to use external evaluators, or even software, for grading student assignments to sidestep the enormous problem of bias in the evaluation process in that context.[13] So far, the problems described may occur with any evaluation processes conducted in any mode. There is an additional concern when evaluations are done using online forms, and that is another version of the negativity bias.

Earlier in the book the tendency towards being more negative in the language used when typing than when speaking or writing longhand was described. Unfortunately, this same bias seems to cloud evaluations conducted online. In a research project designed to explore this exact issue, two groups of people were asked to conduct a peer evaluation appraisal of their teammates after completing a big project. Half of the individuals were asked to rate their teammates on individual paper forms, while the other half were asked to fill out (and return electronically) an identical form sent to them online. Though there was no reason to think the teams themselves differed in any meaningful way, those who filled out their forms online gave systematically *lower* ratings to their peers (on average) than did those who filled out the paper forms. To make sure that the difference observed was truly just a factor of the type of form used and nothing about the teams themselves, the next batch of participants all rated the *exact same* individual performing the *exact same* tasks—in other words, all raters watched the same video of a person at work in his job, and were then asked to rate his performance on identical forms—except one group got the form on paper, and the other got the form online. Again, the online raters gave lower ratings for the man's job performance than did the paper evaluators.[14]

There is no reasonable explanation for this other than the fact that making decisions online encourages people to act somewhat differently than making decisions recorded in other ways. This is not necessarily a problem if all evaluations are done online. Ratings may indeed go down, but it should be an across-the-board effect. In fact, some may argue that this force may be a good balance for the "grade inflation" culture that we live in, whereby anything less than "five star" ratings feels like a failure in many domains. And, as mentioned earlier in the book, people may be more willing to offer bad news in less distorted ways when they can write it online instead of calling or talking face to face,[15] so this may even provide better or clearer information than would a conversation.

There is also the question of fairness. To be considered fair, employees must understand what went into the selection of any particular form of rating or feedback. Too often, and especially in online systems, the focus becomes fixed on a complicated numerical scale with little transparency for anyone about what went into particular decisions. Unfortunately, choosing how to evaluate people is never a fully objective process. In a classroom exercise, MBA students are asked to allocate a fixed bonus pool to six employees with varying performance metrics on several dimensions, including everything from very quantitative measures like "waste rates" and "overall production" to more subjective items like "job effort" and "human relations skills." What's most interesting about this exercise is that *rarely do any two groups ever allocate identical amounts* in their system of dividing the fixed pie among these workers. Even capable people cannot seem to agree on exactly how much each evaluation factor should matter, despite the presence of objective performance data.

To put these concerns into the language of expectancy theory described earlier in this chapter, these feedback problems break both the effort-to-performance and the performance-to-outcome links. Imagine, for example, that the ratings themselves were biased by being overly influenced by events that unfolded in the last month before the end of a 12-month rating period. In that case, effort before the last month of the next rating period might feel unnecessary. And if good performance metrics don't reliably lead to predictable rewards in a transparent way, then motivation to achieve those levels of performance also suffers.

The point here is that it is valuable to remember that evaluations are almost always going to be at least partially subjective. Unfortunately, this allows bias to creep into your decision making (especially when the process is conducted online), and can lower motivation accordingly. If you are in a position where you need to conduct online evaluative ratings, you might want to make sure you have a system for recording true glimpses of the performance of the employees over time, and then step away from the screen and think first about what the decision should be, to avoid these potential sources of bias.

TIP

Know that making your evaluation decisions in front of a computer screen may encourage a more negative slant on your views. Make your decisions based on objective criteria as much as possible to avoid this bias and present a fair decision.

FEEDBACK PART 2: DELIVERY

The appraisal process is not just about choosing your words (and/or rating numbers), but also involves communicating the feedback to the focal employee. This process can occur through a number of communication channels, each with its own set of advantages and disadvantages. The traditional gold standard is the face-to-face conversation. Yet many people, if not most, wince at the prospect of being on either side of this talk.

- From the sending side, managers hate delivering criticism because it risks their relationship with their employees. Many, intentionally or not, even downplay the negative news just to spare your feelings, which could potentially limit your improvement at your job.[16]
- From the receiving side, most people find it just plain miserable to have to hear negative things about themselves. There are those few exceptions who seem to actively seek information about their weaknesses with an eye towards improving them, but these people are the exception and not the norm.

When faced with criticism of any kind, people generally respond with three types of reactions, sometimes in succession. The first reaction can be thought of as bracing for the bad news. Even if the speaker starts with a list of positive attributes about you and your work, you may just be nodding blankly, and waiting for the speaker to get to the "but . . ." and transition into the criticism. While you're bracing and waiting to see how bad this conversation is going to get, you may well miss important content, including well-deserved accolades.

Quotes from the front lines: *"I had a boss once who followed the pattern of 'start out with something good, then slip in the criticism' to the letter. Each time she gave feedback, she'd start with something nice, but these nice words were always followed by the bad news. It started to feel like the first sentences weren't even genuine, but were just a way to segue into the real reason for the conversation, which was for her to air her complaints. Eventually, my colleagues and I noticed that we didn't even listen to the introduction, and only tuned in once we got to Part 2."*

The second reaction type is emotional, whether it be anger, sadness, resentment, or even joy. It is not appropriate to react strongly in a professional meeting, so whatever emotion you may be feeling, your primary job at that moment is to dampen it by masking its effects on your face and body language. Managing an emotional response in this way is hard work. It can take all of the cognitive resources you have available, making you that much less able to absorb and learn from whatever information comes next in the conversation.

Quotes from the front lines: "Once I was in a restaurant in a city and was uncomfortably close to the next table, where a young woman was getting feedback from her boss. He said something nice of course, but then launched into the ways that the more senior people thought her work needed improving. It was so painful to sit there and watch her trying not to cry through this whole conversation . . . I really felt for her!"

The third major reaction is to become defensive and want to explain your side of the allegations. Again, by focusing on formulating your own next arguments in the conversation, your mind is relatively unavailable for listening to and absorbing new information.

Based on this, there is actually a reasonable argument to be made that sending feedback over e-mail is both kinder and ultimately better for learning.[17] Think about it: If you got the same information in an e-mail, you could have your emotional reaction in private and then decide how you would like to respond afterwards. You would know the scope of the feedback (positive and negative) in one quick reading, and then could re-examine the text afterwards for a deeper understanding of all of the points. It might even allow the sender to make the message clearer for you, as that person would not be as concerned with your reactions and could focus on the message itself.

However, in practice clear and effective feedback delivery is more complicated than this. People seem to have an emotional response to the use of e-mail in and of itself for this process. For example, in a research study, participants were asked to imagine that they were an employee receiving feedback that included positive and negative aspects. Examples of the identical feedback that they all received include: "We know that you are a competent specialist and you have proved to be a good manager of your department . . . [and have done some] excellent work" on the positive side, and, "However . . . it has also been recognized that you have a tendency to leap through things without getting into all of the details" on the negative side. The evaluation was summed up by the sentence, "You are a smart and hardworking employee, and we expect you to have many future successes in this company, once you settle down and learn to take time with major decisions." The participant was then informed that the rating received was a "3" out of "5" and the bonus would be adjusted accordingly.

Though all participants in this study read the exact same feedback, some were told that the feedback was given in an e-mail, and others were told that the feedback was given either face to face or on a paper form. In measuring their reactions to the feedback, the study showed systematic differences based on the medium chosen for the message delivery. Those who supposedly received the information over e-mail were the most negative about the feedback itself, the manager, and the whole company. When asked why, participants called the manager a "coward" who was "hiding behind e-mail." They felt it was "aloof, cold, terrible, lame, and harsh" to use e-mail for something like this. Sounds like they all wanted the manager to bite the bullet and have the uncomfortable face-to-face conversation, right? Well, partially. Interestingly enough the *most* satisfied participants were those who received their feedback on a paper form. Paper forms seemed to be the best of both worlds. They had the formality that signaled that the manager was taking this seriously, but avoided the uncomfortable pitfalls of having to stare each other down through the awkward conversation itself.[18] This can perhaps be followed up with a spoken conversation for clarification, a chance for the employee to respond and be heard, and to make sure that the relationship remains intact.

Even when text may be more appropriate and useful than spoken conversation, such as during difficult or emotional conversations, the overall sense that people have that e-mail is first and foremost a tool of convenience can work against you. The image is, unfortunately, of someone dashing something off without serious thought or review, even though that might not be the case at all.

TIP

Uncomfortable or delicate conversations do not belong in e-mails. When text seems kinder or more effective than a face-to-face conversation, write it on letterhead and send it (either digitally or printed out). This touch of formality will remove the concern that you are not taking this seriously.

Lastly, there is one unfortunate tendency that has been noted on the topic of feedback in virtual teams, and it has to do with the type of feedback given (formal versus informal). Managers of virtual teams seem to give *less* informal feedback when their primary channel of communication is e-mail, and instead wait to give formal feedback *only* at the specified times. This is a failure of the system on two fronts:

1. People are not getting the regular, timely, and low-key feedback during the work process itself, which is the kind that actually helps promote positive changes.
2. They are instead getting formal feedback through a channel that makes them less likely to appreciate what's being offered as constructive.

This is a classic lose-lose situation whereby the chance for feedback to do any good is being missed.[19] People need to know whether and how their work is meeting expectations.

The concept of MBWA, or Management By Walking Around,[20] suggests that by simply being physically present now and then in someone's work space, conversations, questions, connections, and feedback would spontaneously ensue. While this is no cure-all as a management technique, there is something real to the benefits of spontaneous conversations. These don't have to be left by the wayside when a team moves to the virtual realm, but it does take more conscious work on the manager's part to keep this kind of informal channel active.

TIP

Give regular, informal feedback and have discussions on what's being done while it's still "in the works" by whatever means available to you—e-mail, phone calls, etc. The kind of thing you might do if you just drop by someone's desk shouldn't get eliminated just because there is no longer a chance to physically stop by.

SUMMARY: THE MOTIVATION AUDIT

Getting and sustaining high levels of motivation from employees is a constant balancing act. When you feel motivation to be waning, use this checklist to perform an "audit" to see if you can diagnose the problem and move towards fixing it.

If people aren't performing, think through:

- Do they understand *how* to accomplish their goals?
- Do they have the ability and resources to perform?
- Do they see the relationship between performance and rewards?
- Do they care about the rewards?
- Do they have appropriate goals (specific, challenging but attainable, and paired with feedback)?

- Is the feedback delivered in a way that they find effective and fair?
- Are their needs getting met?

NOTES

1. Herzberg, F. (1982). *The managerial choice: To be efficient or to be human.* Salt Lake City, UT: Olympus.

2. McClelland, D. C. (1971). *Motivational trends in society.* Morristown, NJ: General Learning Press.

3. Vroom, V. H. (1964/1970). *Work and motivation.* New York, NY: Wiley.

4. Nelson, D. L. & Quick, J. C. (2009). *Organizational Behavior* (6th ed.). Mason, OH: South-Western Cengage Learning.

5. Kerr, S. (1995). On the folly of rewarding A, while hoping for B. *Academy of Management Executive, 9(1),* 7–14.

6. See Buchholz, A. K., Brown, J. A., & Anderson, A. M. (2012). Staggered boards and stakeholder management: The role of myopic loss aversion. Working paper, Rutgers Business School, Newark, NJ.

7. Wiltermuth, S. S. & Gino, F. (2013). "I'll have one of each": How separating rewards into (meaningless) categories increases motivation. *Journal of Personality and Social Psychology, 104(1),* 1–13.

8. Bengtsson, S. L., Dolan, R. J., & Passignham, R. E. (2011). Priming for self-esteem influences the monitoring of one's own performance. *Social Cognitive and Affective Neuroscience, 6(4),* 417–425.

9. Dweck, C. S. (2006). *Mindset: The new psychology of success.* New York, NY: Random House.

10. Dweck, C. (2008). *Mindset, motivation, and leadership.* Stanford Executive Briefings. Mill Valley, CA: Kantola Productions.

11. O'Reilly, III, C. (2001). *How great companies achieve extraordinary results with ordinary people.* Stanford Executive Briefings. Mill Valley, CA: Kantola Productions.

12. McGregor, D. (1960). *The human side of enterprise.* New York, NY: McGraw-Hill.

13. Young, J. R. (2011). Professors cede grading power to outsiders—even computers. *The Chronicle of Higher Education,* August 7.

14. Kurtzberg, T. R., Naquin, C. E., & Belkin, L. Y. (2005). Electronic performance appraisals: The effects of e-mail communication on peer ratings in actual and simulated environments. *Organizational Behavior and Human Decision Processes, 98,* 216–226.

15. Sussman, S. W. & Sproull, L. (1999). Straight talk: Delivering bad news through electronic communication. *Information Systems Research, 10(2),* 150–166.

16. Higgins, E. T. (1999). "Saying is believing" effects: When sharing reality about something biases knowledge and evaluations. In L. Thompson, J. M. Levine, & D. M. Messick (Eds.), *Shared cognition in organizations: The management of knowledge* (pp. 33–48). Mahwah, NJ: Lawrence Erlbaum.

17. Kluger, A. N. & DeNisi, A. (1996). The effects of feedback intervention on performance: A historical review, a meta-analysis, and a preliminary feedback theory. *Psychological Bulletin, 119,* 254–284.

18. Kurtzberg, T. R., Belkin, L., & Naquin, C. E. (2006). The effect of e-mail on attitudes towards performance feedback. *International Journal of Organizational Analysis, 14,* 4–21.

19. Gibson, C. B., Gibbs, J. L., Stanko, T. L., Tesluk, P., & Cohen, S. G. (2011). Including the "I" in virtuality and modern job design: Extending the job characteristics model to include the moderating effect of individual experiences of electronic dependence and copresence. *Organization Science, 6(11–12),* 1481–1499.

20. See Peters, T. & Waterman, R. H. (1982). *In search of excellence.* New York, NY: Warner Books.

EIGHT
Virtual Team Leadership

LEADERSHIP

Do we need managers at all when there's no one in the office? Can you manage people whom you can't see? Fortunately for the worried managers out there, the answer to both questions is a resounding *yes*. Management of virtual teams is not only necessary but also critical for effective functioning. And luckily, an entirely new skill set is not required to do this job right. Many of the ideas and elements that go into successfully managing a face-to-face team apply to this environment as well. For example, one well-known list of the five most important skills for a successful leader to have includes:[1]

- Modeling behaviors by personally acting the ways that you want others to act
- Inspiring others by describing the future and enlisting them in the process of getting there
- Challenging people by seeking out opportunities for experimentation and risk
- Enabling others by fostering collaboration and seeking input on decisions
- Encouraging people by recognizing their successes and the value that they add throughout the work, not just at the end and not just based on the final outcome.

While it is easy to see how each and every one of these areas may still apply in the virtual team context, they will require some adjustment in that setting. Here, these techniques will need to be implemented more explicitly by being concretely demonstrated earlier, more strongly, and more often. The first shift when moving to the virtual world is to stop thinking about managing time; instead, start thinking about managing work and the connections among the team members.[2]

One research study demonstrating this point found that the best predictor of whether individual virtual team members felt connected to their groups was the frequency of reciprocal (that is, two-way) communication with the team's leadership. Why? First, more frequent communication most likely comes with more information about the team's mission, values, and the interests of the individuals and the team as a whole. After all, most of this communication is likely to be about the team's work and its progress towards meeting its goals. Additionally, more frequent communication may also make people feel more included in the decision making of the workgroup, which in and of itself makes people willing to engage more with the team. These researchers concluded that virtual communication can be as effective as face-to-face communication at solidifying team-member engagement, but it needs to be a reliable and often-used channel to have the desired effects.[3]

Quotes from the front lines: *"I had a boss who would just forget to drop us a line when he got news that concerned the team. If you were there in person in his office, he'd tell you what was going on in a heartbeat, as soon as it happened. But he just wasn't any good at remembering to take the time to sit and write to us in messages. He was really hard to work for in that way."*

Imagine that you are heading up a face-to-face team, but of people you don't know well. What would you do first? Probably some combination of team meetings and individual conversations with the team members, in which you would observe each to see if you could get to know something about who each member was as a person, how each person worked, what motivated and excited each one of them, etc. This kind of information is, in many cases, exactly what's missing when a virtual team kicks off. To counter this, team leaders have to reach out in much less subtle ways to get to know the team members.

Telephone calls can be helpful in this situation, as they provide more information about how people are thinking and reacting in real time than you would get from a typed message. Plus, as mentioned earlier, it is *much* easier to call someone and have a good conversation about a work issue if you are already accustomed to speaking to that person on the phone.

However, it can feel awkward to call someone without a true and immediate purpose at hand. It might make you feel foolish, or even potentially alienate the other person if it felt like you were wasting time.

Consider the following method as a tool for helping to get the best out of this potentially awkward conversation. Instead of calling with a hidden agenda to "feel out" the other person, what if instead you came right out and stated your purpose out loud? Something along the lines of this: "I'm calling to chat with you to get to know you a little better. I'm particularly interested in hearing about how you think this upcoming project fits in with your other work and what you'd like to be doing and learning going forward. Also, just so you know, I'd like to have a couple of conversations like this at the beginning, so I can get a sense of how you think about things, and so that we'll be used to speaking with each other if and when we need to discuss issues as the project unfolds." If you didn't want to deliver that speech out loud in the first phone call, you could also introduce these ideas in a message sent ahead of time. In this way, something that might be done subtly and easily in person can still be done, but only through conscious planning and explicit discussions. These types of calls can be encouraged not just from the leader to the team members but also among the teammates themselves.

TIP

Be explicit in forcing early conversations, if for no other reason than to "grease the wheels" for easy communication later.

Identification

In the introduction to this book, the issue of virtuality as a state of mind was raised. In part, this means that people may well feel more or less connected to a team (and to each other) regardless of whether they sit across the hall or across an ocean from each other. The underlying variable of interest when considering this variability is identification. How much does any one person identify with the others on the team, and with the team as a whole? How much does that person identify with the job itself? Sometimes the key to identification is as simple as feeling like you have something in common with the others (such as profession, gender, ethnicity, or political views), which can offer common ground, reduce uncertainty, and provide the benefit of the doubt in terms of trustworthiness.[4] Classic research states that identification with the work hinges on three elements:[5]

1. Experienced meaningfulness: feeling that the work is important, valuable, and worthwhile, and knowing how the individual tasks fit into each the larger project and the organizational goals as a whole
2. Experienced responsibility: feeling personally accountable for the results
3. Knowledge of results: having an understanding, on a regular basis, of the effectiveness of one's performance.

TIP

Make sure that people feel connected to the work they are doing, by reviewing the elements of meaningfulness, responsibility, and feedback with them directly.

In traditional face-to-face work arrangements, the need to feel connected to the work can sometimes be *replaced* by the connections that people feel with their colleagues.[6] In other words, feelings of strong alignment, loyalty, respect, and even friendship between team members can drive motivation right alongside commitment to the work itself. In the virtual setting, this can be harder to establish. It is important for leaders to actively cultivate connections to the work itself and to the other people. And while it is also important for people to feel comfortable with the technology that they are using, if the connections to the people and to the work are solid, then the distance and the use of technology tend to become minor distractions instead of major obstacles. Thus, leaders need to take a hands-on role in making sure that connections remain vibrant. And team members need to simultaneously be doing at least two completely different things at all times: one is moving forward on the tasks themselves, and the second is supporting each other to promote the well-being of the group.[7]

DIAGNOSING PROBLEMS AND CREATING SUPPORTING STRUCTURE

When you turn on a light switch and the light above you shines bright, what caused the light to turn on? There are many different answers that could be considered equally true. You could describe the wiring in the wall that allows electricity to flow to the light bulb. You could speak to the activated electrons in the bulb itself. You could also mention that you have paid your electric bill, which keeps the utility company willing to supply you with power from its plants, or solar panels, or wind farms. Similarly, if you flip your switch and the light fails to turn on, what went wrong? It could be that the bulb burned out, that the wiring is faulty, that the power company has cut you off for failure to pay on time, or any one of a number of other possibilities. When things are not going well in an organizational setting, figuring out what's going wrong can similarly be more difficult than it initially seems.

Who or what gets blamed for problems can sometimes unintentionally be based on the wrong signals. More specifically, it is critical to be able to distinguish between problems where a *person* is at fault, and problems where some of the surrounding context, or *structure*, is at fault. To demonstrate this, some researchers described the true story of a ferry boat that sank in 1987 off the coast of Belgium, a mere half mile away from the dock and in about only four minutes, killing 193 people on board.[8] What went wrong? The mechanical answer is easy: The boat sank because the rear doors of the ferry, opened to load cars on board, were not closed before the boat departed. The boat instantly filled with water, capsized, and sank. Many passengers were trapped in the cabin and died from hypothermia. The more complicated question is, why did this happen? One fact may provide all the answer you need: the assistant boatswain, typically responsible for closing the doors, was on a break after cleaning the car deck, fell asleep in his cabin, and failed to hear the sound that should have alerted him to the fact that the ship was departing. Clearly, the sinking of the boat was this man's fault, was it not? Yes, certainly, but the story is more complicated than this. The first officer's job requires him to stay on deck until he sees the assistant boatswain take over. The officer claimed he saw his replacement approaching, but clearly the assistant (asleep in his cabin) was not seen, and the first officer left anyway. Another boatswain was on deck, but he claimed it was not his job to check the doors, so he did not. The captain of the ship merely assumed that they were closed, since this particular boat was not equipped with mirrors or safety light indicators (which had been requested but were not installed because the parent company did not feel that it was worthwhile to spend extra money just to make sure employees were doing their jobs correctly). Further compounding the problem, the ferry did not fit into the port in question (because this ferry was not on its usual route), and so it had to be filled with dead weight in the lower sections of the boat. Thus, it sank more immediately once water entered the vessel. The design of this type of ferry had a known flaw in it (and two like it had previously had major problems), but it had not yet been deemed unfit for service by either the authorities or the company. Rescue efforts were limited as well, based on the conditions of the rising tide. So was this problem explained away, after all, by a single faulty employee who fell asleep on the job, or is there more to the story that you found relevant?

People are both easier and more satisfying to blame than are structures, even when the truth usually contains elements of both being at fault. The key question used to differentiate between the two is this one: "If this person was fired, and another person put into this role, what are the odds that the problem would recur?" If you can answer with confidence that another person would most likely *not* have the same difficulties, then a personnel issue may be all that is going wrong. More often than not, though, this is an over-simplification of the problem. If you can imagine another person (and remember, *all* people make mistakes) getting into similar difficulties, then you might need to look at the systems in general and see if fixes can be offered through changes in policies and procedures.

Here's another real example (and the last one involving a transportation disaster!). A plane crashed less than a mile from the airport because it had been circling for an hour and ran out of fuel. A transcript of the in-flight recorder demonstrated that a lower-level pilot tried repeatedly to tell the captain about the fuel issue, but the captain didn't respond. Perhaps the captain didn't hear him, or perhaps he had a total failure of competence at a critical moment. Who is at fault here? The captain for sure, but also the military-style culture and policies used among cockpit crews, which prevented an "underling" from shouting down his boss or attempting to tell the tower about the problem himself. To ensure that this never happened again, the correction needed to deal not just with the individual at fault but also with the supporting context.

One last wrinkle on this topic is what's called the *team halo effect*, which means that teams as a whole tend not to be blamed for their failures (yet they are given credit for their successes). Instead, individuals are typically identified as the cause of failures, even if the whole team's performance might have been the more appropriate explanation.[9]

TIP

People are easy and satisfying to blame for problems that arise, but there is usually more involved in solving and preventing problems in terms of the work environment, rules, procedures, and incentives.

Turning back to virtual team leaders, they have a similarly complicated job assessing the causes of the behaviors they observe. In fact, a good leader observes and needs to interpret even very minor issues such as the possible causes of silence, misunderstandings, and delays.[10] For this reason, before the team actually begins its work together, it is critical for the leader to do an inventory of sorts about the structure, or background context, in which this team will be operating. Questions in three different categories may help the leader map out the team and anticipate the areas of strength and weakness:[11]

Team Formation and Goals

1. How was the team formed? Were members recruited or asked to volunteer?
2. Who is on the team? What are their skills and experiences?
3. What does the team need to do? By when? How?
4. Do team members represent different areas within the organization, different regions of the world, etc.?

Organizational Policies and Resources

1. How are team members rewarded? Is it the same for all team members if they are at different locations or in different countries?
2. Is training available for team members?
3. What communication technologies are available? Which do the team members each prefer/which are they familiar with? (See Sidebar 8.1 on adopting new technologies.)

Degree of Complexity

1. Temporal distribution: How easy or difficult is it for teams to communicate in real time?
2. Boundary spanning: Are people from different functional areas? Different organizations? Different national cultures?
3. Team lifecycle: Has the team been created for a single issue, or for ongoing work?
4. Member roles: Is each person there to do *one* thing only, or to serve multiple roles? Do they also have roles outside of this team's work? A greater number of roles tends to be associated with higher levels of negative attitude towards work. Sometimes, leaders even find it useful to line up "alternates" if one person is overly in demand yet also serves a critical function on the team.
5. Work interdependence: How much interdependence does the team need to complete the work? Look at the scale in figure 8.1 below as it moves from the least to the most interconnection among the teammates.[12]

As complexity increases on other dimensions, the need for more work interdependence often also increases. (As an aside, one faculty member

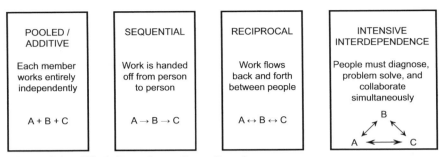

Figure 8.1.   Work Interdependence Levels

has noted that with MBA student teams, the "intensive interdependence" work should be renamed the "pizza stage" since it so often only occurs right before a deadline and when teammates realize that they will need a marathon meeting to finish up the work all together, so they order in pizza! While virtual teams probably cannot share a single pizza, the increase in interdependent work nearer to the deadline probably remains the same.)

Note that the temptation is particularly strong for virtual teams to break their work into smaller, less interconnected (that is, more independent) pieces. This can make the task easier, but it may limit the amount of value that can be realized by having team members work more interdependently. In fact, most teams are created so that the work products can benefit from multiple perspectives on each piece; thus to break the work into a serial-assembly-line type of arrangement may violate the mission of the team. For example, MBA student teams assigned to create a project or case analysis as a group often fall prey to this trap, and the resulting project then contains abrupt and visible seams where the work has clearly been created by different minds and then fails to be fully integrated.

In addition to the problem of integration, working in this way also limits the ability of the team to create something *different* as a group than what they create as a series of individuals. Team synergy research shows that teams can and regularly do surpass the sum of their parts and can create new ideas and knowledge together. A common classroom exercise is used to demonstrate this effect. In it, students are asked to make decisions about which items would be most useful if they found themselves stranded somewhere. Individuals rank the items, and then groups need to come to consensus on what to prioritize. Not only do most teams outperform the average of the individual decisions, but most even outperform the level of the *best* individual, indicating that there is value in both pooling insights and discussing issues.

After assessing the team's context, the next step is to decide what level of relationship will need to be developed for each individual team member.

While of course it seems ideal to have a close relationship with each and every team member, this is not always practical or efficient. In some cases, it pays for the leader to strategically develop sub-teams. Then, the leader can create and nurture close ties with the sub-team leaders instead of trying to connect with every individual on a larger team.

To move towards this view of leadership as a facilitation or coordination effort more than a power position, it can be helpful to recognize that power in the virtual team means something slightly different than it does

---

Sidebar 8.1.   Adopting New Technologies

Virtual teams sometimes must begin with a process of convergence on which technological tools they are going to use. Thus, some members may need to adopt and learn new systems to achieve a common platform for the team. What makes people more willing to try out a new system for communicating digitally? More specifically, what types of introductions make people more or less predisposed to *like* the new system? Researchers in the area of innovation adoptions aimed to answer just this question by experimentally testing different phrases when introducing a new technology. Participants were divided into four groups. Two of the groups were introduced to the technology by hearing about the features themselves, and two heard about what *other people* thought of the technology as a whole. Within the features-specific introductions, one group heard positively framed messages (such as, "This tool works well most of the time, and can be easy to learn") and the other heard equivalent but negatively framed messages (such as, "This tool fails only occasionally, and could be a bit difficult to learn"). The groups that heard about what other people thought similarly had a positive version ("This tool has been widely accepted by others, and the majority have found it invaluable") and a negative version ("This tool has been rejected by only a few people, and only a small minority have found it worthless"). What made the biggest difference? In general, people paid more attention to the sentences that referred to what other people thought than to the ones that described the technology itself. Additionally, people responded more strongly to any kind of negative statements than to the positive ones. So the worst condition was having people hear that others have disliked the tool before, even if the sentence stated that only a small number of people disliked it. And once formed, these impressions lasted long beyond the initial period of trial and learning. Hearing positive statements about the features themselves also had a potential problem—sometimes, expectations were raised too high and the actual features then fell short, leading to disappointment with the tool. The bottom line: the most convincing statements to sell new technology are those that report on the success that others have found with it.

Vishwanath, A. (2009). From belief-importance to intention: The impact of framing on technology adoption. *Communication Monographs, 76(2),* 177–206.

in a traditional team. The real power in a virtual team is driven by what can be thought of as "knowledge power," or the person who is best able to take charge of a project at a particular moment in time. The very best teams transfer this power from member to member as needed throughout the life of their work together. The role of the formal leader is to help the team build trust at the early stages of its work together and then to promote shared understandings among members as the project progresses.[13]

LEADING VIRTUAL TEAMS AS A 12-STEP PROCESS

Leadership means first developing and then monitoring team activities. Policies can also help to set up a successful virtual team, especially when team members reside in different areas (both in terms of physical location and content area). As stated above, one of the most critical insights needed to successfully lead a virtual team is that whatever management techniques you think you need to use with people, you need to use them more boldly and explicitly in the virtual setting. Subtlety simply doesn't come across when you can't see people's faces and don't have the opportunity for spontaneous interactions. What follows are 12 topics with which virtual managers need to contend,[14] presented as a set of problems, and then a list of ideas to help address each issue.

1. **Timing.** The timing of both work and interactions can be unpredictable in the virtual realm. Some things can happen very quickly and efficiently; other times people may wait eight hours for a response to something that is holding them up. Virtual teams also have a natural tendency to be more deadline driven.

   Solutions:
   a. Set expectations appropriately. Make sure all people know to alert each other about when they will give their attention to the work and to each other.
   b. Avoiding timing issues also requires an upfront commitment on the part of the team members to make time for each other as immediately as possible. For busy people, seeing an e-mail from someone not present, but who needs your attention, could mean that you have your assistant schedule a half-hour call two weeks out. This approach is not likely to work for the team as a whole. Instead, have people commit to giving 5 to 10 minutes of attention ASAP once a request has been made.
   c. Virtual teams work better with a more well-defined temporal structure. In addition to concrete suggestions or policies about the length of time permissible between a message sent and the

reply, other formal procedures for accomplishing work will help to regulate the pace of the interactions among the teammates. All of the mechanisms used to manage a team's time, including the use of deadlines, specifying the needs for when and how collaboration of team members (synchronization) should occur, and allocating defined amounts of time for specific tasks can all help to align people's focus and the pattern, timing, and content of their communication for the better.[15]

d. Leaders need to plan well, not just for the team's meetings, but for the times before and after each meeting as well. The process of the work should be on the leader's mind at all times, not just the next deadline or final product.

2. **Evaluation.** Often, team members are divided between their "regular" work and their work on a virtual team, and performance appraisals may only be done by their "regular" managers and not the ones from the virtual team. This imbalance can cause both stress and a lack of dedication to the virtual team.

   Solutions:
   a. As a virtual leader, make sure to evaluate the performance of each team member and communicate this report to the "regular" manager. All team members should be told at the outset that information will be communicated regularly in this way, especially notes of commendation for any job well done.
   b. As much as possible, have each team member's performance evaluation on this virtual team count towards his or her overall performance in the company.
   c. Plain and simple public thank-yous for jobs requiring large efforts should also not be overlooked.

3. **Virtual vs. Face-to-Face Interactions.** Many virtual teams operate by scheduling occasional face-to-face meetings to let people meet or reconnect with each other, and to make progress on the work while members are all together. As mentioned earlier, however, some research has found that this structure can actually *impede* overall progress on the work. The logic is that if these in-person meetings exist, too much work gets pushed off "until we see each other," and then once together, too much time is spent reviewing what has been long forgotten since the last meeting. Some studies even suggest that once accustomed to interacting online, later meetings in a different way (such as face to face) can actually have a negative impact on the relationships, because "modality switching"

can be a source of stress and new ways of relating to each other must be established.[16]

> *Solution:* Contrary to some other perspectives, one option is to ban travel entirely for the occasional face-to-face meeting. Some who have tried this method report that when forced into the 100% virtual status, teams will find better ways to make progress. Personal disclosures or discussions, when offered via text, also tend to have a stronger impact than the same types of comments offered out loud.[17] So, there is something to be said for allowing the relationships to develop electronically, and then leaving them alone in that medium. A middle-ground idea is to have one kick-off meeting in person so that people can put names to faces, and then proceed from there in an entirely virtual way.

4. **Choice of Medium.** Even setting aside face-to-face communication, there may still be disagreement about how to communicate. Some people are just "phone people" and prefer to make a call rather than answer an e-mail. Others prefer text, but have opinions as to which types of programs work best. Still others swear by group platforms that allow for documents and comments to be organized, saved, and accessed by all.

> *Solution:* This one probably needs to be negotiated on a case-by-case basis. By way of example, some teams have chosen to ban e-mail in favor of a group virtual workspace for posting comments, since discussions between only two people can cause more misunderstandings and leave other people out of the loop. Others have chosen to have all members available via an Instant Messaging platform all day long for immediate access to each other. Whatever the team decides, it is helpful to have individuals discuss the pros and cons of each platform at the outset and then establish expectation guidelines.

5. **Development.** Even in the virtual realm, people need challenge, and generally thrive on being stretched. In addition, it is good for the team and the organization to have its employees become proficient at new skills.

> *Solution:* Create policies that reward both the accomplishment of the work itself and the learning and development of the members. While this may include mastery of technologies and processes to work with others virtually, it can also include

developing specific skills and expertise to aid work across lines/ areas within the company. Team members will naturally gravitate towards those activities that give them the most benefits. Be on the lookout for emergent leadership, and support and encourage it.

6. **Role Clarity.** People certainly need to know exactly what they are supposed to be doing, but in addition to that, they also need to know why each, specifically, is on the team at all. For instance, were team members (located in other countries) chosen to represent their country, their department, future customers in their local region, or some other specific expertise? Were they chosen primarily because the leader knew and liked them from previous interactions or personal friendships?

> *Solution:* All team members should be very clear about their independent roles and the roles of other team members. This also means that the "old way" of choosing team members based on whom the leaders already know needs to give way to a more thorough justification of each person on the team (matching a need established in a skills matrix, for example) to ensure the correct fit for the work that needs doing.

7. **Diversity.** The idea that people are more comfortable with others who are like them is well established. Diversity can breed not only a fear of the unknown, but misunderstandings and missed opportunities for effective collaboration.

> *Solutions:*
> a. Identify and discuss differences among teammates early and often. Not all problems will surface before the work starts, but team leaders should reserve (and use) the right to publicize different approaches as they arise. This can include anything from personality-survey type results to different cultural approaches (national culture or even departmental culture) to solving problems.
> b. Encourage members to identify their processes out loud, as in, "I tend to like to discuss things and then take a break to think it all over before I'm ready to make a decision," or even, "I prefer to pick up the phone and discuss an issue as opposed to send an e-mail about it, so expect plenty of calls from me."

8. **Technology.** While it is reasonable to assume that most people are at least functional on tech systems for virtual communication (such

as e-mail), it is not a universal truth and switching platforms can cause all kinds of problems. The big concern is not just that problems will arise, but that they will be hidden from view. Actually getting people to speak up when they don't understand something is a tall order, and a rare occurrence.

> *Solution:* Encourage questions when processes, or the technologies themselves, don't make sense. Monitor what's happening, and be ready to step in if, for example, it seems someone is using the "comment" function on the documents too rarely, or incorrectly. This can be addressed directly, in a one-on-one training session, or indirectly, by pairing the teammate with a more experienced member for a portion of the work. The aim would be to have the two work together in real time and thus the techniques would be demonstrated naturally.

9. **Momentum.** Know that all teams lose steam at some point, and need to be re-energized. It is a normal part of the human experience to lose excitement for a project (or other people) once the newness has worn off and the real challenges emerge. In addition, the "out of sight, out of mind" problem can make virtual teamwork lower on the to-do list for many members.

> *Quote from the front line:* *"Typically when I first start working with a new virtual team their work is solid and the response times are pretty fast, but over time things start to get more drawn out and the work can slip up a little. I think initially there's motivation to demonstrate value, but once they've been with me for a while, they get comfortable and the work suffers.*

> *Solutions:*
> a. Shake things up occasionally by having a different kind of meeting (a more social one, for example). Other ways to change the pace are to invite a guest speaker with expertise relevant to the team, invite someone else in the company to talk about related work, or even work on an irrelevant but fun task or puzzle together.
> b. Note that at about the mid-point of a team's timeline, people are more receptive to stepping back to assess the progress so far and potentially re-group for the plans to complete the work.[18]
> c. Make electronic check-ins and progress updates frequent and mandatory. Find reasons to contact the team regularly with

updates of your own. Encourage team members to send mini-updates (sometimes called "Eureka!" and "Oh Shoot" messages) as they progress through their work, to keep others connected with what they are doing in real time. Don't just wait until there is an official update at a meeting.

10. **Virtual Meetings.** Anything routine can become something that people tune out. So while regular check-in meetings are important for team functioning on lots of levels, they can stop being effective if the meetings lose the attention of the attendees.

   Solutions:
   a. Establish the "rules of engagement" for each meeting. Some conference calls can tolerate people being half-focused and half-distracted, for example, while others need complete and total focus. (Remember that immediate attention can wane as often as every few minutes, and overall burnout for a topic starts after 20 to 40 minutes without a break. After that, you probably can't count on full focus from the meeting attendees.[19] Design meetings to cover only what is critical so as to not drift off into "The Land of Lost Focus.")
   b. Be clear with everyone ahead of time about the expectations for each meeting. This can be as detailed as telling people what and how they are expected to contribute, who is charged with facilitating that particular meeting, who is responsible for recording and posting the decisions made at the meetings, and what sort of follow-up is required.
   c. Each meeting should be ended with three items: a specific to-do list that is posted visibly for all, a defined timetable for people to post their progress on identified tasks, and a plan for what the next meeting should accomplish.
   d. Plan meeting agendas precisely. The ability to "wing it" might work in the face-to-face setting, but doesn't work in the virtual world.
   e. If possible, include the ability for members to vote on items during the meeting, with either Instant Messaging or even good old-fashioned "say 'aye'" types of questions.

11. **Norms.** People are both very social animals and creatures of habit. Both of these traits can work against productive behaviors if the wrong ones are established at any point in time. In other words, it is important to know that any of the team's "rules" can slide if so little as one person, one time, does not follow them and no repercussions

result. People are very attuned to noticing what others are doing and what happens afterwards.

Solutions: Remind everyone, for example, that if you have asked them to check the team's discussion board daily and report on their work, that you expect them to do so and will notice if they do not. Then notice if they do not! Additionally, negative behaviors often happen for a reason, and it is worth the time to see if the norm-breaking behaviors may indicate the need to change processes. Ask lots of questions and listen to the responses before deciding if it is the person or the process that is at fault.

12. **Evolution.** Lastly, understand that no matter how well it has been planned and executed, no team will ever get their processes exactly right on the first try. Teams change, their needs evolve, and the first solution isn't always the best one.

Solution: This can be helped by two different levels of approach—one big picture and one detail oriented.

a. On the big picture side, advocate an attitude of experimentation about all of your processes, and even the technologies themselves. Be prepared to adapt if the original models aren't best serving the needs of the team.

b. On the details, make it a concrete agenda item in meetings regularly to discuss the process issues—what's working and what isn't? Does everyone feel that they are sufficiently kept in the loop about the relevant work progress? If not, what would they prefer to see happen to ensure that the problem is solved? Are the technology choices working, or is (for example) the team over-relying on e-mail for things that should be communicated on a discussion board?

Together, these 12 issues start to paint a picture of what leadership means in the virtual setting. Though not entirely specific to virtual teams, the issues do change and come into focus differently under these circumstances.

EMERGENT LEADERSHIP

Before concluding, it is worthy of note that leadership in teams is not always based on a formally assigned position, but instead can emerge from a team of peers. This process can happen in either a more structured or a more organic way. One study showed that in face-to-face groups, for example, those with assigned leaders (like groups with no leader at all) were actually *less* cooperative with and *less* trusting of each other than were groups who were encouraged to select their own leader.[20] However, this process may be more difficult in virtual teams, as it can take longer to get to know the members' strengths and weaknesses and converge on opinions about selecting a leader. Left to their own devices, online groups may be more likely to have multiple leaders instead, though not necessarily at a single point in time. In these groups, leadership conferral may be a more dynamic process that changes over time as the needs of the group and the expertise of the members becomes more defined.[21] Thus, the structural roles that a leader needs to take, as described above, may still best be served by a single defined leader from the outset. Expertise-based leadership can still be shared among team members as needed.

SUMMARY

Leadership in the virtual world is both the same as and very different from leadership in a face-to-face setting. Thus, while it has much overlap with managing a face-to-face team, it can also require a different focus on managing the process (the relationship between team members and their work) as well as developing and maintaining connections among the team members themselves. Therefore, more frequent and effective communication is a required tool in the manager's arsenal. Virtual leaders must also be cognizant of potential team problems. To avoid future headaches, it is suggested that these managers take the time to assess the team members before the group even begins its work. The 12-step outline can guide virtual team leaders to establish helpful policies so that the teams can be both efficient and successful.

NOTES

1. Kouzes, J. M. & Posner, B. Z. (2007). *The leadership challenge.* San Francisco, CA: Jossey-Bass.

2. Cascio, W. F. (2000). Managing a virtual workplace. *Academy of Management Executive, 14(3)*, 81–90.

3. Gajendran, R. S. & Joshi, A. (2011). Inclusion and identification in virtual workgroups: (When) does leader-member virtual communication matter? *Academy of Management Annual Conference Best Papers Proceedings.*

4. Wilson, J. M., O'Leary, M. B., Metiu, A., & Jett, Q. R. (2008). Perceived proximity in virtual work: Explaining the paradox of far-but-close. *Organization Studies, 29(7)*, 979–1002.

5. Hackman, J. R. & Oldham, G. R. (1980). *Work redesign.* Reading, MA: Addison-Wesley.

6. Humphrey, S. E., Nahrgang, J. D., & Morgeson, F. P. (2007). Integrating motivational, social, and contextual work design features: A meta-analytic summary and theoretical extension of the work design literature. *Journal of Applied Psychology, 92(5),* 1332–1356.

7. McGrath, J. E. (1991). Time, interaction, and performance (TIP): A theory of groups. *Small Group Research, 22,* 147–174.

8. Whittingham, R. B. (2004). *The blame machine: Why human error causes accidents.* Burlingham, MA: Elsevier Butterworth-Heinemann.

9. Naquin, C. E. & Tynan, R. O. (2003). The team halo effect: Why teams are not blamed for their failures. *Journal of Applied Psychology, 88(2),* 332–340.

10. Crampton, C. D. (2001). The mutual knowledge problem and its consequences for dispersed collaboration. *Organization Science, 12(3),* 346–371.

11. Pauleen, D. J. (2003–2004). An inductively derived model of leader-initiated relationship building with virtual team members. *Journal of Management Information Systems, 20(3),* 227–256. Bell, B. S. & Kozlowski, S. W. J. (2002). *Group and Organization Management, 27(1),* 14–49.

12. Thompson, J. D. (1967). *Organizations in action: Social science bases of administrative theory.* New Brunswick, NJ: Transaction Publishers. Also Van de Ven, A. H., Delbecq, A. L., & Koenig, R. (1976). Determinants of coordination modes within organizations. *American Sociological Review, 41,* 322–328.

13. Panteli, N. & Tucker, R. (2009). Power and trust in global virtual teams. *Communications of the ACM, 52(12),* 113–115.

14. Majchrzak, A. & Malhotra, A. (2003). *Deploying far-flung teams: A guidebook for managers.* Chicago, IL: Society for Information Management Advanced Practices Council.

15. Ocker, R., Hiltz, S., Turoff, M., & Fjermestad, J. (1995–1996). The effects of distributed group support and process structuring on software requirements development teams: Results on creativity and quality. *Journal of Management Information Systems, 12(3),* 127–153.

16. Ramirez, A. & Zhang, S. (2007). When online meets offline: The effect of modality switching on relational communication. *Communications Monographs, 74(3),* 287–310.

17. Jiang, L. C., Bazarova, N. N., & Hancokc, J. T. (2011). The disclosure-intimacy link in computer-mediated communication: An attributional extension of the hyperpersonal model. *Human Communication Research, 37(1),* 58–77.

18. Gersick, C. (1991). Revolutionary change theories: A multilevel exploration of the punctuated equilibrium paradigm. *The Academy of Management Review 16(1),* 10–36.

19. Cornish, D. & Dukette, D. (2009). *The essential 20: Twenty components of an excellent health care team.* Pittsburgh, PA: RoseDog Books, pp. 72–73.

20. Naquin, C. E. & Kurtzberg, T. R. (2013). Leadership selection and cooperation in social dilemmas: An exploration of assigned versus self-selected leaders. Working paper. DePaul University, Chicago, IL.

21. Wickram, K. R. & Walther, J. B. (2007). Perceived behaviors of assigned and emergent leaders in virtual groups. *International Journal of e-Collaboration, 3,* 1–17.

NINE

Electronic Decision Making

FACE-TO-FACE TEAMS AND THE PRESSURE TO CONFORM

Before discussing the ways that decision making may change in the virtual environment, it is necessary to explore how decisions get made in teams at all. While even individual decisions can fall prey to any number of biases based on seemingly innocuous details (like which piece of information you happen to see first), decision making in a group is a whole different animal. The first and most influential type of pressure that people unknowingly place on each other is the pressure to conform to the majority. While it makes sense that people might easily be swayed by the opinions and judgments of others when the situation is particularly ambiguous or confusing, the pressure to conform has proven to be even more demanding than that.

A series of experiments, undertaken in the 1950s, demonstrated how persuasive the pressure to conform could be. Participants were taken into a room containing a group of people who, unbeknownst to them, were actually confederates of the experimenter. The group was then asked to make a judgment call. For instance, together they were shown a single line, and then separately were shown three other lines labeled A, B, and C, where one of the three was identical to the first line (let's say it was B), and one was shorter (line A) and one was longer (line C) than the first line. The focal participant was always seated so that the majority of other group members answered the question, out loud, first. For the first few cases, all the confederates gave the right answer, and the focal participant went along with what the majority and common sense dictated. But then the rest of the group started to give the wrong answer. Instead of saying "B" as in the example above, person after person gave the answer "C." This experiment was designed to ask, "What would the focal participant answer"? Now, you are probably thinking (like the vast majority of people would), "If it were me, *of course* I would stand up for what I believe to be the right answer, even if everyone else is saying something else." And, many times, you'd be right, since in these experiments, only 5% of the people conformed every time (that is, agreed with the majority of the group, regardless of what they actually thought). But your resistance to group pressure may not be as complete as you think. On average, only 25% of people *never* gave the wrong answer. That is to say, in 75% of the cases, on some questions they stuck to their personal views and on others they gave in to the pressures of conformity and gave the *blatantly wrong* answer that everyone else was giving. And across many trials, people tended to give the wrong answer about 30% of the time.[1]

Over 50 years later, cognitive neuroscientists followed up on this question and asked a related one: Do people do this on purpose or not? After all, people like to be liked, and if a room full of people all think that Candidate Jones is the perfect choice when you were initially in favor of Candidate Keats, won't they like you better if you also voice support for Jones? Is the need to "go along to get along" so strong that you might just tell a lie to be accepted (or at least to not ruffle feathers)? Perhaps, but people also like to be right! So in this room full of Jones supporters, it may occur to you that perhaps you've overlooked some of the good qualities that Candidate Jones has to offer, since everyone else seems to see them.

Evidence points to a more subtle mechanism instead. What scientists found when doing brain scans of people during these types of experiments was that their brains retroactively changed what they thought they saw. In other words, the brain re-wrote the memory of the length of the line (in the above example) to produce a different image than what they had previously seen before they heard all those other wrong answers. In another stark example of the fact that human beings are very social creatures, we see here that people literally change their minds based on what other people tell them to think about the world, even without meaning to.

The pressure to conform can be a useful instinct. Indeed, sometimes it is safer to trust the group than your own impressions. But this tendency can also bias the decisions of a group. In extreme cases, when the need to agree supersedes all other motives, a condition called "groupthink" can result, with potentially disastrous consequences. Famous examples from history, including the doomed launch of the Challenger spaceship, indicate that the pressure to conform and to self-silence opposing viewpoints can be incredibly risky. The freedom to voice concerns or dissenting opinions is absolutely critical to effective team decision making. And the good news is that it does not take a lot of dissent before the "conformity spell" is broken: if even a single other individual gives the objectively right answer in a task like the line-matching one mentioned above, the percentage of people who will proceed to agree with the wrong answer (even if still given by the majority of people), drops to about 5%.[2]

The pressure to conform also unfolds in a slightly more surprising way. As described above, people are most comfortable agreeing with others, and less comfortable offering differing opinions and thoughts. This behavior also seems to extend into the realm of information sharing in a group setting. Without consciously trying to edit themselves, people have a strong tendency to only discuss things that the others in the group *already know about*, and to resist adding information that is truly distinct. As you can readily imagine, this does not serve the interests of the group well at all. Groups are formed, after all, to capitalize on the pooling of uncommon information, talents, and skills of the individual members. Members themselves enter group discussions with good intentions of sharing their knowledge, yet study after study has shown that the group tends to converge on discussions of *shared* knowledge, and not unique knowledge. The psychological drive for this is the need for acceptance, and the risk that one takes when introducing a new idea is that it will be ridiculed. Again here, many people, upon learning of this tendency, think "Not me! I have no problem speaking up and bringing up new information." Perhaps, but then again, while most people think of themselves as forthright in this way, only a few actually are in a real situation.

To demonstrate this point to MBA students, an activity is commonly used whereby individuals are given various facts about a fictitious murder that has taken place. Each participant reads a set of materials that summarizes the police's findings thus far in the investigation. The police have ruled out all but three suspects and have provided some of the transcripts from the interviews that they have conducted with the remaining suspects. Unbeknownst to the study participants, not all team members have received the same set of transcripts. If the information in all of the transcripts was discussed in the group's meeting, they would, by process of elimination, identify the actual murderer. Should be a no-brainer, right? But, a surprising number of groups (as many as 60%, by some estimates!) don't put all of this together. Why? One reason is the one raised earlier, whereby people feel better and more comfortable talking about the information that the others already know. It's very validating to have someone else confirm what you are saying.

There is a second obstacle, though, and that is the idea of *escalation of commitment*. Many people decide on their opinion or vote on an issue *before* the meeting itself. Instead of learning the perspectives of and listening to information shared by other people, they spend the meeting time trying to refute this new information and convince the others that they had the right idea all along. Thus they hope to convince others to vote with them. How do we know this happens? In the murder task described above, groups occasionally decide that a *fourth* suspect, no longer under suspicion, is actually the culprit, though this one would be clearly ruled out if *any* information shared had been absorbed.

Though the murder mystery exercise is very vivid, it's not very realistic in terms of a business setting. To make these points even more strongly to business school students, a second activity is sometimes used in which a team of people are asked to play senior managers in a company making a high-level hiring decision.[3] Each of three candidates is reviewed for the position prior to the meeting, and again, unbeknownst to the team, each manager has slightly different information about the strengths and weaknesses of the three under consideration (though many facts are held in common). This activity gets more interesting when you realize that taken in isolation, each individual manager's information makes candidate #2 seem like the best choice, but if all information were systematically pooled and compared, there are actually more benefits to choosing candidate #1 (the knowledge of those benefits was more spread out among the managers doing the hiring, so the benefits don't always get considered in total). In other words, let's say each of four managers might know of five benefits for hiring candidate #2, and two for hiring candidate #3. If all the managers already know the same five benefits for candidate #2, that leads to a total of five advantages. But if the two benefits that each knows about candidate #3 are distinct, then there would be a total of eight advantages to hiring that candidate. When doing this activity, a solid 90% of groups end up hiring candidate #2. This is doubtless in part because they fail to realize that there may actually be more benefits to recommending candidate #3 if they had all systematically shared their information and kept open minds about who they themselves wanted to vote for—that is, had they been willing to change their minds and their votes as a result of the discussion and the new information gleaned therein.

Most participants in this exercise prepare for the meeting by thinking through how they will argue for their top choice, convince others that their opinion is the right one, and then "win the day" by getting their top candidate elected. In the meeting itself, most groups engage in the following process:

- They begin by taking some sort of vote, or straw poll, of each member's initial opinion.
- Quickly the group finds out that the vast majority of members (many times, it is even unanimous) prefer candidate #2. Occasionally a group will quit there and hire #2 immediately.
- But most groups take the time to do their "due diligence" and at least have a discussion about the other candidates. They talk some about the pros and cons of each candidate, and, as mentioned above, they tend to reiterate and agree with the things that others have already said. Even if someone does choose to say something that the others do not already know, research shows that these new facts are *less well remembered* by the rest of the team.[4]
- All the team members then feel good about themselves, the process that they used to arrive at their decision, and their teammates. They then proceed to make the sub-optimal decision.

What teams fail to do is two-fold: (1) Keep an open mind before making a final decision—after all, isn't the team gathered for the express purpose of pooling expertise to create something better than what one individual could have done alone? And (2) be systematic in the collection of information, repeatedly asking everyone if they have anything to share that hasn't already been covered. These two tools together can help tremendously in avoiding this trap.

TIP

Don't firm up your opinions before a meeting, and don't ask others to commit to their opinions at the outset (in other words, don't vote too early). Use the meeting itself to systematically gather all information from everyone, repeatedly soliciting remaining thoughts.

Similarly, even when sharing new knowledge, people are much more likely to tell their peers things that *relate* to something that they already know about. Called *incremental knowledge*, these ideas build on conversations or topics that have already been established, and thus feel more approachable. Brand new knowledge or ideas are of uncertain value, and thus may feel riskier to offer. In fact, research shows that entirely new ideas are most often discussed with superiors instead of with peers—these ideas seem to need to be vetted from above before they are raised in the team itself.[5]

Quotes from the front lines: *"I was in a meeting once where some opinions were raised that made me question my original plan for an important vote. But I felt truly uncomfortable flipping that quickly the decision I had come up with during my preparation based on the objective materials I had studied ahead of time. I ended up voting the way I had planned to, but to this day I'm not sure it was the right thing to do."*

TIP

Consider separating meetings for sharing information from meetings for making a decision (or allow for final decisions to be made at a later point in time). People are much more comfortable both accepting new information and changing their minds after they have had a chance to get used to new ideas.

Now consider these concerns in light of the fact that team members engaging in electronic conversations have an even weaker tendency to share information at all (especially at the beginning of their work together),[6] and the problem for virtual teams becomes quite clear. Team members need to be encouraged to share ideas and thoughts that might, or might not, end up useful in the end. This can be accomplished through dedicated time in some team meetings, or (in line with the strengths of virtual interactions) virtual teams can utilize a postings page for ideas that might or might not be relevant to others, just to get more ideas circulating.

TIP

Find ways to specifically invite all ideas to surface, especially on virtual teams.

A final problem is meeting participants who do not speak up at all. Often, this is driven by a power dynamic. Look around the room at the people speaking the most often, and you will probably be able to correctly identify those with the highest positions of power. In addition, even a single person with great expertise on a topic, or one person offering a strong argument, can be enough to unintentionally intimidate and silence others at the table.

Quotes from the front lines: *"At my first job, at big meetings, the top-level managers always sat around the conference table and talked, while the more junior-level associates sat on chairs pushed back against the walls of the room and said nothing unless specifically asked. At my second job, everyone sat around the table together and joked and talked. The senior people even solicited opinions from the more junior ones before they them-selves voiced their opinions, so they could speak without the fear of dis-agreeing with a superior."*

Especially in virtual groups where team leaders might not know all of the members well at the outset of the project, soliciting opinions from every person is a critical step. In fact, some argue that this process is actually easier in a conference call or an online conversation than it is in person. Face-to-face meetings have the extra burden of politeness to con-tend with, whereas virtual meetings of any kind are afforded a level of directness, out of necessity. For example, oftentimes, in person, people will nod along with a statement, due to politeness more so than agree-ment. This confusion is avoided if people (a) don't see each other and (b) have a chance to have the floor and state their thoughts and opinions.[7]

The conformity pressure in groups can also make people feel "egged on" to make more extreme choices than they would be willing to commit to on their own. The extreme choices can go in either direction, more risky or more cautious (or even less ethical). There are four parts to the explana-tion of why this tends to happen.

1. Accountability is spread out when more than one person is associ-ated with a decision. People are just more willing to "take a flyer" on a wild position if they feel that others also believe in it.
2. There is a general tendency for group discussions to intensify the actual opinions held by the individual members. Hearing other peo-ple agree with you can make you that much more sure that you were *so right* in the first place. And who doesn't like being right?
3. Both actual and imagined conformity pressures exist, as discussed earlier. Pressure to conform can certainly be real, but it can also stem from what is called *pluralistic ignorance* (but could also easily be called *mistaken* conformity pressure instead), which is the sense peo-ple have when they think that "everybody else wants this," even if in fact each and every group member is only going along with a

decision because each feels the others want it, and not because of an internal belief in it.[8]

4. Lastly, conformity pressure can also manifest itself in the faulty decision to "stay the course" when instead change is warranted. This is another version of the *escalation of commitment* effect, and this problem identifies the strongly held desire to stick with a decision or course of action once it has been established.

How to fix this? Personal accountability is one answer, but beyond accountability for the outcomes, research shows that having to be responsible for the *process* used to make decisions also leads to better decision making.[9] Another element in the solution has to do with what is called *psychological safety*, or the feeling that the team is characterized by open, supportive communication, speaking up, and risk taking.[10] Studies show that teams that can create this atmosphere are less likely to fall into many of the pitfalls presented by the virtual team structure, and these teams are more likely to have innovative end products to boot.[11]

One conclusion drawn by some researchers is to do away entirely with consensus as a goal of any decision-making process, to avoid the added conformity pressure. More specifically, striving for consensus can easily lead down one of two fruitless paths.

- It can lead to endless haggling as members try in vain to shout down others with opposing viewpoints and fail to adequately consider changing their own minds. Prolonged haggling such as this can result in either a minor annoyance or a major problem whereby decisions are delayed unreasonably. Individuals may also become so embroiled in the fight that they end up disenfranchised and look to leave the team (or even company).
- It can lead to a *false* consensus, whereby people cave in to the majority opinion because they simply do not care enough to have the fight over their true opinion. In this latter case, what passes for consensus may actually be disengagement with the task. It can be hard to know whether consensus is truly indicative of harmony or whether it is actually just a display of apathy.[12] In particular, decisions that come too easily or too quickly are candidates for being re-examined.

Using a "majority rules" decision criteria is the other most popular norm. Yet this too can be problematic, as it can encourage coalitions and politicking internally to get the majority on one's side, as well as an unhappy minority.

Yet before a decision is simply handed down from above, people do need to have a sense of fairness about the process by which their opinions are heard, even if they do not translate directly into the final decision. To help ensure that false consensus isn't driving the results, it is important to make sure that all perspectives have been heard. A few suggestions for making this happen are presented here.

- Appoint a "devil's advocate," or someone specifically assigned to argue for a point of view contrary to the ones already on the table. Rotate this role so that no one person gets associated with being overly negative.
- Make sure that all people understand that it is part of their responsibility to create and present options that satisfy not only their own point of view, but also the needs of the rest of the team as well. To get in this habit, people can occasionally be asked to represent and speak up on behalf of a different constituency, just for practice in changing frames.[13]
- Give chances for new perspectives to be raised. Ask questions like, "Are there any perspectives we haven't heard yet or thought through completely?" If you feel that ideas may fail to surface in the group setting (even at something dedicated to the process like a "second chance" meeting), poll people privately to make sure relevant concerns are aired.
- End the discussion of decisions with the question, "Who can't live with this proposal?" This can help pave the way for buy-in even for non-preferred ideas.[14]

Remember that the ultimate goal is not consensus for its own sake, but having integrated team perspectives that will likely encourage better solutions.

TIP

Consensus is a nice outcome, but not a required one for good decisions (and striving for it may even hamper the process at times). Make sure a decision structure is in place to move decisions forward with input, but without the blind need for unanimity.

Finally, a related problem (and one that is especially relevant to virtual teams) is having the right people involved in the decision at the time it is being made. Too often, in virtual situations, people end up having smaller phone conversations or e-mail exchanges in pairs and omitting the input of people relevant to the topic.

Quotes from the front lines: "In my experience, decision making goes badly on virtual teams because of the joint problems of miscommunication, not having the right decision makers in the right meetings, and not having the right data/information at the right times to make good decisions. As a result, things get decided, then reversed, then confused, then changed again as better information and relevant people get included."

VIRTUAL DECISIONS

Earlier chapters in this book have discussed the ways in which moving to a virtual setting from a face-to-face one can change the nature of conversations, relationships, and even judgments. Decision making is no exception, and it is important to understand how the psychological distance afforded by virtual interaction can change both the processes and the outcomes in predictable ways.

Certain tasks are better suited to the electronic realm. To begin, a theory in psychology called *construal theory* explains that people have different tendencies towards thinking in more concrete or more abstract terms (on a number of dimensions) depending on how close or how far away they are from the topic in question.[15] People tend to think in very general terms about an event that will occur far in the future, for example, but will think in very detailed terms about an event on the immediate horizon. Imagine that you are planning a conference for a year from now. Your thinking at this point in time will probably center on the overall goals of the conference. A week before the conference is to take place, however, your thoughts are much more likely to be focused on the logistics of the event instead.

While this example demonstrates the shift from abstract to concrete thinking as you approach the event in terms of time, further studies into this effect demonstrate that the same shift in thinking can happen for other kinds of relative distance as well. Physical distance from others can trigger the same kinds of responses, as can feeling socially connected or disconnected from others in a conversation (such as in-group and out-group members). This has great implications for virtual teams, who are nearly always separated from each other on at least one dimension, and often more. More abstract thinking (or "higher level" construals) tends to be less detailed, but may be capable of synthesizing and representing ideas and processes in new ways. Research has shown that distance can thus inspire greater objectivity, less emotion, and clearer big-picture thinking than can people who are close to each other in physical or psychological ways.[16]

TIP

Understand that distance can change thinking style towards the more abstract and away from the concrete. When detailed tasks arise, make sure the individuals in question first renew their sense of focus on each other and the task to help facilitate this frame of mind.

Creativity in the Virtual Setting

One distinction made in the decision-making realm is between divergent and convergent tasks. Divergent tasks are idea-generation tasks (like brainstorming), and have the specific goal of generating many different options for consideration. Convergent tasks involve the selection of ideas, or the narrowing down from a whole field of options to choose the most viable one(s) for proceeding. A review of the research in this area comes to a clear conclusion: computer-mediated discussions are not only effective, but are potentially even *more* effective than their face-to-face counterparts at divergent tasks, but are less effective on convergent tasks.[17]

A classroom exercise on brainstorming gives some clues as to why idea generation might happen more effectively online. In this activity, a class is divided in half, and each half consists of a number of distinct teams of about four people (let's call the two halves of the room Side One and Side Two). All teams are given the same task to do, in which they have 20 minutes to develop as many ideas as possible for applications for a brand-new technology (for example, electronic ink that can be programmed from afar to change its message at any time).[18] Side One is told to use a typical brainstorming process whereby they discuss ideas out loud and have at least one person act as a recorder to capture all ideas on a list. Side Two is told to engage in an activity called *brain-writing* instead. In this process, all four team members are asked to start with a piece of paper and a pen, and during the allotted 20 minutes, each person writes down an idea and then passes the paper to another teammate. Upon receiving a new piece of paper, each team member reads what is already on that paper, and then adds a new idea (related or unrelated to the other ideas on that page). Students on Side One may have more fun laughing and talking aloud, but those on Side Two nearly *always* end up with more ideas collectively. Some of the reason is the more efficient use of time, since everyone is working at once, but it is also due to the increased stimulation that each person gets by being exposed to more of each other's ideas. The text-based format that many virtual teams use for communicating is more closely aligned with the brain-writing task than the traditional out-loud brainstorming.

When it comes to the topic of innovation, having communication and interaction happen across time and space also affords people the opportunity to get used to ideas. To understand the potential strength of this opportunity, the problem must first be explained. A paradox has been discovered in the area of creativity, whereby people often *say* that they support and seek novel ideas, but in reality they *resist* them when actually presented with them. In fact, even with full support from the top for the concept of creativity, both creative ideas and creative people seem to meet more than their share of opposition. Though it is not openly acknowledged, people seem to have an implicit bias against creativity.[19]

The reason this is so hard to spot, even in yourself, is because this is what psychologists would call an "approach-avoidance" problem. Your instincts are, at the same time, telling you to approach and to avoid creative ideas. This problem seems to be rooted in people's inherent discomfort with uncertainty. New ideas, by definition, present a challenge to the status quo. Though everyone may like the idea of innovation, when it actually comes time to heave out the set of ideas and processes (and even people) that have been in place, it can make them uncomfortable. Instead of recognizing this discomfort for what it is, many people end up blocking the recognition of creativity. In other words, one might say, "Of course I'm in favor of creative ideas and innovative methods, but this particular idea just wasn't the right one." Those placed in the role of decision maker suffer from this affliction even more strongly, and unfortunately tend to signal to those below them that practical ideas will "sell" better than novel ones.[20]

Fortunately, the processes used by virtual teams can mitigate this bias. To make new ideas seem less uncertain and less groundbreaking, they can be introduced early and often. As described above, given time to get used to an idea, it will become familiar and may cease to be as intimidating as it might otherwise have been. Termed the *familiarity* or the *mere exposure* effect by psychologists, it has been well documented that while the unknown creates a fear response in all types of organisms, the known creates a sense of well-being. Studies on this effect range from those on baby chicks, who will gravitate towards certain musical notes that were played before they hatched, to people attributing better moods after observing the same set of Chinese characters they had previously seen, to people attributing more positive traits to pictures of others after repeated viewings. The effect is so strong that some argue that it drives an instant emotional response to either like or dislike a particular stimulus. This reaction is quite hard to break once set.[21] Based on this, it is a grave mistake to wait until ideas are fully polished before introducing them to others who will need time to buy in.

TIP
Everyone needs time to warm up to new ideas. Introduce ideas early, and repeat the discussions on them until the concepts feel comfortable and familiar.

Another reason for the relative success of brainstorming in the electronic realm is that people feel more comfortable "speaking up" in this format. Whether communicating with peers, subordinates, or the boss's boss, when online most people seem to lose the sense of intimidation or inhibition that might hold them back when face to face. In this way, electronic conversations seem to promote more equality of contribution, which is a strong asset for these types of interactions.

Quotes from the front lines: "Questions that you don't dare ask someone in person can be done through e-mail. For example, you can ask a question almost as a faceless person (especially if you haven't met face to face yet). Later, even when you cross paths, they won't remember that you were the one who needed to ask about those things."

E-MAIL, PHONE CALL, VIDEOCONFERENCING: WHAT TOOL TO USE WHEN?

Oftentimes, team members may have a choice as to how they contact one another, and so it is worth reviewing the potential effects of this selection. As noted earlier, face-to-face encounters are the most "rich" channel, allowing for immediate give-and-take and for visual, aural, and linguistic signals to be sent and received. However, this does not tell us whether all these channels are actually *necessary* for effective communication at all times. Modern life has provided us with the means to explore this question in detail, as some channels (such as instant messaging) provide the more immediate give-and-take feature of speaking without the visual cues or tone of voice, for example, while e-mail can also remove the element of synchronicity.

Research on this topic has shown that the choice of medium can matter in some cases, but not in others.[22] Right away, this indicates that the general perception that face to face is always the preferred medium is not accurate. Perhaps not surprisingly, the choice of medium seems to matter the *least* when the team has a solid base of cooperation and goodwill on its side. With trust and a clear sense of what they need to accomplish, teams are equally effective at making high-quality decisions through any communication medium. Thus, groups with high levels of cooperation seem to be able to perform well even without seeing, hearing, or immediately responding to each other. However, for groups with a negative orientation toward each other and toward their path forward (that is, one where at least some group members feel antagonism), having more cues available actually seems to *hinder* effective outcomes! This is thought to be because antagonism can be incredibly contagious, and the ability to see or hear this negative attitude can inspire it in others, leading to a cycle by which it exacerbates the negative attitudes present in all. Thus, neither phone calls nor face-to-face meetings seem like good choices in this case. Not that this open antagonism is different from the way more mundane messages may be interpreted as more negative than intended as discussed in Chapter 1.

In short, it seems that the filters provided by e-mail can actually help to diffuse a negative situation and keep it from getting derailed, to help preserve the team's focus on a productive path forward. Only when team members started out neutral (that is, neither positively nor negatively predisposed towards the team and the work) did the richer channels seem to help. This is consistent with the commonly held notion that meeting team members in person (or at least on video) is important early in the team's interaction. However, once the team has reached a level of cooperation and mutual respect with each other, leaner media such as e-mail can suffice. More conversational turn-taking can help to build rapport and trust. What is potentially new here is the idea that when things get hostile, more is not always better in terms of the interaction. Sometimes it may be best to hope that the anger and hostility get "lost in translation" to give each person more distance from these negative emotions.

TIP

Having richer communication (like face-to-face or video) helps when team members start out neutral towards each other and the task. It doesn't add anything when the team is already positive, and it can actively hurt the process if the team is already negative. Be thoughtful about what you need to use when.

BIG PICTURE STRATEGIES AND DECISION-MAKING MODELS

Teamwork is based on the ability of the members to identify and solve problems together. Since you can't solve a problem that you don't understand, experts on topics from teamwork to creativity to negotiations all recommend starting with defining the problem (from the perspective of all relevant parties). The main theme in this book has been to make everything explicit in the virtual team setting, and figuring out how to define not only the problem itself but also all of the relevant contextual factors is one of the most important jobs that a virtual manager has. An analogy can be found in the new product development literature. Years of research has yielded a codified process to make sure that the decisions reached are thorough and effective. This allows it to be repeated with more consistent results. In addition, it also allows it to be carried out more independently, since each person is very clear on where the project is, where it is headed, and what the expected jobs are at each point in time. These features make this model very useful for a manager of a virtual team—and many of the identified features are indeed copies of topics covered elsewhere in this book, but are worthy of review here. The initial planning is the biggest and most critical hurdle for most virtual project teams. General and specific questions you might want to use to guide you in this stage include:[23]

- General/Initial Planning Phase
  - Who will use the end products that we are going to create? What needs do they have that this project will fulfill? Is it possible to have these outsiders involved at key points to make sure the team stays focused on the right goal?
  - What features, attributes, or characteristics will make our final product be a big success, and what would make it merely adequate (or worse, useless)? Separate out the list into "must have" and "would like to have" elements.
  - What limitations do we have economically, logistically, politically, or otherwise to accomplishing our work? Are resources committed initially, or do they have to be re-earned throughout the project?
  - What is our overall timeline, and at what points do we need to lift our heads and make sure we're working towards the right ends? Who gets to decide if the whole project isn't working and needs to be re-grouped? Based on what criteria, specifically?
- Specific/Rules of Engagement
  - What are the tasks assigned to each member of the team? Does each member understand the role not just of him/herself but also

of each other person? Are team members responsible for more than one role? Is there a defined and accountable team leader?

o What elements are "due" at which points in time? What are the criteria for success for each of these stages?

o What decisions are the team members authorized to make, and for what others are they merely in an advisory role?

o Is decision making done by consensus? Majority? Leader finalized but based on the input of the team? Will all team members share the responsibility for implementing the decisions?

o How are team members supposed to collaborate—circulate virtual documents for comments, for instance, or engage in collective brainstorming sessions, or use more of a sequential relay approach where work is passed from member to member, or a silo approach where each works independently and the product is assembled at the end?

o When and how are team members supposed to be available to each other? Are there "phone hours" when calls are expected? What is the meeting schedule and type?

o Are various communication technologies to be used for certain types of needs? For example, e-mail for sending reports, chat rooms for discussing project issues?

Having a list of this sort completed, and understood, by all team members at the outset of the team's work together is incredibly important, and sidesteps all kinds of "dead in the water" traps that can otherwise impede progress or successful completion.

SUMMARY

People have a natural inclination to want to be on common ground with each other, both in terms of the information that they share and the decisions that they make. Coupled with the pressures to have consensus in decisions, this can result in an unintentional bias away from good decision making. To counteract this problem, people need to be encouraged at various points in the process to express their views, in a more private setting if necessary. Virtual discussions tend to encourage people to take a bigger-picture view of problems, which can be useful or problematic, depending on the circumstance. Similarly, creativity can cause psychological conflict in people because of the competing needs for familiarity and novelty. Choosing the right channel for the right topic is important, but it is good to know that most topics and most conversations can thrive in most settings, especially if the group members already have a solid foundation with each other.

NOTES

1. Asch, S. E. (1956). Studies of independence and conformity: A minority of one against a unanimous majority. *Psychological Monographs, 70(9),* 1–70.

2. Bond, R. & Smith, P. B. (1996.) Culture and conformity: A meta-analysis of studies using Asch's (1952b, 1956) line judgment task. *Psychological Bulletin, 119,* 111–137.

3. Peterson, R. (2006). *PB Technologies.* Case published by the Dispute Resolution Research Center, Kellogg School of Management, Northwestern University, Evanston, IL.

4. Stasser, G. & Titus, W. (1985). Pooling of unshared information in group decision making: Biased information sampling during discussion. *Journal of Personality and Social Psychology, 48,* 1467–1478.

5. Schultz, M. (2001). The uncertain relevance of newness: Organizational learning and knowledge flows. *Academy of Management Journal, 44(4),* 661–681.

6. Hinds, P. J. & Weisband, S. P. (2003). Knowledge sharing and shared understanding in virtual teams. In C. B. Gibson & S. G. Cohen (Eds.), *Virtual teams that work: Creating conditions for virtual team effectiveness* (pp. 186–206). San Francisco, CA: Jossey-Bass.

7. Majchrzak, A., Malhotra, A., Stamps, J., & Lipnack, J. (2004). Can absence make a team grow stronger? *Harvard Business Review,* May, 1–9.

8. Thompson, L. L. (2004). *Making the team: A guide for managers* (2nd ed.). Upper Saddle River, NJ: Pearson Prentice Hall.

9. Doney, P. M. & Armstrong, G. M. (1996). Effects of accountability on symbolic information search and information analysis by organizational buyers. *Journal of the Academy of Marketing Sciences, 24,* 57–65.

10. Edmonson, A. C. (1999). Psychological safety and learning behavior in work teams. *Administrative Science Quarterly, 44,* 350–383.

11. Gibson, C. B. & Gibbs, J. L. (2006). Unpacking the concept of virtuality: The effects of geographic dispersion, electronic dependence, dynamic structure, and national diversity on team innovation. *Administrative Science Quarterly, 52(3),* 451–495.

12. Eisenhardt, K. M., Kahwajy, J. L., & Bourgeois III, L. J. (1997). How management teams can have a good fight. *Harvard Business Review,* July–August, 2–10.

13. Druskat, V. U. & Wolff, S. B. (2001). Building the emotional intelligence of groups. *Harvard Business Review,* March, 80–90.

14. Susskind, L. (2005). Breaking Robert's Rules: Consensus-building techniques for group decision making. *The Trading Zone, Harvard Negotiation Newsletter, 8(4).*

15. Trope, Y. & Liberman, N. (2010). Construal-level theory of psychological distance. *Psychological Review, 117(2),* 440–463.

16. For a review, see Friedman, R. & Belkin, L. (2013). The costs and benefits of e-negotiations. In M. Olekalns & W. Adair (Eds.), *Handbook of research in negotiation. (pp. 357-384).* London, UK: Edward Edgar Publishing.

17. DeSanctis, G. & Monge, P. (1999). Introduction to the special issue: Communication processes for virtual organizations. *Organization Science, 10(6),* 693–703.

18. Amabile, T. M. & Archambault, S. (1999). E Ink. Harvard Business School Case #800143.

19. Mueller, J. S., Melwani, S., & Goncalo, J. A. (2012a). The bias against creativity: People desire yet reject creative ideas. *Psychological Science, 21(1),* 13–17.

20. Mueller, J. S., Burris, E., & Kamdar, D. (2012b). The proactivity paradox: The tradeoffs of behaving in ways to generate and implement creative ideas. Working paper, University of San Diego, San Diego, CA.

21. Zajonc, R. (2001). Mere exposure: A gateway to the subliminal. *Current Directions in Psychological Science, 10(6),* 224–228.

22. Swaab, R. I., Galinsky, A. D., Medvec, V., & Diermeier, D. A. (2012). The communication orientation model: Explaining the diverse effects of sight, sound, and synchronicity on negotiation and group decisionmaking outcomes. *Personality and Social Psychology Review, 16(1),* 25–53.

23. Cooper, R. C. (1998). *Product leadership: Creating and launching superior new products.* Reading, MA: Perseus Books.

TEN
Cross-Cultural Complications

THE OBVIOUS AND THE SUBTLE

Teams with members from multiple countries go by many names, including international, global, transnational, cross-cultural, geographically dispersed, multinational, and multicultural.[1] Whatever they are called, they contain different cultures, which are defined as "characteristic ways of thinking, feeling, and behaving shared among members of an identifiable group."[2] Their use has not only arisen out of convenience or economic efficiency, but also to promote better work products. Indeed, researchers have found that culturally heterogeneous teams tend to outperform single-culture teams on many tasks, including identifying problem perspectives and producing higher-quality ideas and solutions. But others have observed that information sharing drops significantly in these teams, and decision making can suffer as a result.[3] Before proceeding, note that this chapter does not aim to identify how specific cultures act and react; it instead generalized areas of misalignment are presented that can trip up the multinational team not seeking to sidestep these pitfalls.

Some may think that as global interaction becomes more commonplace, the problems that result from cross-cultural interaction may naturally lessen, as all people become more familiar with the way things are done in different places. However, others have observed that increased globalization can actually make people become *more* entrenched in their own ways, leading to more divergence between cultures and customs.[4] Even now, you can't use an American appliance in a European outlet without an adaptor—similarly, behaviors need adaptation to function properly in other settings.[5]

Why does culture cause problems? There are both obvious and subtle issues at work here. First, on the broadest level, there is the innately human tendency to react to anything different from oneself as "weird" or "wrong."[6] Even once this reaction is overcome, cross-cultural interactions require a whole extra layer of thought about each interaction. In a single-culture discussion, your job is to think through the content of the topic at hand, and form and share your opinions on it. In a cross-cultural situation, you have the added task of piecing together what the other side has understood of your statements, and how accurately you have understood the other side. As discussed below, language itself as well as silence and "agreement" can be used to signal very different things in different cultures, so what you might be used to taking for granted could need to be double-checked when an international dimension is added to the team.

One of the most immediate difficulties encountered with cross-cultural interactions is having different languages present on the team. While teams do, of course, generally manage to find a common language with which to get their work done, it doesn't come without a cost. Those working in their non-native languages are at an incredible disadvantage. It takes them longer to communicate both in terms of getting their own messages across and in understanding what's being said to them and around them. Words don't always translate precisely. The ideas of non-native speakers are likely to come across as more simplistic than they probably deserve. They get less credit, and they are often treated with less respect.[7] And even if the language itself is fluent, speaking with an accent is often enough to derail a meeting or conference call. Lastly, even emoticons are used differently in the East and West! Together these problems are cumbersome, but they are also readily recognized by most everyone, as are the best solutions: tolerance and a willingness to ask for clarification. This is especially important because if information is difficult to interpret, it tends to lead to less experimentation overall on the team, and a subsequent lowering of the quality of decisions and final products.[8]

TIP

Take your time and give others the benefit of the doubt about what they are trying to say. Follow up on either side when things don't flow easily or don't make sense. More specifically, the following practices should be encouraged:

- Rephrasing
- Checking for comprehension by asking concrete questions and asking listeners to explain back ideas
- Repeating information with different words
- Using visual aids
- Following all spoken interactions with written follow-up material (written while thinking as the reader, not as yourself).[9]

A second obvious problem is the fact that global teams work in different time zones, and have trouble coordinating their efforts. In fact, one researcher mapped the entire globe in terms of time zones and working hours and noted that "the American workday is a terrible time to try to get the rest of the world on the phone."[10] And the stakes are even higher in terms of getting it right—delays in responses can end up meaning lost days instead of just lost hours in this context.[11]

Quotes from the front lines: "The time-zone problem does not end when we find a workable time to have a phone call. It also creates problems because where your head is at 7 am from home is just not the same as where your head is at 1 pm from your office. People who are out of sync just don't engage with each other to the same degree."

Similarly, different rules and regulations can cause problems in coordinating work and setting goals. Clearly, different countries have different laws that guide business activities, and not having the relevant elements laid out at the beginning can cause tremendous difficulties later down the line.

Quotes from the front lines: "Sometimes our foreign colleagues do not understand the laws or procedures that are required and have difficulty in accepting our requirements as this is not something they would need to deal with in their own country. Whether it be a pricing issue or a compliance issue, it has led to some long conversations, and even some lost business, because the foreign colleague cannot properly explain or understand the requirements."

Again, though these types of problems are cumbersome, most teams manage to find solutions (even if not optimal ones) that can work, since many of the problems themselves are so readily apparent.

Additional complications can sneak up on people, though, and catch them unaware. A major source of these complications is one's unspoken expectations about how things should be done, based on different standards of what is customary and acceptable in different cultures. Though these are not necessarily the miscommunications associated with not understanding one another's words, they are similar in the sense that they reflect different assumptions that parties may hold about how to express ideas. To illustrate this point,[12] first consider the costly error made by two teams of NASA scientists, called the "metric mixup," which resulted in the Mars Climate Orbiter disintegrating entirely. The spacecraft position was miscalculated due to the fact that the flight system software was written to take data using one set of metric units (Newtons) while the software on the ground that generated those instructions used a different unit of measure (Imperial pound-force).[13] This example mirrors the issue of speaking different languages discussed above. Here, these two groups were using different scales, or "rulers," to measure force and thrust.

Global teams may also be using different rulers of other sorts for measuring all manner of work issues. For example, how long is a week? Is it five days, six days, or seven days? How long is a workday, even? What does the calendar of the year look like, in terms of who is able and willing to take vacation at what times? What time is "on time"? Does a team meeting mean that all stay until the work is done or that people do their part and then leave? It is easy to imagine different cultures having different assumptions about the right answers to each of these questions, and that these problems might not be identified until after they have already tripped up the team's progress. Take the very vivid example of the team asked to estimate how long their project should take: members from one country estimated that six weeks was an appropriate timeframe, while those from a different country estimated six months instead![14] Similarly, what does it mean when someone on a conference call is silent? Is it a sign that the silent party:

- Needs a moment of "think time"
- Doesn't understand what's been said
- Is waiting to be invited to share an opinion
- Is expressing implicit dissent with what's been said?[15]

This problem is complicated by the fact that not all cultures feel comfortable with open discussions, or with being put on the spot when specifically asked to comment. Additionally, reaching "agreement" may, for some, mean the absolute end of discussion on the topic, while for others it may be considered wholly appropriate to revisit the topic yet again further down the line.

TIP

Be explicit about the ways that discussion will progress, including telling everyone ahead of time if each person will be called upon to voice an opinion on the matter being discussed.

Americans, along with some other cultures, are known for their work-work-work tendencies and their assumption that vacation can only be taken during "slow" times at work. Other cultures have no qualms about shutting down an entire project while the team (and indeed, sometimes the whole country!) takes the month off. U.S. culture also has a tendency towards terse e-mails, coupled with expectations of rapid replies, while others may find this process rude and ill-advised.[16] These issues can become very problematic if the differing assumptions aren't fully understood.

Quotes from the front lines: "I do feel that the culture in the United States of doing everything as quickly as possible and treating everything as massively important does not translate around the world. The laid-back culture found in other countries has caused slow downs and obstacles that we must factor into our timelines in order to properly plan our projects."

TIP

Especially with issues of timing and communications norms, err on the side of spelling out expectations.

Besides just the concrete issues of timing and planning, many other areas of work can reasonably be done through many different approaches. One prime example of this is the difference between cultures about how important a personal relationship is to a business interaction. In some places, it is perfectly reasonable to enter into a business discussion, and even a complex deal, with a total stranger. In others, the topic should not even be broached until a solid personal relationship has been founded.

Quotes from the front lines: "*It took us some time to learn that relationships are crucial to our foreign partners for doing business, and need to be established before any work-related issue is addressed. If it is not, the work results will be noticeably less than expected.*"

Beyond the effects of relationship building on business practice, this topic also relates to the differences cultures display when engaging in trust development.[17] Different cultures rely on very different mechanisms for deciding whether others are trustworthy. For one thing, right at the outset there may be differences in whether strangers are assumed to have good intentions until proven otherwise, or whether trust is non-existent until earned. And over time, while some cultures rely more on performance as the basis for trust, others may lean more heavily on the personal connections such as shared meals and lengthy discussions on non-work topics to build trust. Similarly, some cultures routinely use intermediaries to make trust-building go more smoothly, in part because of the endorsement and lending of one's reputation when introductions are made, while others prefer directly making one's case to new contacts. Use of intermediaries may persist far past the point of introductions in some cases.

Even conflict itself can go unrecognized in cross-cultural settings. Like other aspects of human perception, the decision of when and whether a conflict exists (not to mention how it has been handled) can exist in the eyes of the beholder. For example, one person may believe that a meeting contained a lively discourse, while another member of the same meeting might have felt entirely attacked. Even asking directly for one's opinion can feel confrontational to some but necessary and productive to others.[18] Similarly, one may feel that a conflict between team members was resolved appropriately using the utmost delicacy while the other side felt that a more direct apology was required. One's "direct addressing of a problem" can be seen as aggressive behavior by another. One's polite withholding of criticism can be interpreted by another as passive and non-contributory resistance. One may phrase rejections in such delicate and positive language that they may be misinterpreted as agreements by another.[19] Even how loudly you speak is often culturally determined! A related issue is the use of meetings—are they used to hash out issues and decide on a course of action, or do they exist to solidify a decision that's already been made? Different answers to these questions will result in very different expectations about what is appropriate interaction and progress in a meeting.

TIP

If possible, consider allowing team members to observe/listen in to a meeting within a single (other) culture before they are asked to join in meetings across cultures. It will give each person a chance to understand what the others will be expecting.

One last tip seems worthy of mention, since it seems to be universally agreed upon.

TIP

Avoid humor in international settings. It rarely translates.

In addition to general observations about the individual features of different cultures, there is also a wide-ranging school of thought about how various cultures align or misalign on whole clusters of dimensions. Thus, research has established that there tend to be groupings of traits that coincide, which can be used as a shortcut for beginning to understand cross-cultural issues. What follows is a description of one of the larger groupings identified, and how that relates to work in a global virtual team.

INDIVIDUALISM AND COLLECTIVISM

It is certainly true that every person on earth is a unique individual with particular needs, tastes, and work-style preferences. It is also true that depending on what country you are from, there is a strong chance that your preferences will have much in common with those around you. This is not to say that you are completely like any other person, just that the chances are high that you will have more similarities in the way that you act and react to situations with someone from your own country than with someone from across the globe. Researchers in the area of cross-cultural studies have taken these ideas and created a useful set of generalizations and categories on which to base explanations of typical behaviors in various areas around the world.

One of the most common groupings described is the difference between individualism and collectivism.[20] *Individualist* cultures (like most Western countries, America among them) are defined by members who primarily think of themselves as unique and independent beings, with the right and the expectation to promote their own well-being. *Collectivist* cultures (like most Eastern countries), by contrast, emphasize the *interdependence* of people, and stress the importance of the group's goals as opposed to the individual's goals. Social cohesion is strongly valued in these cultures. In addition, there are several other traits that tend to coincide with this individualism-versus-collectivism distinction. Collectivist cultures tend to have more respect for hierarchies and for people in positions of power than do individualist cultures. They also tend to use more "signaling" in their communication patterns. That is, as opposed to asking a lot of questions to size someone up or to understand a message, for example, they can learn from the context (dress, bow type, facial expressions, etc.) who someone else is and what is being communicated without the need for as many words.

The terms individualism and collectivism are used as a shortcut for two distinct styles that seem to pervade many business interactions. Given these distinct fundamental viewpoints, it should come as no surprise that everything from communicating to motivating to resolving conflicts may require a different approach to make each cultural type comfortable. What follows is a description of some of the main differences that may interrupt the workflow for a global virtual team with members from diverse cultures,[21] and then a list with a summary of the major points. Suggestions for trying to prevent these potential problems follow afterwards.

Motivation. People the world over all have some common elements to what they find motivating (such as striving for a feeling of self-efficacy, which is defined as a sense of one's own ability to complete tasks and reach goals). However, motivating workers from different perspectives can require very different messages. Individualistic workers, driven by their own personal goals and aspirations, show an increased willingness to work with others toward a collective goal based on how much that goal coincides with their personal goals. These goals can include reaching one's own full potential, as self-actualization is highly prized. Put another way, it is much more important for team members from these cultures to see "what's in it for me." On the contrary, collectivist workers consider group goals as their number one priority and realign or subordinate their personal goals to the team goal. They find virtue in dedication to the team; loyalty, solidarity, and self-sacrifice are of utmost importance.[22] Furthermore, collectivists are most comfortable receiving goal direction from superiors, whereas individualists prefer to feel in control of their workflow and choices.[23] Even the risk of failure evokes different motivations along the individual/collective continuum. Individualists view failure as destructive to their own self-worth ("I am not good enough"), whereas collectivists see it as a threat to group harmony ("No one will want to work with me").[24]

Rewards and Recognition. While individualists prefer rewards such as promotions that recognize their personal input (and independent thinking) and will help them move ahead, collectivists tend to prefer having rewards equally distributed among the group, and fear that individual recognition will upset the harmony that they strive for. This is also reflected in the fact that collectivists are much more tuned into their level of satisfaction with their supervisor, while satisfaction with the work itself and promotions are what seem to drive an individualist's level of commitment to the organization.[25] However, it should be noted that collectivists may adapt to a more individualistic style of rewards if they are working with strangers and have no sense of long-term connection to the others. It is only when the relationship becomes more salient that they are willing to forego individual rewards for the sake of the group.[26] Lastly, it is important to make sure that rewards are offered on the same scale, and timeline, in various locations. One team member being evaluated quarterly while another is evaluated yearly can cause problems.

Communication. It is often assumed that people prefer face-to-face communication, but this is not always true. In essence, since individualists tend to be more concerned with the nature of the task and being able to complete it independently, they tend to be more comfortable with impersonal communication styles (such as the use of e-mail messages) because they enable the fastest and most efficient contact. Conversely, collectivists may prefer face-to-face and other close-contact communications to create emotional ties and build relationships. These preferences are also consistent with the image of individualists as more verbal and direct, so they can transfer and solicit the information they need from phone and written communication. Collectivists, on the other hand, are generally less verbal and prefer to have visual interaction to pick up the contextual clues that indicate concern, satisfaction, needs, and unspoken preferences.[27]

Teamwork Metaphors. Individualists tend to think of teams as a means to achieving each individual's goals, and therefore can move fluidly from one team to another as the need arises. Collectivists, on the other hand, are more likely to form and stay in a few stable and close-knit groups.[28] Consistent with these patterns, a unique study demonstrated that different cultures were likely to employ different metaphors for the way a team should operate. In the study, it was observed that people from individualistic cultures used more competitive and task/goal-focused types of metaphors to describe how a team works together, such as the image of a sports team, while collectivistic cultures tended more towards metaphors about the relationship among the teammates, such as a family or community.[29] The researchers made a compelling argument for why it matters in today's business setting, stating that one's expectations are set by the larger metaphor utilized. If one is expecting a manager to act like a sports coach to provide clear, competitive objectives for a specific task, but instead the manager thinks of the team more like a community and is not as task-focused, that manager may be deemed ineffective at accomplishing objectives. Or on the other side, a manager overly focused on the end results will likely confuse a team member expecting more support and guidance throughout the process.

Conflict. As described earlier, conflict within a group is usually a hindrance to completing work, regardless of culture. Yet even here, cultures may differ in both when they perceive conflict and what to do about it once it arises. For example, individualistic cultures may see conflict arise based on a violation of an individual's rights, whereas a collectivist culture may generally see conflict as the result of a violation of duties.[30] The two may also use different mechanisms to cope with and resolve conflicts. Individualistic cultures prefer to directly address the conflict and use their own skills, experiences, and rational appeals to reach a resolution. As might be expected, collectivists take a different approach—avoidance and withdrawal. These avoidance strategies do not necessarily fit the Western notion of avoidance (neglect); rather, avoidance is used in many Eastern cultures out of concern for the other party.[31] Certain withdrawal techniques can be very proactive, such as seeking a third party to help mitigate and resolve a dispute. Yet here there is also an example of where the dichotomy between individualism and collectivism may be too simplistic: even within individualistic cultures, some may prefer to work things out by accounting for the interests of both sides, while others may like to refer to existing rules and regulations.[32]

Decision-Making Style. Individualist cultures like to hash out the issues based on rational arguments, choose one, and move on. This is sometimes called the "checklist" approach, as each issue is generally only discussed once. Collectivist cultures prefer a more holistic style, circling back to issues and making sure all are comfortable with the package on an emotional level as well as an intellectual one before proceeding. Until well understood, this can cause great frustration for both sides.[33] Teams may do well to try out different styles at different points in time and see what works.

TIP

Understand that those from different cultures are likely to respond best to very different types of management: individualists prefer to understand and value their end goals as worthwhile accomplishments not just for the team but for their own career path, whereas collectivists prefer to feel that they are working in harmony with the group.

SUMMARY OF INDIVIDUALIST VERSUS COLLECTIVIST TENDENCIES

- Goals
  - *Individualists:* Stretch the self professionally
  - *Collectivists:* Meet the needs of the team
- Rewards
  - *Individualists:* Proportional to individual contribution
  - *Collectivists:* Equally distributed to all group members
- Communication
  - *Individualists:* Comfortable with more impersonal communication (text)
  - *Collectivists:* Prefer more context to understand message (visual connection)
- Teamwork Metaphor
  - *Individualists:* Sports teams
  - *Collectivists:* Family
- Conflict
  - *Individualists:* Typically look for solutions/decisions that include key members
  - *Collectivists:* Typically refer to authority or external source to resolve
- Persuasion Style
  - *Individualists:* Rational appeals
  - *Collectivists:* Emotional appeals
- Decision Making
  - *Individualists:* "Checklist" approach
  - *Collectivists:* Holistic approach

HARNESSING MULTIPLE CULTURES

Somehow and at some point, the different approaches on the team need to be reconciled and a path forward needs to be decided on. Adjusting one's speech seems to be an intuitive place to start, as in one study, a full 80% of people reported doing so (such as speaking more slowly, clearly, pausing, and inviting responses). It is interesting to note that people were more conscientious about changing their spoken language when interacting with those from other cultures than they were about changing their written language, even though written communication is just as prone to misinterpretation, if not more so.[34] All people seem to increase these types of adjustments the longer they were on the team, giving more weight to the idea that teams should stay together as long as possible once formed.

> **TIP**
> Encourage modification of not just speech but written language as well. For example, in both forms people should ask each other open-ended questions to confirm understanding to avoid taking a "yes" answer at face value.

There are three very different models for how a reconciled approach can be chosen: the *dominant coalition* model, the *integration-identity* model, and the *fusion* model.[35] The dominant coalition model is essentially a process whereby one ideology is declared (either explicitly or implicitly) the official policy of the team and all dissenters must find a path to support it. This can be through a "majority rules" process, a leader decision, or by some other means. The integration-identity model assumes that for the team to function effectively, its members must be interconnected by a common set of motives, ideas, values, and goals that all can relate to. This may be thought of as the "melting pot" approach, whereby the team seeks to blend each person's approach into one soup, though not always uniformly drawing from all inputs. In practice, this approach can sometimes end up more closely resembling one culture at the expense of others. Overall, both approaches risk losing some of the other cultural perspectives present in the team. In the dominant model, other views are specifically rejected, and in the integration model, the overarching goal of consensus may inhibit dissent from surfacing.

Finally, the fusion model presents something different. Named after the fusion style of cooking, this perspective maintains that distinct pieces from each culture can be lifted, intact, for the benefit of the entire group.

Different approaches can even be thought of as a menu of choices, to be used or substituted at different points in time as the need arises. The resulting combination of styles may actually yield something not only functional, but also surprising and pleasing both to the members themselves and in terms of the effective creation of work products. Decisions are not made by an authority or by consensus, but instead by staying focused on multiple criteria at all times. Indeed, for some teams, it might be very freeing to stop trying to force everyone onto the same page at all times. Instead, the group can think of the various components of the work process as better fits for one or another approach and then strive for coexistence instead as the model for effective teamwork. Sub-groups can even be embraced in this model, as a method of preserving a specific approach to work and encouraging more information extraction, to be later combined with other areas on the team.

TIP

Let team members remain in their comfort zone when possible and consider the multinational team as a series of blocks that can fit together in different ways at different times.

Regardless of model chosen, if there is one silver bullet to a global team's challenges, it is the use of frequent, spontaneous communication among team members. This seems to universally increase positive results in multinational teams. This alone is related to increased trust, a better sense of the shared context, a greater feeling of shared identity, and more productive conflict handling in multinational teams.[36] Indeed, virtual teams (communicating primarily through electronic text) may actually have an advantage in the cross-cultural dimension, since electronic messages can be an equalizing force that promotes individual contribution even from those in cultures who might typically defer to the group.[37] But how can you encourage spontaneity, which by definition needs to arise without pre-planning? When held to the letter of the definition like that, of course you can't. But as discussed in other areas of the book, you can encourage frequent informal communication through three different means:

1. Tell people that this is important and is expected on the team
2. Tell people it is part of their job to respond to others who reach out to them as immediately as is possible
3. Model it by engaging people in frequent informal conversations yourself.

It also can't hurt to mention that frequent communication seems to be one of the best predictors of success.

> **TIP**
>
> Team members need to feel like "insiders" with each other, and they won't get there without a lot of time spent in contact. Encourage spontaneous communication within the team, especially if the team is multinational.

SUMMARY

Operating in a global business environment has created the opportunity for culturally diverse teams that are capable of performing at higher levels than their traditional counterparts. However, cultural diversity comes with its share of complications. There are fundamental differences between cultures that will influence the behaviors of team members. Recognize how collectivist and individualist societies differ to prevent problems from developing within the team. Overall, this type of culturally diverse environment requires just a bit of extra effort: tolerance, clarity, and follow-up will save the group time in the long run.

NOTES

1. Connaughton, S. L. & Shuffler, M. (2007). Multinational and multicultural distributed teams: A review and future agenda. *Small Groups Research, 38,* 387–412.

2. Gibson, C. R. & Gibbs, J. L. (2006). Unpacking the concept of virtuality: The effects of geographic dispersion, electronic dependence, dynamic structure, and national diversity on team innovation. *Administrative Science Quarterly, 51,* 451–495.

3. Watson, W. E., Kumar, K., & Michaelson, L. K. (1993). Cultural diversity's impact on interaction process and performance: Comparing homogeneous and diverse task groups. *Academy of Management Journal, 36,* 590–602, and Williams, K. & O'Reilly III, C. A. (1998). Demography and diversity in organization. In B. M. Staw & R. I. Sutton (Eds.), *Research in Organizational Behavior, 20* (pp. 77–140). New York, NY: Elsevier/JAI.

4. De Mooij, M. (2003). Convergence and divergence in consumer behavior: Implications for global advertising. *International Journal of Advertising, 22(2),* 1–20.

5. Hall, E. & Hall, M. (1989). *Understanding cultural differences.* Yarmouth, ME: Intercultural Press Inc.

6. Avruch, K. & Black, P. W. (1993). Conflict resolution in intercultural settings: Problems and prospects. In D. Sandole & H. van der Merwe (Eds.), *Conflict resolution theory and practice integration and application* (pp. 131–145). Manchester, UK: Manchester University Press.

7. Behfar, K., Kern, M., & Brett, J. (2006). Managing challenges in multicultural teams. *Research on Managing Groups and Teams, 9,* 233–262.

8. Hollingshead, A. B. (1998). Communication, learning, and retrieval in transactive memory systems. *Journal of Experimental Social Psychology, 34,* 423–442.

9. See Janssens, M. & Brett, J. M. (2006). Cultural intelligence in global teams: A fusion model of collaboration. *Group and Organization Management, 31(1),* 124–153.

10. Segalla, M. (2010). Why Mumbai at 1pm is the center of the business world. *Harvard Business Review,* October. Reprint F1010Z.

11. Kumar, J. (2006). Working as a designer in a global team. *Interactions, 13,* 25–26.

12. Swaab, R. I. & Meyer, E. (2012). *Managing global virtual teams.* Managing Global Virtual Teams Programme, INSEAD. Fontainebleau Cedex, France.

13. NASA Mars Climate Orbiter Mishap Investigation Board Phase I Report, November 10, 1999 (http://sunnyday.mit.edu/accidents/MCO _report.pdf), as described in Swaab, R. I. & Meyer, E. (2012). *Managing global virtual teams.* Managing Global Virtual Teams Programme, INSEAD. Fontainebleau Cedex, France.

14. Behfar, K., Kern, M., & Brett, J. (2006). Managing challenges in multicultural teams. *Research on Managing Groups and Teams, 9,* 233–262.

15. Anawati, D. & Craig, A. (2006). Behavioral adaptation within cross-cultural virtual teams. *IEEE Transactions on Professional Communication, 49(1),* 44–56.

16. Lipnack, J. & Stamps, J. (1997). *Virtual teams: Reaching across space, time, and organizations with technology.* Hoboken, NJ: John Wiley & Sons, Inc.

17. Asherman, I., Bing, J. W., & Laroche, L. (2000). Building trust across cultural boundaries. Regulatory Affairs Focus, May, http://www .itapintl.com/facultyandresources/articlelibrarymain/buildingtrust.html.

18. Meyer, E., as quoted in Stillman, J. (2012). Cross-cultural teams: Solving the communication challenges tech can't fix. http://gigaom .com/2012/05/25/cross-cultural-teams-solving-the-communication -challenges-tech-cant-fix/.

19. Anawati, D. & Craig, A. (2006). Behavioral adaptation within cross-cultural virtual teams. *IEEE Transactions on Professional Communication, 49(1),* 44–56.

20. Triandis, H. C. (2001). Individualism-collectivism and personality. *Journal of Personality, 69(6),* 909.

21. Gelfand, M. J., Erez, M., & Aycan, Z. (2007). Cross-cultural organizational behavior. *Annual Review of Psychology, 58,* 479–514.

22. Chen, C. C., Chen, X. P., & Meindl, J. R. (1998). How cooperation can be fostered: The cultural effects of individualism and collectivism. *Academy of Management Review, 23,* 285–304.

23. Iyengar, S. S. & Lepper, M. R. (1999). Rethinking the value of choice: A cultural perspective on intrinsic motivation. *Journal of Personality and Social Psychology, 76,* 349–366.

24. Bagozzi, R. P., Verbeke, W., & Gavino, J. C. (2003). Culture moderates the self-regulation of shame and its effects on performance: The case of salespersons in the Netherlands and the Philippines. *Journal of Applied Psychology, 88,* 219–233.

25. Watsi, S. A. (2003). The influence of cultural values on antecedents of organizational commitment: An individual-level analysis. *Applied Psychology International Review, 52,* 533–554.

26. Chen, C. C., Chen, X. P., & Meindl, J. R. (1998). How cooperation can be fostered: The cultural effects of individualism and collectivism. *Academy of Management Review, 23,* 285–304.

27. Ibid.

28. Ibid.

29. Gibson, C. & Zellmer-Bruhn, M. (2001). Metaphors and meaning: An intercultural analysis of the concept of teamwork. *Administrative Sciences Quarterly, 46,* 274–303.

30. Gelfand, M. J., Nishii, L. H., Holcombe, K. M., Dyer, N, Ohbuchi, K. I., & Fukuno, M. (2001). Cultural influences on cognitive representations of conflict: Interpretations of conflict episodes in the United States and Japan. *Journal of Applied Psychology, 86,* 1059–1074.

31. Gabrielidis, C., Stephan, W. G., Ybarra, O., Pearson, V. M., & Vilareal, L. (1997). Preferred styles of conflict resolution: Mexico and the United States. *Journal of Cross-Cultural Psychology, 28,* 661–677.

32. Tinsley, C. H. & Brett, J. M. (2001). Managing workplace conflict in the United States and Hong Kong. *Organizational Behavior and Human Decision Processes, 85,* 360–381.

33. Behfar, K., Kern, M., & Brett, J. (2006). Managing challenges in multicultural teams. *Research on Managing Groups and Teams, 9,* 233–262.

34. Anawati, D. & Craig, A. (2006). Behavioral adaptation within cross-cultural virtual teams. *IEEE Transactions on Professional Communication, 49(1)*, 44–56.

35. Janssens, M. & Brett, J. M. (2006). Cultural intelligence in global teams: A fusion model of collaboration. *Group and Organization Management, 31(1)*, 124–153.

36. Hinds, P. J. & Mortensen, M. (2005). Understanding conflict in geographically distributed teams: The moderating effects of shared identity, shared context, and spontaneous communication. *Organization Science, 16*, 290–307.

37. Rosette, A. S., Brett, J. M., Barsness, Z., & Lytle, A. L. (2012). When cultures clash electronically: The impact of email and social norms on negotiation behavior and outcomes. *Journal of Cross-Cultural Psychology, 43*, 628–643.

Conclusion

Virtual teams are nearly ubiquitous already, and their use is on the rise. And while of course this steady increase is based on solid business advantages, the virtual process inherently creates "holes" compared to the way people are used to interacting with each other.

- Holes form in the way people express themselves (that is, more unconsciously negatively) when typing to each other versus speaking or writing on paper.
- Holes form when people who prefer to meet in person, and enjoy sharing stories and jokes from their lives, suddenly have to communicate with faceless strangers.
- Holes form when quick questions cannot be asked (or answered) about what exactly is supposed to be accomplished.
- Holes also describe the feeling that team members may have that they are out there on their own (referred to as "situational invisibility").[1]
- Finally, holes result from the new tensions that arise in virtual work: the tension between being ignored and being overly visible (such as having to be available on a chat function all day long); the tension between having the work be too divided and expecting people to circulate every idea and document within the team; and the tension between local culture and the team's expectations.[2]

These holes can amplify the naturally occurring problems of virtual teams. This book has set about explaining and analyzing these holes, with direct and concrete actions suggested throughout the text to help to fill them in. As you have read, successfully leading and participating in a virtual team is a combination of familiar and unique skills. All teams need time to get to know and trust each other, need clarity on what needs to be done and how, and need to adjust over time. Virtual teams have the unique added burden of identifying problems by what *doesn't* present itself: silence, delays, and problems that remain hidden. Who have you *not* heard from? What *isn't* happening? Why?

As a conclusion, what follows is a review of 10 key ideas that have been presented to help fill in these gaps. Each is aimed at creating and guiding virtual teams to their best advantage, from the initial policies through the ongoing "tune-ups" for successfully managing both the content and the relationships in these teams.

EARLY TEAM DEVELOPMENT

1. First moments have a long-lasting impact, so you want to use them wisely by setting expectations during the "first day of class."
   - Right up front, ask each team member for patience, tolerance, and a "benefit of the doubt" attitude. Commitment on this overarching concept can help avoid problems before they arise.
   - Recognize the specific challenges some team members will face out loud and early (reporting to multiple teams and managers, for example, or needing to be available for team meetings at typically "off hours" times).
   - Make sure to require broad participation at kick-off meetings (if that is to be a goal later down the line).
   - The tone of the first e-mail messages can be as important as the first meetings—enthusiasm and a positive outlook can set the team on the right course.
   - Make sure there are strong "drop everything and respond" norms in the team when someone reaches out. Waiting until it's convenient to reply will shut down the impulse to ask again.
   - Give guidance on what makes for good written communication, understanding that most messages get skimmed instead of read. Remind people to think as the reader while they write.
   - Say/write everything explicitly. It takes practice to remember to reliably write down your ideas and send them to others, but the habit is critical.
2. It's too hard to get to know a whole group of people together at once, especially over the phone.

- People are much better at speaking one on one than in large groups, so make "getting to know you" more intimate by pairing people up. This makes introductions the most effective.
- Use ice-breakers that connect people to each other in a way that is meaningful both personally and professionally. People generally only seek help from someone they are on friendly terms with, so forging relationships that allow for this type of interaction can have significant rewards.

3. Phone calls can be especially important at the very beginning, to make sure that people get in the groove of speaking with each other.
- Don't over-rely on occasional face-to-face get-togethers, since waiting for these can impede progress on tasks the rest of the time.

4. When you can't see each other, initial trust is largely based on reliability (being able to count on someone to answer you promptly as well as to produce promised work).
- Norms of responsiveness and "small wins" are both routes to achieve this.

ONGOING ADJUSTMENTS

5. Make sure the division of work is clear and understood by all.
- Team members should be more than just names on a list. Each person should understand who is on the team and why. In addition, each should know how everyone's work fits into the larger group project, as well as the other team members' individual goals, expectations, and priorities.
- Share updates on the whole project to make sure everyone keeps track of how their parts fit into the bigger picture at all times.
- Make sure all know how the project fits into the larger organization's goals and success.

6. Create accountability in writing to increase commitment.
- Remember that motivation stems from the right balance of knowing what to do and being permitted to decide for oneself how to do it.

7. Schedule meetings at very regular intervals, and manage them to make sure the content is covered in an efficient manner.
- Ask team members to do nothing else during conference calls; remember that a distracted mind is working sub-optimally.
- Minds wander every few minutes, so recap often. Keep the overall meeting as short as possible to avoid burnout. And don't

forget this touchstone of good communication: If it's important, say it twice!

- Give people notice when they are going to be "called on" by using their names at the outset of the question.
- Don't have some people in a room and others on the phone. If everyone can't be together, have everyone on the phone.

8. Don't be afraid to adjust, and as the group progresses, give others the voice to do so as well.

- Virtual teams hide problems better than others do. Seek out sources of hindrance, and invite bad news regularly.
- Make it explicitly acceptable to ask for help.

EFFECTIVE PROCESSES

9. Good decision making requires careful planning and a delineated process in which everyone knows the rules of both the contribution and the final decision stages before discussions even begin.

10. Cross-cultural issues make everything more complicated. A combination of tolerance and patience is needed to make sure team members get aligned and stay aligned on their work.

- Remember that different approaches might be valuable to the team in different ways.
- Pairing people up across naturally occurring "fault lines" can help to bridge different sub-groups.

Lastly, a note on the role of technology. Technology has been evolving faster than human nature, so we find ourselves playing "catch up" when trying to form relationships, interact well, and make good decisions in ways that are unique to us. As options change and develop, so (in all likelihood) will the ways virtual team members interact. In particular, keep an eye on technological advances that make people feel more present with each other both during conversations and during regular work time. Such an example includes online avatars that indicate availability or even movement during conference calls,[3] or maintaining active links throughout the day to be able to check in with others spontaneously. Companies are also beginning to use in-house social media sites for connecting people through "social awareness streams" that help to provide a sense of who knows what without the benefit of in-person conversations.[4] These are examples of tools that are specifically aimed at filling some of the holes left by virtual interactions. They undoubtedly create some new problems as they solve existing ones, and need to be managed to make sure that the balance between focus and connection can be maintained for each team member. It is all an ongoing process of evolution.

In general, keep an open mind and continue to fine-tune your own skills, because being a successful virtual team member or leader is a key competency in giving you the ability to succeed. Sincerely wishing you the best in your future virtual interactions!

NOTES

1. Cramton, C. D., Orvis, K. L., & Wilson, J. M. (2007). Situation invisibility and attribution in distributed collaborations. *Journal of Management, 33(4),* 525–546.

2. Gibbs, J. (2009). Dialectics in a global software team: Negotiating tensions across time, space, and culture. *Human Relations, 62(6),* 905–935.

3. Zhao, S. (2003). Towards a taxonomy of copresence. *Presence, 12(5),* 445–455.

4. As described in Gibbs, J. L., Rozaidi, N., & Eisenberg, J. (2013). Overcoming the "ideology of openness": Probing the affordances of social media for organizational knowledge sharing. *Journal of Computer Mediated-Communication, 19(1),* 102–120.

Additional Resources

BOOKS ABOUT DECISION MAKING AND SOCIAL PSYCHOLOGY

Blind Spots: Why We Fail to Do What's Right and What to Do about It, by Max H. Bazerman and Ann E. Tenbrunsel (2012). Princeton, NJ: Princeton University Press.

Influence: Science and Practice, by Robert B. Cialdini (2001). Needham Heights, MA: Allyn & Bacon.

Judgment and Managerial Decision Making, 8th Edition, by Max H. Bazerman and Don A. Moore (2013). Danvers, MA: John Wiley & Sons.

Mindset: The New Psychology of Success, by Carol Dweck (2006). New York, NY: Random House.

Mindwise: How We Understand What Others Think, Believe, Feel, and Want, by Nicholas Epley (2014). Forthcoming from Brilliance Audio.

Thinking Fast and Slow, by Daniel Kahnemann (2011). New York, NY: Farrar, Strauss, & Giroux.

Yes!: 50 Scientifically Proven Ways to Be Persuasive, by Noah J. Goldstein, PhD, Steve J. Martin, and Robert B. Cialdini, PhD (2008). New York, NY: Free Press.

BOOKS ABOUT TEAMWORK AND LEADERSHIP

Do Nothing!: How to Stop Overmanaging and Become a Great Leader, by J. Keith Murnighan (2012). New York, NY: Penguin.

Getting Disputes Resolved: Designing Systems to Cut the Costs of Conflict, by William L. Ury, Jeanne M. Brett, and Stephen B. Goldberg (1988). San Francisco, CA: Jossey-Bass.

Groups That Work (and Those That Don't): Creating Conditions for Effective Teamwork, edited by J. Richard Hackman (1989). San Francisco, CA: Jossey-Bass.

Hidden Value: How Great Companies Achieve Extraordinary Results with Ordinary People, by Charles A. O'Reilly and Jeffrey Pfeffer (2000). Cambridge, MA: Harvard College.

Leading Teams: Setting the Stage for Great Performances, by J. Richard Hackman (2002). Boston, MA: Harvard Business School Publishing Corporation. Also see http://www.team-diagnostics.com/ to take the survey about effective team functioning.

Making the Team: A Guide for Managers, by Leigh L. Thompson (2004). Upper Saddle River, NJ: Pearson Prentice Hall.

Teaming: How Organizations Learn, Innovate, and Compete in the Knowledge Economy, by Amy C. Edmondson (2012). San Francisco, CA: Jossey Bass.

BOOKS ABOUT CREATIVITY AND INNOVATION

Creative Conspiracy: The New Rules of Breakthrough Collaboration, by Leigh Thompson (2013). Boston, MA: Harvard Business School Publishing.

Creativity: Flow and the Psychology of Discovery and Invention, by Mihaly Csikszentmihalyi (1997). New York, NY: Harper Collins.

Creativity in Context: Update to the Social Psychology of Creativity, by Teresa M. Amabile (1996). Boulder, CO: Westview Press.

How Breakthroughs Happen, by Andrew Hargadon (2003). Boston, MA: Harvard Business School Publishing.

The Progress Principle: Using Small Wins to Ignite Joy, Engagement, and Creativity at Work, by Teresa Amabile and Steven Kramer (2011). Boston, MA: Harvard Business School Publishing.

Winning through Innovation: A Practical Guide to Leading Organizational Change and Renewal, by Charles A. O'Reilly III and Michael L. Tushman (2002). Boston, MA: Harvard Business School Publishing.

BOOKS ABOUT INTERPRETING AND PRESENTING INFORMATION

How PowerPoint Makes You Stupid: The Faulty Causality, Sloppy Logic, Decontextualized Data, and Seductive Showmanship That Have Taken Over Our Thinking, by Franck Frommer (2012). New York, NY: The New Press.

The Cognitive Style of PowerPoint: Pitching Out Corrupts Within, 2nd Edition, by Edward R. Tufte (2006). Cheshire, CT: Graphics Press.

The Signal and the Noise: Why So Many Predictions Fail—But Some Don't, by Nate Silver (2012). New York, NY: Penguin Group.

The Visual Display of Quantitative Information, by Edward R. Tufte (2001). Cheshire, CT: Graphics Press.

BOOKS ABOUT CROSS-CULTURAL ISSUES

Culture's Consequences: Comparing Values, Behaviors, Institutions and Organizations across Nations, by Geert Hofstede (2001). Thousand Oaks, CA: Sage Publications.

Managing Global Organizations: A Cultural Perspective, by Rabi S. Bhagat, Harry C. Triandis, and Annette S. McDevitt (2012). Cheltenham, UK: Edward Elgar Publishing.

Multinational Work Teams: A New Perspective (Series in Organization and Management), by P. Christopher Earley and Cristina B. Gibson (2002). Mahwah, NJ: Lawrence Erlbaum Associates, Inc.

Negotiating Globally: How to Negotiate Deals, Resolve Disputes, and Make Decisions across Cultural Boundaries, by Jeanne M. Brett (2001). San Francisco, CA: Jossey-Bass.

BOOKS ABOUT TECHNOLOGY, DISTRACTION, AND MULTITASKING

The Man Who Lied to His Laptop: What We Can Learn about Ourselves from Our Machines, by Clifford Nass and Corina Yen (2012). New York, NY: Penguin Group.

Organizations and Communication Technology, edited by Janet Fulk and Charles W. Steinfield (1990). Newbury Park, CA: Sage Publications.

Peopleware: Productive Projects and Teams, by Tom DeMarco and Timothy Lister (1987). New York, NY: Dorset House Publishing.

Index

ABOUT THE AUTHOR

Terri R. Kurtzberg, PhD, is associate professor of management and global business at the Rutgers Business School Newark and New Brunswick at Rutgers University in New Jersey, where she teaches negotiations and organizational behavior. She received her PhD from the Kellogg Graduate School of Management at Northwestern University, Evanston, Illinois. Kurtzberg has received multiple teaching and research awards. She is the author (with Charles E. Naquin) of *The Essentials of Job Negotiations: Proven Strategies for Getting What You Want* (Praeger, 2011). Her articles on negotiations and electronic communications have been cited by *Fortune* magazine, *The New York Times*, CNN.com, BBC World Service Radio, and CBS Radio. Her work has been published in journals such as *Journal of Applied Psychology*, *Organizational Behavior and Human Decision Processes*, *International Journal of Conflict Management*, and *Group Dynamics: Theory, Practice, and Research*.

	DATE DUE		

01/97

How Men

and Women

Can Overcome

Communication

Barriers—and

Increase Their

Effectivness

at Work

FRAMES OF

REFERENCE

Carol Rudman, Ph.D.

PETERSON'S/PACESETTER BOOKS
PRINCETON, NEW JERSEY

Dedicated to the memory of my father,
Abraham Arthur "Artie-for-short" Friedman,
who always knew I would write a book some day.

Library of Congress Cataloging-in-Publication Data

Rudman, Carol
    Frames of reference : how men and women can overcome
communication barriers and increase their effectiveness at work /
Carol Rudman.
      p. cm.
    Includes index.
    ISBN 1-56079-532-8   1. Business communication. 2.
Communication—Sex differences. I. Title.
    HF5718.R836   1995
    302.2—dc20   95-30147
                                             CIP

Creative direction by Linda Huber
Cover design by Susan Newman
Cover illustration by Joe Fleming
Interior design by Cynthia Boone

Printed in the United States of America

10 9 8 7 6 5 4 3 2 1

Visit Peterson's Education & Career Center on the Internet
(World Wide Web) at http://www.petersons.com

ACKNOWLEDGMENTS

I want to express my thanks to the following special people:

To Yetta Friedman, my courageous mother, who by now knows every airport in the New York City area like the back of her hand.

To my children, Samuel and his wife Susan, Meryl, and David, who are unfailingly loving and "supportive."

To Rochelle Green, my kid sister, for paying me to write her English papers.

To Dr. Susan Pickman—"Thank you" doesn't begin to cover it.

To Andrea Pedolsky, my brilliant and challenging editor, who never pulled her punches.

To Milly Murphy, nurturing friend forever. To Dr. Isabel Davis, Vera Parisi, Gloria Benitez, Judith Beckman, Elizabeth Drewry, Laurel Brett, and Sara Kaplan, wonderful friends who miraculously are still speaking to me.

To Linda Jacobson, business partner and friend, who continues to teach me many things.

To Dr. Herbert Cooper, Tom Hendrickson, Jim Monk, and Bob Pokorney, the Presidents' Club gang, who keep me on my toes.

To Maddy Epstein and George Kowalchuk, who helped this book happen.

To my colleagues, clients, and many workshop participants who generously shared their stories and their insights, especially

Lila Brown, Rosetta Bailey, Pat Cohen, Donna Ferrigno, Loriann Hoffman, Sean Galin, Charlie Hensel, Nick Igneri, Kenny Lavigne, Steve Shivak, Kevin Sullivan, and William Pedersen.

CONTENTS

INTRODUCTION

Where There's Dialogue, There's Hope

I t's become conventional wisdom that men and women communicate differently. Despite this, the differences are intriguing as they play themselves out at home and at work. In fact, a whole industry has developed around gender, with social scientists, psychologists, linguists, communication specialists, and biologists entering the fray. On any given day, pick up a newspaper or magazine or tune in to a radio or television talk show, and you're likely to encounter at least one segment relating to gender.

All this commotion has shown that there are many opinions about why men and women communicate differently, with scenarios ranging from "it's hard-wired in the brain" to "men as oppressors, women as victims." Many questions are raised; however, few answers are given. While those of us who care peel away the layers of complexity and scrutinize them, business continues, and men and women still have to deal with each other every day and get things done. They have to talk one-on-one, participate in meetings, give presentations, and instruct each other on various matters. They have to get along.

Generalize—Don't Stereotype

Though both are convenient and sometimes necessary ways to organize large amounts of information, generalizations differ from stereotypes. Stereotypes start from the inside out. You make up your mind about what you will see before you actually observe anything. Since expectations tend to justify themselves, you see what you expect to see—not necessarily what's in front of you. Stereotypes tend to be rigid; if something you observe doesn't match, you discard the observation as "an exception" or "unique." You say to a man or a woman behaving in an unexpected way, "You're different." And the stereotype lives on.

Generalizations, on the other hand, move from the outside in. Many observers collect data and make assessments based on what everyone has observed. If future observations yield something different, generalizations change.

In this book, I generalize about gender communication rather than stereotype women and men. As men and women change their behavior, I expect my generalizations to change. In fact, I'll discuss some generalizations that are changing even as you read this. I'm not offering rigid ideas about how people "should" behave. Rather, I'm sharing generalizations that I encourage you to confirm by your own open-minded observations. Paying attention—in essence, that's what *Frames of Reference* is all about.

It Isn't Easy, But . . .

Every day at work you face many different experiences specifically relating to the challenges of men and women communicating with each other. Often these events are emotionally charged, and you're too caught up in them to have any kind of perspective or to learn very much from each other about how to make them work better next time. Instead, you come away with hurt feelings, a bruised ego, and the firm conviction that whatever happened, the resulting mess was certainly not your fault. The miscommunications that result can put companies and individual workers in precarious positions. They can cost serious money in both the value of lost employee productivity and sizable legal fees to attorneys expert in defending against sexual harassment charges. Make no mistake: Learning how to communicate across the gender divide is a bottom-line issue.

The Dance Must Change

Men and women living together at home make a kind of tacit agreement about how they will be a couple. Over time they work out a mutually acceptable pattern of relating to each other, almost like a metaphorical dance: One partner behaves a certain way, and the other automatically moves into an expected response. For instance, if a man and a woman at home are discussing something and he constantly interrupts her, rarely letting her finish a sentence and never soliciting her opinion or drawing out her point of view, she might decide to keep the peace by keeping quiet. Keeping the peace might be more important to her than either asserting her general right to speak without being interrupted or airing her views on the particular topic at hand, at least for the moment. She might prefer to wait for another opportunity to speak up, or she might decide not to address the topic. A conversational dance is developed in which he interrupts and she retreats, he airs his views, and hers often go unremarked. If such a pattern works for them, that's their private business.

On the job, however, such a pattern becomes the company's business. If a male employee always interrupts a female coworker and she decides to "keep the peace" by keeping quiet, the company is losing her input. Raising the topic later is most likely going to be raising it too late, so her effectiveness and value to the organization diminish. Therefore, on the job, his constant interruptions and her silent retreat are not acceptable. In the workplace, the dance must change. He has to learn when and how to share the air time; she has to learn when and how to claim it.

"That's well and good," my many seminar participants have said over the years, "but exactly *how* do we do that?" And so arrived the impetus for my search for an approach, a way to teach people how to *think* about how they communicate—as well as how they think their colleagues, staff, and bosses communicate: a way to help us get inside of each other's frame of reference.

Tuning in to the Technology

The search ended the night I sat down to watch a movie I had videotaped. For the whole evening, the remote control "clicker" hardly left my hand. When I missed a point in the movie or thought I might have misunderstood something, I rewound the tape. When I wanted to answer the telephone or put another bag of popcorn in the microwave, I hit "Pause." Waiting for the popcorn to pop, I would find myself thinking about the scene I had just watched, considering its implications and speculating about what would happen next. How great to be able to control the events in your own life this way, metaphorically speaking, of course. How wonderful to have a power tool like a magic "clicker" that would let you stop the action to think about it, rewind the tape to review a situation if necessary, and then decide how you wanted to behave.

And so was born the three-step approach to overcoming communication barriers that I've used ever since:

❑ FREEZE FRAME

❑ REFRAME

❑ COLLECT SNAPSHOTS TO REFLECT ON

FREEZE FRAME The first step to increasing your communication effectiveness is to develop some degree of objectivity about what's going on. Step outside of your emotional involvement for long enough to see what might be derailing the situation; mentally hit "Pause," and stop your imaginary videotape: freeze frame. That is, stop for a mental moment. Back off from the event you're involved in to examine the communication and its surroundings, or context. Ask yourself exactly what *is* going on? What is the speaker saying or not saying? What are you failing to say or hear?

The following pages will address several issues of gender communication, and you'll read stories that illustrate them. The following situations will be discussed:

- ❏ being interrupted
- ❏ giving and taking criticism
- ❏ expressing ideas
- ❏ disclosing personal matters
- ❏ using humor to reduce stress
- ❏ expressing emotions
- ❏ negotiating
- ❏ decoding nonverbal messages

To help you get started, each chapter includes a **PIC-TURE THIS** scene depicting workplace situations you're likely to find familiar. You'll use freeze frames to pinpoint the various gender communication differences in each story and to ask specific questions about how to reconcile them. Then, you'll begin developing some answers.

REFRAME To pinpoint cross-gender communication differences, it's necessary to notice frames. Think for a moment of picture frames. Although picture frames aren't always noticed, they contribute to a picture's total impression. Putting the same picture into another frame can change the picture's effect entirely. What's more, a frame change may cause people who overlooked the previous frame to notice the picture now and respond to it differently. Thus, framing affects behavior.

In communication, "frame" is another word for "context." If you want people to notice your message and respond to it, you have to "frame" it so that it has meaning to them. When you ask a question, for example, you try to phrase it in a way that your listener understands, so you'll get an answer you can use. If that does not happen, you ask the question in a different way—you reframe it—trying to get a more helpful response.

Reframing, as used in *Frames of Reference*, means re-positioning communication for maximum effectiveness. You reframe your own conversation, if necessary, and also that of other people. In each chapter, you'll read about workplace incidents I've either witnessed or been told of by clients and colleagues. You'll use these stories to learn how to reframe.

After considering several aspects of gender communication, you'll rewind your metaphorical videotape and revisit the people you met in **PICTURE THIS**. You'll replay the scene and see which reframes work best.

Reframing helps you respond thoughtfully rather than react reflexively. A good, practical use of the technique is to defuse a potentially volatile situation. For instance, a coworker makes an insulting remark. Before hurling a nasty remark in return, you think, "Wait a minute. Maybe he didn't mean to insult me. Perhaps he's upset about something else. What's my next best move?" Instead of reacting from habit, you're now responding from choice. You calmly ask, "Did you mean that the way it sounded?" and wait to see what happens.

COLLECT SNAPSHOTS TO REFLECT ON

Remember how pleasurable it can be to page through a family photo album or your high school yearbook and recall all the fun you had at last year's Memorial Day picnic or the prom you went to with your high school sweetheart? The pictures help you remember the event and give you a reason to do so. Although the purpose here is improved communication and not nostalgic recollection, using "snapshots" to recall events *is* very much to the point.

At the end of each chapter, you'll be asked to look back on your life at work and collect specific freeze-frame stills, moments of your life and thoughts about gender communication. In that way, you'll create a mental "scrapbook" of communication mishaps and successes to use as a reference tool for the future.

Although it can be hard to get a perspective and switch gears during an actual conversation, you can still reflect on the event afterwards. Then you can think about reframes you might have made and different ways you might handle similar situations in the future; you can rescript your behavior. If you do not reflect and at least consider rescripting, you're likely to repeat the same behavior in a similar situation next time, and that may not have a productive effect either on your working relationships or on your career.

Murphy's Law Revisited

You know Murphy's Law: Anything that can go wrong will—and usually the worst possible thing at the worst possible moment. But Murphy's Law has a little-known corollary: When things go right, nobody notices. If you're serious about building your communication skills, it's just as important to begin noticing what you do *right*.

When things go wrong, you're more likely to review them in some detail afterward because you want to make them happen better next time. But when things go right, you rarely look back. If you scrutinize your successes as conscientiously as your failures, you're more likely to be able to duplicate the good stuff. Triumphs can be a valuable learning tool, so be sure to add them to your scrapbook.

Take Whatever You Need

When I began writing *Frames of Reference*, I set out to be even-handed yet persistently concerned with gender spin. As the book took shape, however, my generalizations seem to have developed even more exceptions. I'm happy about that because it makes me hopeful that soon I'll have to reconstruct many of them entirely because men and women are learning so much with and from each other.

Keeping a friendly dialogue going, both about gender differences in general and about how men and women communicate in particular, may not provide all the answers, but it certainly adds opportunities to reach mutual understanding. In any communication situation, where there's dialogue—there's hope.

And so this book became increasingly about communication in general, albeit with a gender spin where applicable and where helpful. Whatever your style, take what you need.

It Gets Easier

With a little practice, the process of reframing will become automatic, taking no more than a couple of seconds. You really won't need to think it through point by point. When you are actually involved in a conversation, you'll learn to keep on with it while at the same time doing some quick freeze frames to get a perspective on what's happening. Then you'll be able to try some instant reframes to see how the message might look from a different perspective. Eventually, you'll be able to do quick freezes and instant reframes, switching gears on the spot. Trial and error is the best way to expand your style. Try things and see how they work. If you're not satisfied, you can make adjustments. In that way, you become the director of your life.

If how you communicate at work is jeopardizing your personal success and your employer's bottom-line concerns, then you have to learn how to communicate differently, how to understand other frames of reference and navigate successfully around them. Your magic video clicker becomes an important communication power tool. Roll the tape!

ANATOMY OF
INTERRUPTIONS

used to think the reason men were always interrupting other people was hormonal. The commonplace that women are more easily and frequently interrupted in conversation than men, and that when they are interrupted, men typically bounce back into the discussion but women back down from it—I thought hormones might be playing a role there, too. Be that as it may, the generalization about women's conversational vulnerability and men's comparative volubility is changing all around us.

See for yourself. The next time you're meeting a colleague for lunch, for instance, and you get to the restaurant early, use the waiting time to do a few freeze frames. Pan the room and periodically hit your mental magic clicker to stop the action. At each spot, observe who's talking, who's listening, who's perpetually interrupting and who is always being interrupted. What you would have seen ten years ago is a number of men who looked like the stars of their own personal talk shows, with women for the most part composing their attentive audiences.

Now, however, many women have learned to counter interruptions and claim air time, and many men have learned to share it. Observing this change encourages my belief that cross-gender workplace communication can improve in other areas as well. Still, change takes a long time, and many people have only just begun the process. Keep reading and see how reframing can help you speed it up.

There are two basic kinds of interruptions: conversation and work process. Since conversation interruptions are more familiar because they are more abundant, we'll start there. Scene I and Scene II below display different kinds of conversation interruptions. Let's see what they are and what are the possible repercussions of each.

❏   ❏   ❏

PICTURE THIS

Scene I
Conference room, Matrix
Manufacturing, Inc.

Characters
Alice Anthony, Jake Burns,
Beverly Chung, Jim Goldberg,
product managers

The Matrix management team has put their collective heads together to prepare the annual report, an important project requiring everybody's full involvement. Naturally, each product manager wants to highlight his or her own staff's performance, so the dialogue is immediately lively. Soon, however, it becomes apparent that every statement Alice or Beverly tries to make is cut off by Jake or Jim. Each man seems to have undertaken a mission to allow no sentence initiated by someone else to proceed to completion.

While the two men seem to be enjoying the highly charged give-and-take, the two women are looking increasingly glum, and they are saying less and less. Finally, the female voices recede into the background because by now the women are muttering between themselves if they're saying anything at all, and the male voices—still loudly interrupting each other at every possible opportunity—prevail.

❑   ❑   ❑

PICTURE THIS

Scene II
Employee lounge, Matrix
Manufacturing, Inc.

Characters
Louise Morales, Helen
Collingwood, Mara Porter,
assembly workers

Over coffee, Helen and Louise are heatedly debating the proposed union benefits package. Each time Louise starts to say something, Helen nods her head emphatically and finishes Louise's sentence for her. Before Helen can draw breath to start a sentence of her own, Louise jumps in to capture and carry the conversational ball forward in the same general direction. She repeats a word or phrase of what Helen has said, elaborates on it, offers a few additional remarks, and frequently asks Helen what she thinks. For her part, Helen answers questions, asks Louise other questions, interjects opinions, and often interrupts Louise's statements to finish them for her.

Enter Mara, who sits down at the table, listens for a moment, and then joins animatedly in the discussion, which smoothly opens to accept her. Mara's voice soon becomes part of the general chorus.

Throughout, the three women bind the conversation together with an undertone of "um-hums" and "ah-hahs," weaving a tapestry of talk in which it becomes increasingly difficult to separate who said what first. Though they interrupt each other repeatedly, nobody seems to mind, and nobody withdraws from the discussion. Even though they ultimately disagree on the value of several points in the union contract proposal, they all walk away smiling, feeling good about the conversation and about each other.

❏   ❏   ❏

FREEZE FRAME What's going on at Matrix Manufacturing? Must a discussion with Jake and Jim always become a fight to the finish?

Is their sole aim to seize and hold conversational control? Do Alice and Beverly always start out as participants but quickly turn into a disgruntled audience?

If interruptions usually damage the dialogue the way you've seen them do among the product managers, then what about the assembly workers? Among them, interruptions abound, but the conversational atmosphere and outcome are very different. What's going on here?

Interruptions to Control and Redirect

In Scene I, Jake and Jim are interrupting to seize conversational control. Each tries to get his own particular point across, give the topic a different spin, or change it altogether. Each apparently expects the other to fight to gain or keep control, and both seem to be having a good time turning the discussion into what sounds like a verbal duel to the death. They're enjoying the game. But Alice and Beverly aren't even playing it any more. It's a pattern that's very common: Men interrupt to seize conversational control, and women yield it to them. The pattern can be costly.

Given that only half the project managers' team is contributing fully to its development, the annual report is not going to look as thoughtfully constructed and as balanced as it should. This will reflect badly on the whole team. Moreover, Alice and Beverly are not doing wonderful things to highlight the efforts of their respective product groups. Their failure to do so may come back to bite them later on, when they want to negotiate resources for future projects and have to find proof to justify additional expenditures.

There are also relationship costs. One way of ending Scene I might be to depict Jake and Jim leaving the meeting slapping each other on the back and gloating about having run away with the conversation. By using interruptions to dominate the situation, in effect they have captured the annual report to showcase their own project teams and their own work. On the other hand, Alice and Beverly might be shown smirking complacently because although Jake and Jim did do almost all of the talking and most of the work, the two women are still going to receive half the credit for the report.

The reality is this: Everybody is frustrated, not only because the meeting went badly, but because they've done this dance before, and it's gotten old. Jake and Jim come away feeling resentful because as they see it, they had to hold up the entire conversation; Alice and Beverly once again abdicated responsibility for contributing and seemed to be contentedly willing to sit back and take a free ride.

Are Alice and Beverly pleased with this "free ride"? No way! The two women are actually angry. They're annoyed with themselves for getting tired of battling to complete a thought or finish a sentence and for backing down as usual when dealing with Jake and Jim. And they're angry with the two men for having staged yet another conversational contest.

It's not likely to be pleasant for anyone to be in a room with these four people anytime soon. You'd probably enjoy yourself a lot more having coffee and conversation with the assemblers from Scene II—Louise, Helen, and Mara. In their conversation, interruptions abound, but judging from the outcome, they are interruptions of a different kind.

Interruptions to Support and Enhance

Louise, Helen, and Mara are "tapestry talkers," speakers (of either gender) who generally don't mind being interrupted because their idea of a conversation is everybody talking at once. Tapestry talkers are accustomed to being interrupted and will allow the intrusion or not allow it, depending on how they feel at the moment. Being interrupted is therefore no big deal, especially since most of the interruptions that occur tend to be supportive rather than competitive.

When the three women interrupt each other, they do so not to seize conversational control or change the topic but to agree with, support, and elaborate on what the other person is saying. So, rather than attempting to displace, their interruptions are meant to help the speaker along. Most women interrupt in this way. Even if the speakers disagree entirely about the topic at hand, tapestry talk helps each speaker air her views in turn. In fact, the speaker is often grateful for tapestry talk interruptions because they enhance her idea and also give her a chance to breathe. And a good time is had by all. In general, women use tapestry talk more frequently than men.

Interrupting Interrupters

When you decide that being interrupted is not acceptable to you—you'll lose your train of thought, for instance, or lose the floor to a compulsive talker whose views have already had more than enough air time—try the following:

❏ **Straighten your posture,** look the interrupter directly in the eyes, and say calmly, *"Please don't interrupt."* Then raise your voice slightly and keep on talking.

This is a simple sentence, but you may already be having palpitations contemplating such an action: *"Oh, I could never do that."* Most men and many women have learned to say this with style. It's a powerful, pointed phrase that gets easier to use with practice.

❑ **Put your hand out,** either waist or chest high, palm out and facing the interrupter, indicating, *"Stop."* Since nonverbal signals speak louder than words, most people will notice and respond to them.

❑ **"Level" repeated interruptions.** Leveling means bringing something out into the open, stating it directly so you can deal with it directly. For example, you might say, *"I've been interrupted six times in the last ten minutes, and I'm losing my train of thought. I'd like to finish what I have to say, and then you can respond to it."* You're leveling the way the dialogue is being conducted, and you're explaining why you want to continue in a different way.

❑ **Manage the inevitable.** Sometimes the interrupter is giving you a strong signal that he simply cannot listen anymore but needs to talk now or he'll explode. If he's not going to be listening, why keep talking? Trust your own instincts to tell you when this is happening; a cue is when the listener draws in his breath sharply, leans abruptly forward, or puts his hand on your arm.

At such a time, rather than lose your pacing or your patience, you can graciously allow yourself to be interrupted by saying something like, *"Let's stop for a moment. What issues are coming up for you now?"* That way, you stay in control since you're deciding what to do next.

❏ **Designate a conversational ally.** If you're going to be discussing a touchy subject or speaking to a particularly tough audience, enlist the support of a coworker before the meeting. Brief him or her on what you're going to say and ask for help in turning the talk back to you when you need to continue explicating your ideas. That way, your ally can help deflect the interruptions and you can stay focused on the point you're trying to make.

If you witness someone else struggling to finish a sentence or complete a thought, you may eventually watch them withdraw from the discussion. To help prevent that, you can become a self-designated conversational ally. Reframing a colleague's withdrawal not as an abdication of conversational responsibility but as an understandable reaction to a perceived attack, you can help her re-enter the conversation and participate fully in the dialogue. Here's how:

❏ **Become a gatekeeper.** That is, interrupt the interrupter and deliberately turn the conversation back to the person who was speaking. You're opening the way for her to continue. Asking the speaker a direct question works well. For example, in Scene I, Jake might say, *"Just a second, Jim. Alice didn't finish her point. Alice, how exactly did you propose we format the document?"* Continue gatekeeping for as long as it takes to help the speaker fully express herself.

Interrupter—Know Thyself

If your enthusiasm causes you to jump into conversations too often and too fast, your coworkers have probably let you know that already, either by repeatedly telling you to be quiet or by backing down and becoming quiet themselves. If nobody has said anything to you, then ask directly for their feedback. Or, during your next several conversations, listen for whether you hear your own voice too often while someone else is also talking.

If you habitually interrupt people, admittedly it's a real challenge learning to stop yourself. But if breaking the habit makes other people more comfortable and productive when they're talking with you, if it facilitates rather than discourages their input, it's clearly worth the effort. You can begin to share air time by trying the following:

❑ **Breathe before you speak.** Inhale for 4 slow counts, hold for 3, exhale for 4. As you breathe deeply, listen to what the other person is saying. Then decide whether it would be most productive for you to speak now or to wait. The point here is that rather than reflexively interrupting all the time, you're making a conscious choice about whether and when to do so.

REFRAME Let's see how reframing the different kinds of conversational interruptions can help the product managers in Scene I develop the best annual report and solidify a productive working relationship in the process.

Alice and Beverly recognize that like many men, Jake and Jim have a different conversational rhythm from their own. Apparently, men don't consider interruptions to seize control "rude," but rather expect them to occur and even enjoy it when they do. So men have considerable practice in dealing with such interruptions confidently. Following their example, when anybody interrupts Alice, she no longer reflexively backs down.

If Beverly wants to continue making her point, she raises her voice slightly and simply keeps on talking. For emphasis, she also raises her palm and says, "Wait a minute, Jake, I was explaining something here." Reframing interruptions as challenges to rise to, rather than attacks to withdraw from, allows both women to use such strategies without becoming hostile to the interrupter. They make their points not with a scowl but with a smile.

Alice has learned how to consider the validity of an interrupter's remark. If it is valid, she might decide to explore it with, "Oh. Interesting idea, Jim. What do the rest of you think?" She maintains conversational control by making the decision to move in the new direction.

For their part, Jake and Jim have learned to monitor their own behavior, often by taking a few deep breaths while deciding whether to speak. They consciously try not to interrupt to control when they think doing so might cause the speaker to withdraw. Both men contribute a great deal to keeping the conversation lively and flowing. When they cannot remain quiet a moment longer, they have learned from the women how to interrupt to support, so they tapestry talk, and nobody seems to mind that.

Also, these workers receive another kind of help from each other. When the heat of the moment causes Jim to interrupt Alice, for instance, either Jake or Beverly gatekeeps by turning the conversation back to her. Sometimes Alice decides to let go of her point anyway, but the choice is hers. Both men have reframed gatekeeping not as coddling but as making a valuable contribution to the team effort by helping a coworker express herself, so they do it willingly when it's called for.

Alice and Beverly realize that when they interrupt Jim and Jake occasionally and wrest the topic from their hands, neither seems to get offended. What's more, both women are beginning to have a good time barging in and plunging on, having their say. But they're willing to back down if a speaker lets them know that interruptions at a particular moment are not okay.

Most importantly, even when the conversation heats up, nobody withdraws from it. This time, the whole team leaves the meeting feeling satisfied that everybody has contributed as fully as possible to making the annual report a solid piece of work—a true collaboration they can all be proud of.

Interruptions of Work Process

Another kind of interruption that frequently occurs in the workplace has to do with work process. People sometimes rush to rescue other people—most frequently women—prematurely. That is, a manager may interrupt a staffer's efforts at solving a problem or learning how to do something by moving in too quickly to help him or her. Like conversation interruptions, poorly timed interruptions of a work process can prevent people from learning what they need to learn and from contributing as fully as they should. Conversely, people sometimes allow others—most frequently men—to struggle too long trying to figure something out on their own, when they really should be helped.

Consider what would happen if you as a manager habitually rescued an employee prematurely. Both your good intentions and your justifiable impatience notwithstanding, you would be depriving the staffer of a chance to develop problem-solving skills and habits of self-reliance, persistent effort, and follow-through. And you'd be bruising the employee's self-esteem in the process. Although people tend to rescue women more quickly than they do men, nobody's doing anybody any good by throwing them a lifeline just as they're learning to swim on their own.

"Rescuing" should be a conscious decision, not a knee-jerk reaction resembling a chivalric gesture from a male manager or a maternal gesture from a female supervisor. In either case, repeated premature rescuing creates and perpetuates a dependency relationship. It encourages the belief that the employee can safely make a mess and simply wait for someone else to clean it up, or it reinforces the habit of looking for help from a "magical" rescuer. Before you rush to rescue anybody, do a quick freeze frame and ask yourself: Am I about to rescue this person prematurely? Reframe your actions and think about what would best promote employee growth.

A young engineer related to me how she needed data from a male colleague to complete a report and prepare an important presentation. Her boss, male and ten years older than she is, called from abroad to inquire about the status of the project. She told him, "I'm waiting for the material from Bob. He said he'd have it to me on time." Immediately, her boss said, "Switch me upstairs, and I'll get the stuff for you." "Wait a minute," she countered. "I appreciate the offer, and yet I need to develop a relationship with Bob. We're going to be doing a lot of these reports, and he and I need to get things organized between us. I'll call him myself." She admits she believes her boss meant well, but she did not think he'd have rushed so quickly to rescue a male colleague.

When it comes to work process interruptions, men have their own set of troubles. Sometimes men hesitate to let themselves be interrupted; that is, they don't ask for help when they should. Instead, they feel tremendous pressure to figure things out on their own. This pressure causes them to reinvent many wheels and to waste valuable company time doing so, whereas if they had asked the right person the right questions earlier on, their helper might have offered the necessary answers, saving everybody a lot of time and effort, and saving the company a lot of money.

Because many managers fail to notice when it's time to offer help to men, the male employees are left to flounder unnecessarily. When you delegate a new task or project to an employee, arrange a status check meeting scheduled in advance and put it in writing. For instance, you both decide to meet every Friday afternoon, from 2:00 to 2:15, and mark your calendars accordingly. This gives you a planned opportunity to decide whether you need to step in to suggest mid-course corrections. At each meeting, if you don't see the results you're looking for or hear the employee ask questions suggesting that he's reaching out for the help he needs, freeze frame and think about whether you're letting him struggle too long alone.

Rescue Me—In a Few Minutes

If you think you're being prematurely rescued, that is, offered help before you want or need it, try the following:

❏ **Explain what you're trying to do and where you think your efforts are going wrong.** Then ask the person helping you to work with you instead of for you. Ask your coworker to teach you how to think it through on your own, not to solve the problem. That way, you'll be learning how to approach similar situations in the future, and the helper can still feel justifiably virtuous and appreciated for having come to your rescue.

- ❏ **Use the "And yet" twist:** "I appreciate your offer, **and yet** I need to wrestle with this on my own for a while longer." "And yet" sounds less contrary than "But." After all, you don't want to sound contrary because you aren't ready for help now, and yet you may need rescuing from the same person in the future.

If you're struggling with a problem but are unaccustomed to asking for help, try the following:

- ❏ **Set yourself a finite time limit.** Calculate how much the company is paying for you to struggle on your own, and decide if your efforts are worth the price. Think about whether you'd pay for the effort out of your own pocket. If you haven't solved the problem in an hour, for instance, at an out-of-pocket cost of $_____, then "interrupt" your struggle and get help.

- ❏ **Ask for and accept the kind of help you need.** If you want the answer, ask for that. If you want to learn how to solve the problem yourself next time, ask your rescuer to teach you. Know what you're asking for. And if it's at all acceptable, take what you get. That is, if what the person produces is not exactly what you might have envisioned but it gets the job done, accept it. If you tinker with it too much, your helper is not likely to rush eagerly to your rescue the next time.

COLLECT SNAPSHOTS
TO REFLECT ON

❏ Picture a time when you were at a meeting, found yourself being constantly interrupted, and escaped from that by talking only to the person next to you. How did you feel about the interrupters? How might you now reframe their actions?

❏ Recall a time when you walked away from a conversation feeling annoyed at having had to keep the dialogue going almost single-handedly because the people in the room were not contributing as much as you thought they should. Freeze frame and see if you encouraged others to enter the discussion, or if your interruptions might have contributed to shutting them out of it. If you could rewind the videotape and do the conversation over, how might you change your own behavior?

❏ Picture a time when you were working on a project and someone "rescued" you. Freeze frame and see whether being rescued at that precise moment helped or hindered your development. Did you let yourself be rescued prematurely, or did you wait too long to ask for help? If you could play the scene again, how would you change your timing?

❏ Picture a time when you "helped" an employee finish a task or make a decision. Freeze frame and see whether the employee's gender might have affected your actions. If you could play the scene again, would you rush to the rescue at the same time?

2 DIRECTION AND INDIRECTION

It seems that nothing can be done without having a meeting, forming a committee, creating a work group, or building a team—cross-functional, self-managed, or otherwise. Everybody has to have input. Everyone has to express their ideas and champion their viewpoints, resolve interpersonal conflicts, and persuade others to act. Everyone has to contend with new management tools, such as multiskilling and 360-degree feedback.

In fact, in the new, flattened organization, people who have had little or no supervisory training often find themselves in situations where they have to perform such supervisory functions as issuing orders to peers, giving instructions to temporary employees, and criticizing the efforts of coworkers.

These interpersonal activities are tricky business in the best of times. What further complicates them is the gender difference, which is often overlooked because of the concentration on content, not on approach. Men and women frequently differ in approach, more specifically in degrees of directness. Most men value direct statement and prefer to "tell it like it is" rather than "waste time beating around the bush"; women, on the other hand, tend to be circuitous, or "polite." So it's not surprising when men and women frequently misread each other's directness or the lack of it. This difference in approach can have considerable and costly impacts in two areas of interaction: (1) giving and receiving orders or instructions and (2) giving and receiving constructive criticism.

You'd probably have little difficulty believing a situation where because an order was ignored or instructions misunderstood, a company lost thousands of dollars. But misconstrued criticism can be costly to a company. When a supervisor or manager gives constructive criticism to an employee, she is trying to teach the employee something valuable. Her purpose may be to pinpoint and correct behavior that isn't up to par or to acknowledge and reward good stuff so that it happens again. But if the employee doesn't "get it," whatever worthwhile intention the manager had is lost; the positive result the manager was looking for is gone. Company time has been wasted. What's more, if the manager's helpful attitude and thoughtfully considered remarks are genuine, then the relationship between the two people, which could and ideally should have been improved by the well-intentioned criticism, can be eroded instead.

Let's roll the videotapes and see what reframes you can create to help you effectively give orders and instructions that get the results you want and offer criticism that helps others grow.

❑   ❑   ❑

ORDERS AND INSTRUCTIONS— GIVING AND TAKING

Heaving more folders onto a corner of her already overcrowded desk, Ingrid begins searching frantically for a file she needs right away. When she can't find it, she calls her assistant, Gilbert, to come and help her. She needs to read a particular file to prepare for her next court session, and she's asked him on three different occasions to retrieve it from the file room. Each time, she patiently explained how to use the

P I C T U R E   T H I S

Scene
Bradford Junction City
Attorney's Office

Characters
Ingrid Griffin, Senior
Prosecuting Attorney
Gilbert Ochoa, Paralegal

double code numbers to locate the file, and each time he claimed he understood what she was saying. "When do you think I'll have the material?" she'd politely inquire. "Right away," had been the reply. But apparently he still hadn't put the folder on her desk. If she ever does get her hands on the material, Ingrid will now be able only to glance at it briefly before she has to appear before the judge.

So she takes a deep breath and tries one last time. Speaking in words of one syllable and barely controlling her rising anger, she slowly and carefully instructs Gilbert yet again on how to use both locator codes. *"If one of the guys had asked Gil for something, he would have had it long ago,"* she thinks, not because she's touchy about possible sexism but because she has observed that her male colleagues are more successful in getting results from the paralegal whose support services they all share. Meanwhile, Gilbert shifts around uneasily in front of her desk. *"Doesn't she think I know anything?"* he wonders. *"Why does she have to talk down to me like that? And who does she think she is anyway, my mother or something?"*

"I don't believe this," Ingrid thinks. *"Gil looks as if he's hearing all this for the first time!"* Finally, she loses her cool, pounds a fist on the desk, and insists in no uncertain terms that he use both locator numbers and GET THE FILE THIS MINUTE! "Okay, okay" he says, backing slowly out of the room. "You never said it was an emergency. And why didn't you explain in

the first place that I couldn't locate it unless I used both codes? I thought I could use either one."

As Ingrid begins slowly tearing her hair from her head, Gilbert considers how he can repair his wounded self-esteem. He'll show her she'd better treat him well; he'll take his own sweet time. And he saunters in the general direction of the file room.

❑   ❑   ❑

FREEZE FRAME Good grief! Who wants to go through this kind of scene twenty times a day? Does communication have to break down so completely whenever Ingrid tries to give Gilbert orders or instructions? What will it take to get them on the same wavelength?

Are You Asking Me or Telling Me?

Apparently acting on the unstated assumption that the best way to get a message across is to spit it straight out whenever possible, most men tend to speak in statements. *"If I state it directly, my want or need is unmistakable,"* they think, *"so therefore I will get what I want."* Although being direct doesn't guarantee you'll get what you want, often it does improve your chances. That's not to say that men are always dictatorial or even that every statement that sounds like an order is actually an order—some may be requests or possibly slight preferences and open to discussion. But to many women's ears, men whose jobs require them to give a lot of orders or instructions sound like they're always making demands. Whereas other men would perceive them as straightforward, women see them as authoritarian and sometimes abusive, hardly a coworker or manager that a typical employee would rush to work with.

In contrast, women often speak in interrogatories, using actual questions or ending sentences with upward inflections that sound like questions. To men's ears, women thus sound tentative and uncertain, or at least uninformed. For example, Lila says to her employee Fred, "You'll be at Friday's preconference meeting, won't you?" Although Lila certainly expects him there, her phrasing makes it possible for Fred to contemplate answering, "No, I hadn't planned on it." Even if Fred says nothing further and the dialogue ends, he may not realize that his boss definitely wants him at that meeting. On Friday morning Lila says to Fred's buddy Hank, "Fred's coming to the preconference meeting, isn't he?" This causes Hank to wonder why Lila hasn't demanded that Fred be present, and if she has, why she's unsure that he'll obey her orders. Even though she knows exactly what she wants, Lila sounds tentative and uncertain to Hank's ears, too. This does not do good things for her reputation as an effective manager.

Learning to Learn from Each Other

Think of a story you could tell about when a direct or indirect style of giving orders caused confusion and dismay. I think of Mary, who today is a transportation fleet management supervisor for a large utility. Mary told me about the time when she was the first and, for several years, the only woman working in the company garage. Shortly after she started working for him, her boss Barry screamed at her in public, dressing her down loudly and long for forgetting to put on her hard hat. "Shouting at me like that, he gave himself apoplexy, and he almost gave me a heart attack," she remarked. "I hid from him for weeks afterwards. Why didn't he just ask me, 'Please put your hard hat back on'? I'd have done what he told me."

But how was Barry supposed to know that? If he had done as she wished, Mary might indeed have put the hard hat back on, but the rest of the crew—all men and unused to such "gentle" treatment— would have wondered about Barry.

Because he had worked almost entirely with men for his whole career, Barry needed some time to learn how to supervise a woman. He didn't like the idea very much, Mary recalls, but he was a practical man. He wanted Mary to be productive, and he knew that more women would be coming into the garage. So he learned from experience and from discussions with Mary that a somewhat less direct approach allowed her to hear him better than she could when he barked orders. Men often are more accustomed to or willing to accept the military model of having orders and instructions barked at them; women usually are not. Men usually simply hear commands to be obeyed; women may hear abuse.

That's not to say that Barry—or any male manager— should withhold his comments from Mary—or from any employee. Indeed, men sometimes shy away from offering feedback to a woman because they're "afraid of hurting her feelings." That's unfair to the woman because she'll be deprived of potentially valuable input. If Barry wants to improve his chances of having a productive impact on Mary, he should not dilute his message. But he can use reframes to help him moderate his delivery.

Fortunately for both of them, Barry was open to learning from Mary, and she was a natural reframer, alert to the possibility that when you communicate, the meanings people derive are not necessarily always the same ones you intended for them to understand. Mary learned a lot from watching Barry, which is a good thing, too, since most of the drivers she manages are men. Mary saw that her indirect way of giving orders and instructions confused many men. She's learned how to be more brusque and to the point. She doesn't shout because she doesn't like to, but when it's necessary, she directly tells her men: "Put your hard hat on now." Her male employees have learned to reframe as well. They know that even if Mary were to be indirect and say, "Why do you think we give you hard hats, so you can make planters out of them?"—that really means they had better put the hats back on. And they do.

Giving Orders and Instructions That Get Results

Sometimes when you give an order that appears to you to be luminously clear or an instruction that is unmistakable, it can seem almost bizarre how radically the results differ from the outcome you had every reason to expect. In such circumstances, women tend to blame themselves for giving faulty instructions; men tend to blame the recipients for failing to understand. To increase your chances of getting good results when you give orders or instructions, here are some suggestions:

❏ When giving nonnegotiable orders to anyone, **be direct**. Women can learn how to do this from men, many of whom seem to excel at it. Don't require people to wonder if you "really meant what you said." Men will understand your direct approach, and women will come to appreciate it as they begin to reframe it as clarity rather than abuse.

❏ **Use labels** until people get to know you: *"That's an order." "This is a request." "I'm making a suggestion." "I have a slight preference."* Such labeling might sound artificial, but it will help both men and women learn how to "hear" you. Also, it helps listeners feel more confident that they're "getting it." Once people have learned to understand your style, you can discontinue the labels.

❏ **Determine "musts" and "mights"** in your own mind before giving instructions, and be sure you mean what you say when you label them as such. Say, *"You might want to try X,"* only when you mean it's really okay with you if the person decides not to do so. Otherwise, if *"doing X"* is a must, then say that.

❏ Men can learn from women how to **be somewhat indirect** when giving orders to more timid or insecure employees, whatever their gender. If they hear you as authoritarian, they may retreat behind the barricades, and you'll have a hard time finding out exactly how well they understand your instructions and whether they have any questions or concerns about the task at hand.

❑ **Instead of asking "Do you understand?" encourage paraphrasing.** It's usually people who understand you the least who are also the least likely to say, "I haven't a clue what you're talking about." They will say, "Sure, fine, no problem." But what they really mean is, "If you'll get out of my face, maybe I can sit here and figure out what this mess is about." Then you are no longer in control.

❑ To check for understanding, ask them to **paraphrase.** Paraphrasing means they're using their own words to describe what they think you've just told them to do. That way, you can clear up any possible misunderstandings before your employees go rushing madly down the wrong road. To lead them into a paraphrase, try something such as *"Where can I clarify?"* or *"So that we're sure we're on the same wave length, tell me how you think you're going to approach X."*

❑ **Watch for telltale signs of noncomprehension** from both men and women, such as blank stares or repeated requests to "explain it again." Women are more likely to ask for further clarification when they need it, so be ready to answer their questions without framing repeated inquiries as nitpicking and the questioners as pains in the neck. Men are more likely to try to mask their confusion, so don't wait for them to ask a direct question before you offer a fuller explanation.

❑ **If you think your instructions haven't gotten through,** don't push harder in the same direction. Rather, try another method: draw a picture; show a chart or graph; encourage the listener to take notes. People have different styles of receiving and retaining information, so be willing to do whatever it takes to get your message across and get the results you want.

With minor adaptations, these same techniques also help when you are receiving orders or instructions:

❑ When communicating across genders, **ask for labels** to help you understand what's going on. When a man is shouting, for instance, rather than getting upset, a woman can reframe his commanding tone, hear it as something other than a demand and calmly ask, *"Is that an order or a preference?"* When a woman is being indirect, a man might reframe what seems to be uncertainty as a possible order and then ask, *"Is this a 'must' or a 'might'?"*

❑ **Instead of saying "I don't understand," para- phrase.** To avoid either the suggestion that you weren't paying attention or the implication that the instructions were ineffective so you have to reinterpret them, lead in to your paraphrase with something like, *"Just to be certain I've understood you clearly, here's what I'm going to do . . ."* You're using your own words to explain what you think you are hearing and seeing. This gives the instructor the opportunity to validate your accuracy and correct you if necessary. Using a question mark at the end of your paraphrase makes it less likely that the instructor will take offense.

❑ When taking instructions, it's helpful to **make room for your preferred learning style** by pinpointing it. Say *"I need to take notes," "Show me the diagram," or "I learn best by listening."*

REFRAME Let's get back to Ingrid and Gilbert and see which reframes rescue Gilbert's self-esteem and save Ingrid's sanity—along with the hair on her head.

Gilbert understands that his boss has a lot on her mind and sometimes forgets to tell him things, so when she asks him the first time if he would please retrieve a file for her as soon as possible, he says, "Specifically when do you need this?" Ingrid reframes his question not as a challenge to her authority but as an aid to prioritizing his time. "It would make me feel better to have it right away so I don't have to worry about it any more," she admits, "but I can see you're busy now. Specifically, I need to review it for at least an hour to get ready for my court appearance tomorrow morning at 9:30. Any time before you leave today would be fine." Gilbert now reframes her polite and seemingly offhand request into a direct order and an immediate priority.

When Ingrid hurriedly mentions something about two locator numbers, Gilbert doesn't worry about who's to blame for the lousy instructions. Instead, he says, "Wait a minute. I'm going to take notes so I'll be sure to remember exactly what you need." He reframes Ingrid's dismissive tone to a probable indication of the pressure she's under rather than a putdown of his intelligence, and he gets on with helping her instruct him clearly so together they can get the job done.

For her part, Ingrid has learned how to be more direct when giving orders to both men and women, and she tries to make herself as clear as possible by carefully labeling "musts" and "mights" and by using labels to distinguish orders from preferences. "Use both locator codes," she directs. "One alone won't work." Reframing Gilbert's failure to take immediate action as an instructional event that needs fixing, Ingrid concentrates both on the goal at hand and on finding the instructional technique that works best with him.

When he quietly slides the files onto her desk later that afternoon, Ingrid says, "Thanks for the quick work, Gil. We're becoming quite a team!"

CRITICISM—CONSTRUCTIVE AND DESTRUCTIVE

Degrees of directness also can affect the impact of constructive criticism and even change it entirely. Although the word "critical" usually has a negative spin, it actually means "making judgments," both positive and negative ones. When you assert "That's great," you are exercising your critical skills as much as you are when you announce "That stinks."

Too Much or Too Little of a Good Thing

Women can sometimes be too direct and too frequent with praise. Many men hear frequent praise as insincere, apple-polishing at worst, and at best suspect. Consequently, if a woman praises a man too often, he'll uneasily mutter "Thanks" or "It's just my job" the first few times. Thereafter, he may hear her effusions as gushing or silly, if he hears them at all. In either case, if she's trying to reward his behavior so it will continue, she's not going to achieve her desired result. Rick, an associate in a large consulting company working on a team project, told me how his colleague Rina seemed to have a salt shaker of "Attaboys" that she sprinkled over everybody. "I always wondered what she was trying to prove," Rick explained, "or what she was trying to pull. But I didn't take her praise seriously. After a while, I didn't even hear her any more. Nor did anyone else."

Men can be too indirect by *not* offering praise frequently enough, especially when they're dealing with women. That's because women generally assume that if you don't say anything, it means you don't like their work. If you offer praise indirectly, you may inadvertently wind up demoralizing an already bruised coworker who experiences your remarks as more blows to her shaky self-esteem. For example, Eunice, director at a large transportation agency, told me about the first time Ward, her brilliant and energetic boss, grabbed a red pencil and "attacked" an extensive report she had submitted for his review. Eunice watched him in horror.

Then she went home and spent a sleepless night seriously thinking about quitting the job. After long hours of agonizing, she decided not to do that. Instead, she came in the next day and began the laborious project of restructuring the entire report. "If I didn't have a strong ego," she said, "I'd have been out of there. I really felt awful." When she submitted the new document to Ward, he asked why she had bothered to rewrite it. The original one had been fine, he said; it simply needed a few minor adjustments. "If I don't say anything, it means I like it," he explained. "If I didn't think it was good work, I wouldn't have taken the time to edit it like I did." Until she learned to reframe his style, Ward's indirect way of praising her work was lost on Eunice, and it had an opposite effect from what he intended.

Many men seem to work from the unstated assumption that if you still have your job, then that is sufficient recognition of achievement in that job, and little more should be required. But as anyone will tell you, that kind of oblique recognition does little to contribute to a motivating environment. And as most of us—men included—will admit, it really does feel good to hear sincere praise sincerely delivered. Not all the time—but once in a while.

Notice What Is Noteworthy

To help you decide when praise is in order and also to prevent you from overdoing it, take the word "noteworthy" literally; that is, is the behavior you've observed worthy of your making a note of it? If people are doing their jobs, that's not noteworthy. You'd have nothing to write down even if you wanted to. A simple "thank you" here and there is enough. If a colleague does something noticeably over and above what designates average daily performance, however, that's noteworthy. If you were writing that person's performance appraisal, would you want to make a note of this? If your answer is yes, it's time to offer praise.

If you want to use the power of praise to your best advantage, here's how:

❑ **Be specific.** Although in the short run, it's easier to say a general, *"Nice work,"* you're not helping the recipients learn much about what worked and what they should do again the next time. Say instead, *"That meeting was excellent because . . ."* or *"What I appreciated most about your teaching Joe how to mend the press web was. . . ."*

❑ **Be brief.** Though men generally start to feel this way sooner than women, after a point everybody starts wondering why you're being so effusive, and sincere praise begins to sound perilously like manipulative flattery with an ulterior motive.

❑ **Widen the circle.** You add impact to your praise by pinpointing how the work benefited others. For example, say, *"The system you designed for maintaining lateness statistics is really helping the folks in Human Resources. Thanks for taking care of it so quickly for them."*

❑ **Put it in writing.** Although sometimes men are reluctant to admit to this, people like to see their names and their accomplishments acknowledged in print. Take a moment to write a note, remembering to be specific and brief and to widen the circle if possible. Writing something down also extends the impact of your praise over time.

If you decide that you need and deserve a reassuring word, try these techniques:

❑ To encourage others to praise your efforts and let you know what they consider most valuable about your work, you can use **the "More of" opener.** That is, ask, *"What exactly should I try to do more of at the next committee meeting?"* You're helping them help you.

❏ Try **positive inquiry** to get specifics. If a coworker just says, *"Nice work,"* try: *"Thanks. I want to be able to do it as well next time, so tell me, what two things stood out most for you? What two aspects did you like best?"*

I Praise Yours, You Praise Mine

There's yet another way to approach praise that can distance men and women at work. In response to someone praising their work efforts, women frequently respond in kind, apparently working from this premise: "Since you've said something nice about my work, I'll say something positive about yours in return, or at least I'll pay some thoughtful attention to it."

Most men, however, do not feel similarly impelled to reciprocate, and their male colleagues would probably not expect them to do so. If women expect and therefore wait for such reciprocity, they're likely to wait a long time. And they're going to be disappointed by and even angry with the man who responds, "Yes, you're right. This widget I designed *is* a true beauty!" and strides off down the hall without even acknowledging his female colleague's contribution to the design effort at all, much less praising its worthiness.

In general, if you want to offer praise, do so unconditionally. That is, be helpful by saying what you want and by pinpointing specifics, and don't expect a reply in kind. Reframing what might be seen as thoughtlessness or arrogance into evidence of the belief that for some people accepting a compliment carries with it no perceived obligation to return one will help women think more kindly of the men they work with. It will even help them deal more comfortably with people who *are* thoughtlessly arrogant.

On the other hand, if a coworker has been extremely helpful, consider reframing her compliment as both a sincere recognition of your contribution and a gentle reminder that perhaps mutual recognition is in order, and it might indeed be time to praise her noteworthy achievements.

"This Stinks!"

If you really mean to offer constructive criticism where your intent is to help someone grow, you don't want to waste time beating around the bush. Tell it exactly like it is. But too direct an approach to criticism may cause some people, primarily but not only women, to recoil from what they hear as blunt or even brutal delivery. As they curl up in metaphorical horror, they're not likely to learn very much from whatever insight you're trying to share.

A client of mine told me about how he almost destroyed what turned out to be a very valuable working relationship because he didn't recognize what was going wrong. The difficulty had to do with his ultra-direct style of delivering criticism. Vice president at a small Connecticut newspaper, John was having problems with Ilene, his human resources manager, whom he was grooming to be his successor. "I blew this one," he lamented to me. "I thought she would take hold, but I don't think she's cut out for the job after all. You have to be tough to succeed in this business. You have to be able to make decisions under pressure and stick to them. Ilene can't stand up for her ideas. Whenever I challenge her, she crumbles."

As John continued in the same vein, I reframed the picture he was describing. "Oh," I said, "I think it's wonderful that you're mentoring her. But maybe your methods could use some softening. I know that if you didn't think Ilene were worth the bother, you wouldn't be taking all the trouble you take with her work in the first place. I see that you're toughening her up so she'll know how to play in the big leagues. But does she know your intentions? I'm betting she doesn't understand that you're trying to make a human resources vice president out of her! I'm betting she thinks she's about to lose her job."

Admittedly, it was easier for me to recognize John's intent and Ilene's confusion because I was emotionally separate from the situation. Before he lost an excellent colleague, John decided to approach Ilene to be sure she knew how satisfied he was with her work. He was surprised to learn that she hadn't understood he was grooming her for a big next step. She wasn't quite ready yet, he admitted, but she was getting there. Reframing would help John recognize that his blunt style of delivering criticism wasn't working. It's a good thing he did so before he lost a valued protégé.

Don't Do That Ever Again, Please!

Saying something obliquely, even sandwiching a negative comment between two positive ones, which is a technique many of us have been taught to use, can be dangerous.

Molly, a friend who teaches at a local university, told me how she learned this the hard way. Meaning to convey that an extensive report a male graduate student had submitted contained too many errors, lacked sufficient supportive data, and consequently would have to be rewritten, she said, "You make several strong points, Rob. There's a lot of good stuff here. You need to be careful about accuracy, and it's really helpful to back your assertions up with sufficient data." For his final project, Rob submitted the same paper without rewriting a word, and he was astonished when he received a failing grade in the course. Molly's oblique criticism would probably have gotten through to her female students, who would have asked for more specifics and then made the desired changes. Rob simply didn't get it.

What women experience as heavy-handedness, men often hear as helpful directness. Unless women with a style like Molly's use reframes and begin to see that the direct approach is more appropriate with men like Rob, they will most likely be ineffective in coaching sessions, performance appraisal discussions, and even disciplinary meetings. Let's see what reframes are in order.

Offering Criticism Constructively

Whatever your gender and whatever your position in the organization, if you want to help your teammates improve, here are some suggestions for criticizing them with maximum benefit:

❏ **Don't pull your punches**. You have valuable insights to share, and you owe it to the company to share them. When criticizing women, reframing may lead you to soften your tone somewhat, but don't dilute the message.

❑ Whatever the recipient's gender and whatever your own style preference, **be direct about indicating the consequences of poor performance.** If people must get their act together or risk losing their jobs, don't imply it; say it directly. People have a right to know clearly what they're facing. Then be a willing resource for helping them figure out how to improve their performance.

❑ **Be specific. Stick to the facts.** Carefully document behavior or the results of behavior and discuss only that. For example, if you say, *"You're getting sloppy,"* you're not offering anything concrete. But if you say, *"That Anderson report you submitted yesterday had seven errors that I've circled on the draft. That's an unacceptable error rate,"* the originator of the Anderson report now knows that the report was unacceptable and exactly what has to be done to improve it.

❑ **Criticize the work, not the person**. Remember that you are in fact criticizing just the work. Trust your coworkers to learn not to take your well-intentioned remarks as insults to them personally.

❑ **Offer your criticism in writing**. While you're building your flexibility and learning when and how to be more or less direct in your conversational style, try jotting down on paper the remarks you want to share. Giving recipients a written critique before you meet with them allows them time to consider your comments in private, gather their thoughts, and deal with whatever emotional reactions they may have. Then you will both be more comfortable when you meet to discuss specifics and answer questions.

Taking Criticism Professionally, Not Personally

Criticism is always a gift if you let it help you learn something. Even if it's invalid criticism, you still learn something, mostly about the critic. That is, you're recognizing that this colleague sometimes offers criticism for reasons other than helpfulness. If you have to continue working with that person, the more you learn about his or her behavior, the better chance you'll have of learning how to cope.

If the criticism you're receiving is valid, you want to be able to hear it without defense so you can learn the most from it. When receiving criticism, try the following:

❑ If the critic is shouting at you, reframe the directness as an inappropriate if well-intentioned approach, and **listen past the delivery for the content.** This is not going to be easy when someone is yelling in your face, but with practice it is possible, and it's frequently productive.

❏ **Ask for specifics.** Whether the critic is being indirect or overbearing, focusing on facts and asking for specifics will still help you. Nobody learns anything from a comment like, *"This product is terrible!"* Try asking, *"What two things should I change first?"* Asking questions moves your responsiveness from your gut, which is twisting, and your heart, which is breaking, to your head, which is trying to learn something. You're gaining a degree of objectivity you didn't have before. Keep asking questions until you get specifics and have a clear idea of the next steps to take.

❏ **Postpone responding.** If you feel yourself getting defensive, say something like, *"Thank you for your input. I need to think about what you've said."* That way, you won't be cutting yourself off from future criticism by making the critic uncomfortable in the face of your tearful or angry reaction.

COLLECT SNAPSHOTS
TO REFLECT ON

❑ Recall a time when you gave orders or instructions to a colleague and were amazed at how little the resulting work resembled what you thought you were asking for. Freeze frame and think about how gender differences in directness might have complicated the event. Which reframes would help you modify your approach? What would you do differently to increase your chances of a successful outcome?

❑ Freeze frame the last time you mistook a "must" for a "might," or vice versa. How does reframing help you understand what the instructor's intentions could have been? How does reframing affect your feelings about the event? If you could rewind the tape and play the scene again, what questions would you now ask the instructor?

❑ Picture a recent coaching discussion with your boss. Freeze frame a moment when gender differences in directness affected how criticism was being offered or how you were receiving it. How would reframing help you profit more from the criticism being offered?

❏ Recall a time when you praised a coworker sincerely. Freeze frame and ask yourself: How specific were you? How did your colleague respond? How do you think gender affected your delivery style? How do you think gender affected the recipient's response?

3 To Be Succinct, Or Not to Be

Experience has taught men to value and demonstrate a succinct conversation style at work. In business, where time really is money in a way that is different from private life and where people have to deal with so much information from so many sources each working day, the point of most discussions usually has to be immediate. Succinctness is therefore a cost-effective skill everyone needs to cultivate. What's more, a succinct delivery style suggests an inner self-confidence, a kind of "clearly I know what I'm doing so I don't have to explain myself" attitude that enhances one's professional image.

Succinctness has its downside, however. Someone who asks for or offers few details can overlook crucial ones or make promises that cannot be kept. Questions remain unasked and flaws in logic go unnoticed and therefore uncorrected. Still, "cut to the chase" or "just give me the bottom line" are phrases that can be heard resonating through company corridors around the country, usually coming from men and frequently directed at women.

That's because many women prefer to offer abundant and time-consuming detail and generally require the same density of material from others, or they have the uncomfortable feeling that they're missing something. Sometimes it is indeed productive to examine all the relevant details (key word: *relevant*); for instance, you might want to learn how the speaker's mind works. Such insight can be helpful in dealing with her in the future. Or you might want to know how a particular viewpoint developed, or how a particular problem was worked out, again for future reference. Also, detailed exploration allows you to discover and correct inaccuracies before you go public with anything embarrassing.

Dwelling on details has its downside, too. It can lead to analysis paralysis, or a constant search for more information, which generates more data and generates more questions in need of answers, all of which also generate a well-earned reputation for indecisiveness. Many women still have to learn that it's not always necessary to understand something fully before going ahead with it.

Voluble speakers and detail seekers have a reputation for calling meetings that nobody wants to attend. Faced with the likelihood of having to listen to endless details, a lot of busy people scramble frantically for substitutes to send in their place. Then it's unlikely that the decision makers will attend. Or if they do attend, they'll arrive with a hurried air and a hostile edge. Since hurried and hostile do not make for either effective listening or productive participation, the meeting will probably take twice as long as it should and yield half as many action items as everybody would prefer.

Most important, insisting on full details all the time suggests a lack of confidence, both in your own achievements and in the capabilities of others. Offering detailed explanations can sound like defensively justifying a course of action in advance because you expect people to take issue with it and find it wanting. This seeming lack of confidence does not enhance anyone's professional image. For example, a client of mine explained how when her boss asked, "Why did you choose that vendor?" she launched into an elaborate explanation of her decision in a defensive tone. Then she agonized for weeks, wondering why her boss doubted her judgment. He later said he was only asking a casual question and would have been content with a word or two, just so he knew what was going on. "A man would have simply answered, 'I think they're the best people for us,' and come across as supremely self-confident," she said. I agree with her.

Requiring detailed explanations from others can put them on the defensive. "Why does he have to double-check everything I do?" people wonder. "Why doesn't he think I know how to take care of business?" Such thinking does little to enhance an employee's self-esteem.

So it seems that there are times to be succinct and times to be expansive. The trick is to learn when to expand the use of detail and when to contract it, as well as how to do each with style.

❑   ❑   ❑

PICTURE THIS

Scene I
Executive Conference Room, Global Money Managers, Inc.

Characters
Michael Markowitz, Executive Director, Global Marketing

Dan Wilson, Managing Director

Emma Doyle, Senior Director

Speaking in an increasingly impassioned voice and breathless manner, Emma expounds on her plans for a new product offering. Her excitement about the new concept and her team's exemplary efforts in developing it are clearly evident. But neither Michael nor Dan seems to be sharing her enthusiasm. Although Dan recognizes that what she's saying is valuable information, he still finds himself wondering why she's droning on and when she's going to stop. *"I should have never let her get started,"* he thinks. *"I should have given this presentation myself."*

As Emma slaps yet another transparency on the overhead projector and expands on yet another aspect of the concept, which she is intent on proving will make the company more competitive in an area where they've been losing money recently, both men shift uneasily in their chairs and even occasionally roll their eyes skyward and furtively consult their wrist watches.

Emma is aware of their behavior. And she's desperately concerned by it, since she needs their immediate support for the additional resources she's about to ask for. Thrown off in the pacing of her remarks by what she interprets as evidence of their still uncaptured imaginations, Emma valiantly adds more fascinating data to a presentation that both men already perceive as dead and drowned under overabundant detail. *"Enough already,"* thinks Michael Markowitz, even as Emma launches yet another rococo argument to justify her request for increased funding.

Michael never hears her ask for more money because he stopped listening a while ago. Instead, he's wondering why Dan hasn't yet coached his employee properly on how to give briefings to busy senior people like himself. Finally, Michael has to leave to attend another meeting, where he fervently hopes that the speaker will be better prepared—translate that to mean able to get straight to the point.

Believing that she has let him down in front of the boss, Dan stands glaring at Emma. She glares intrepidly back, wondering how long she's going to continue working for a man like Dan, who clearly doesn't stand behind his employees and is not going to help her get the resources she needs. For the moment, at least, this project's future is still uncertain, and Emma is furious. *"No wonder the company lost money last year,"* Emma fumes, as she heads for her office, where she knows two of her subordinates are waiting to meet with her. *"Maybe I'd better update my résumé after all."*

P I C T U R E   T H I S

Scene II

Senior Director's office,
Global Money Managers
Inc.

Characters

Emma Doyle, Senior Director
Eric McWilliams, Director of
Global Marketing, Asia
region
Jeff Balesteros, Assistant
Director

❏　　　❏　　　❏

Still steaming from her meeting with Michael and Dan, Emma wrenches her mind away from rehearsing what she'd really like to say to both of them to inquire about the status of Eric and Jeff's newsletter project. They've been having considerable difficulty communicating their needs to Benitez Advertising, and Emma has had enough of fielding irate calls from the folks over there. She's also lost patience with worrying about why Eric and Jeff are telling her so little about what's going on, and she's wondering exactly what they are trying to hide. She does not want to micro-manage, so she tries to carefully monitor how much detail she expects from them. Still, how can she support their efforts if she's not confident that she has the complete picture?

But when Emma asks how the last advertising planning meeting went, Eric insists everything is fine. "This month's newsletter is good to go," he announces. When she specifically and persistently asks how things are going with the folks at Benitez, Jeff tersely informs her that she has nothing to worry about, all deadlines will be met. *"Doesn't she think I can handle those people?"* he wonders. *"Eric's not such a stickler for details. He doesn't grill me on every conversation I have. He knows I can do the job, and he just expects me to get on with it. Why doesn't she trust that I know what I'm doing?"*

Emma is emotionally exhausted from her encounter with Michael and Dan and extracting information from these two men has begun to feel like pulling teeth. But if she doesn't persist, she'll keep on wondering when she's going to get the next call from Benitez Advertising and which new crisis she'll have to avert. So she continues throwing questions at them, beginning to sound even to her own ears like the Grand Inquisitor. Eric and Jeff reluctantly divulge information—a little piece at a time.

All told, a conversation that could have taken 5 minutes takes 35, and everybody walks away dissatisfied with the meeting's skimpy outcome and with each other as well.

❏   ❏   ❏

FREEZE FRAME   Ouch. People at Global seem to spend a lot of time in meetings and get little accomplished. Has Emma's addiction to detail finally blown her pet project and her future relationship with Dan and Michael? How will Dan's career suffer from his failure to coach Emma effectively? Also, how can Eric and Jeff learn to use their time with their boss to better advantage?

When Less Might Be More

In general, you can determine when to be succinct and when to be expansive by factoring in three elements: (1) why you are having a particular meeting, (2) what the listener's information needs and preferences are, and (3) how much time you have to spend.

First, determine your purpose. If you want to explore an issue thoroughly or if you think it's necessary to demonstrate carefully how you got from point A to point Z, for example, you're naturally going to offer considerable detail. In most situations, however, you should share the big picture and two or three salient details that prove your points most forcefully. In the interest of everyone's time and attention span, err on the side of succinctness.

To develop your ability to do what's most appropriate for your purpose, know your own style and either say more or say less than you would like to. If you freely admit that you're a detail junkie, indulge yourself in private with a consenting friend. But when you are in public, say less than you want to. If you tend to omit detail, say more than you originally planned to. Actually, "more" or "less" are only what your remarks are apt to feel like to you, given your habitual approach. In fact, you will most likely be saying enough to make your point thoughtfully and well.

Next, let the listeners lead you. After you've succinctly made your point, encourage listeners to ask questions. People who want to understand your thought process will ask broad, general questions. This will give you the opportunity to expand somewhat and also to offer information they didn't know to inquire about. Listeners who want more details will ask for them. Listeners who prefer to skip the details will ask for summaries. Whatever your preferences, you'll be more effective if you give listeners what they want and take their preference for brevity as an indication of their own style rather than as a lack of interest in what you're presenting or as a rejection of you personally.

If you're speaking to several people at once, concentrate on figuring out what the decision makers' preferences are. You can do that by paying attention to the kinds of questions they are asking. Then play to those preferences.

Finally, think about how much time you have allocated or have been given for the meeting and how to use it most productively. In a 1-hour meeting, for example, you can obviously present more explicit detail; for a 15-minute briefing, you might want to use a chart or graph to help you summarize. Here are some additional suggestions for expressing yourself so people profit from your remarks.

When you are the speaker:

☐ **Get direction.** If you have to brief a specific individual, ask a coworker who knows that person's preferences well how best to proceed. If necessary, actually ask the intended listener. Try something like, *"If I want to convince you that we should invest in* *developing the Agate prototype, what would it take?"* People will usually be willing to tell you in advance how much detail they prefer and how much time they have to give you. Then you know how best to organize your remarks.

❑ **Structure your remarks and mark your structure.** To organize, try the **Three T's: Tell them** what you're going to tell them; **Tell them**; then **Tell them** what you told them. Then mark your structure. That is, if you have two main points to make, say so and then make only those two points. Label each point: *"First. . . ."* If you have three reasons why you propose a specific action, say, *"I have three reasons,"* and present only those three.

❑ **Use the Rule of Three.** Often, one or even two reasons may not make your point forcefully enough, and four will beat it to death. Three generally does the job. So even if you have seventeen salient details to support your opinion, select three. If you have twenty-five specific examples to prove your point, pick your best three. (As an effective set of labels for three points, try, *"first,"* *"next,"* and *"finally."*) If your audience needs more details, they'll ask for them.

❑ **Select interest barometers.** When you're speaking to a group, visually scan the audience at least once every

5 minutes. People who are physically restless from the moment they enter a room are not likely to be helpful barometers of audience interest, so overlook them. Instead, watch for patterns of behavior change in people who were visibly attentive but who are now acting differently. For example, a person who had been sitting forward in her seat and nodding at you is now slouching back. Two men who were sitting still and looking in your general direction are now shifting around and glancing frequently and longingly at their briefcases. When you start to see such patterns, check them out by providing a verbal opening for the listeners to lead you. Say something like, *"Let's pause for a moment. What issues are coming up for you now?"*

❏ If you're speaking to one other person, you're more likely to be aware of nonverbal signals of continuing interest or incipient boredom. Since women often look interested even if they are not, use the same techniques as you would for a group. Provide a verbal opening for them to lead you to understand the level of detail and length of explication they prefer.

❏ **Label limits.** If you find yourself losing audience attention but you still have a few vital points to make, tell the audience how much time you're going to need:

"Five more minutes will wrap this up." If they no longer have to wonder when you're going to get finished, most people will willingly pay attention for a few minutes more.

Getting the Details You Need

As a listener, it's important to know how to lead speakers effectively to meet your information needs. Such skills become especially valuable when you cross gender expectations; that is, if you are a woman who prefers succinctness or a man who embraces detail. Speakers often take their cues from generalizations about men and women and overlook the preferences of the specific individual in front of them.

Start by reframing your role as a helpless victim into one as a collaborator in the creation of a productive dialogue. To help you do your part with style, try the following:

❏ **Ask leading questions.** Use questions that will give you the kind of answers you want. Here are some examples.

Clarity: *"Will you explain exactly what you mean by standard trade discount?"*

Specifics: *"You said our customer representative was*

rude. Can you be more specific? Did she raise her voice? Ignore your questions? Leave you on hold for too long? Refuse to connect you with her supervisor?"

Feedback: *"What specific concerns do you have about our ability to meet this deadline?"*

Agreement: *"If I delete all service charges, what more will you need from us so we can do business?"*

Opinion: *"Tell me, what did you think of that trade show?"*

Creativity: *"What if we donate the material and use it as a tax write-off?"* In a "What if" question, the wilder your own example, the more creative others are likely to be.

Summary: *"Let's see if I've got your point. You said that . . ."* and then paraphrase what you heard.

❏ **Tell why you're asking.** People respond more readily to any question when they know why you're asking it. So to improve your chances of getting the kind of answers you want, give your questions a context. For example, say, *"So that I can get accurate information into our memo about this meeting, precisely why are you unable to meet the deadline?"*

❏ When people are rambling, **time-frame the discussion** and **use the broken-record technique** to keep bringing them back to the point: *"I have another* *meeting in 10 minutes, so tell me briefly how this relates to X."* Repeat a version of *"How does this relate to X?"* as often as you need to. You *want* to sound like a broken record. By the time your persistence gets annoying, the speaker will most likely have answered your question.

REFRAME

Scene I

Now we're ready to get back to Emma, Dan, and Michael. Start the videotape again and let's see how each of them can use reframing to salvage their meeting as well as their future work relationships.

A "big-picture" person, Dan values Emma's attention to details because he can happily leave them all to her. His confidence that Emma will overlook nothing leaves him free to think about other things. He also knows, however, that Michael only wants to hear about the big picture. So when Emma asks Dan how best to approach Michael, he advises her, "Use a bottom-line opening. Start by telling him exactly what your bottom line is, exactly what you want, in twenty-five words or less. Then explain briefly why you want it. If he wants more details, trust him to ask for them."

Although Emma would prefer to share her wealth of fascinating information so she can be sure of making her point with Michael, she acknowledges Dan's greater experience in dealing with his boss. So she reframes Dan's suggestion not as discounting the value of her thorough research efforts but as offering a helpful technique she would do well to learn, and she prepares her remarks accordingly. Emma recognizes that her thorough research functions not as a source of information she necessarily needs to share but rather as a source of confidence for herself. So she'll continue to do her research because it makes her more comfortable, and she doesn't feel cheated when circumstances neither permit nor require her to tell all.

"I'm going to convince you that Marquis Money Fund can bail us out and it deserves a greater up-front investment to the tune of $50,000," Emma begins, "And here are three reasons why." As she is explaining her second point, she notices Michael begin to shift in his chair and glance at his wristwatch. Rather than being thrown off by his restlessness, Emma chooses to reframe it not as rejecting her ideas but simply as a signal that he has other meetings to attend. So she doesn't lose her pacing or her place. She has one crucial point still to make, and she wants his attention, so she calmly announces, "Three more minutes of your time is all I need," and keeps talking.

Michael appreciates this signal, which he interprets as respect for the numerous demands on him, and he decides that he can manage to keep listening for 3 minutes more. Emma concludes by strongly repeating her request for additional funding. Michael nods, shakes her hand and Dan's, and says, "Good going, folks. You've got my vote. Go for it." Then he rushes from the room. "Great, Emma," says Dan, as he shakes her hand and smiles.

Now Emma returns to her own office, where Eric and Jeff are waiting to discuss the newsletter project.

REFRAME

Scene II

We've just seen Emma's skill in letting the listener lead (through nonverbal behavior, in this case) convert her meeting with Michael from a disaster into a success. Let's see how reframing allows Eric and Jeff to achieve a similar turnaround in their meeting with Emma.

Knowing that their boss feels most comfortable discussing issues in detail, Eric has instructed Jeff to pay close attention to what the people at Benitez said at their most recent meeting, so he'll be ready to recount the dialogue for Emma, if she should ask him to do so. "It's not that she doesn't trust you to take care of things," he told Jeff, offering his subordinate a way to frame Emma's persistent questions as indicating something other than lack of confidence in Jeff's abilities. "It's her style, that's all. I know you sometimes feel like you're in the witness box, but she'll be able to back us up better if she knows exactly who said what."

Eric can speak with authority on this point because Emma explained it to him just last week, when he had said to her, "I want to be able to coach Jeff about how best to update you on the newsletter project. So tell me, why is it important for you to know all the details of what the folks at Benitez said?" Emma had willingly explained the reasons for her persistent questioning because she understood that Eric and Jeff would most likely frame her numerous inquiries as indications that she distrusted them, which was not a message she wanted to send.

So now when Emma asks, "Give me a 3-minute capsule of how things went at the meeting with Benitez. I don't need to know everything, but I do need to know what they're probably going to call me to complain about," Jeff is prepared with the information and feels comfortable about sharing it with her. Although Emma might prefer an even more detailed explication than he delivers, she is ready to compromise because she knows that Jeff's own preference would be to say, "Things are fine," and leave it at that. "Okay," Emma says, "now that I understand more about what's happening, exactly what kind of help do you want from me?"

Reframing Emma's question not as a challenge to his interpersonal skills but as a sincere offer of support, Jeff tells her, "This month's newsletter is good to go, but if Benitez calls to complain about the deadline, remember that I told them precisely what we needed and when we needed it and gave them enough lead time. Back me up on that." "Sure thing," Emma replies. "I know advertising people can be touchy. You guys are doing a great job." Handshakes all around, and this brief and productive meeting ends with everybody smiling and feeling good about themselves and about each other.

COLLECT SNAPSHOTS
TO REFLECT ON

❏ Do you fall within the generalizations about men's succinctness and women's expansiveness, or do you cross gender expectations? Freeze frame three moments from the last time you gave an informal presentation. What effects might gender differences have had on both your own style and the audience response?

❑ Picture a recent formal presentation that you gave. How did the degree of detail you offered feel to you? How did you know you were meeting the listeners' needs? If you could give the presentation again, what would you do the same way, and what would you change?

❑ Recall a recent conversation you had in which the results were exactly what you wanted them to be. Freeze frame your questions and see if you can pinpoint which ones worked for you and which did not. See how well both you and the other speaker let the listener lead. If you could replay the discussion, which questions would you ask the same way? Which would you ask differently?

❑ Recall a meeting you attended where you did not have to participate very much. Freeze frame and think about whether you became an interest barometer—a listener whose behavior changes offered a perceptive speaker clues to audience attentiveness. Were other people also restless? Did the speaker pick up on your behavior? What role do you think gender might have played in how the speaker did or did not respond?

USING PERSONAL DISCLOSURE

Personal disclosure means sharing information about yourself and demonstrating an interest in learning about other people as well. As such, it plays an important role in the workplace. Management trainers suggest that exchanging a few personal remarks is a good way to begin a coaching session or performance appraisal discussion because doing so helps to make the conversation less stilted, freer, more two-way. A more collaborative dialogue will be a more productive one. Experts on team building encourage us to know each other by sharing facts about ourselves and listening to what others have to say, in order to uncover shared values. Shared values bind and motivate people to work hard to reach shared goals and increase loyalty to each other and to the organization.

A truism of negotiation is that the process works better when the participants consciously invest the time to build and solidify good relationships with each other. Ignoring the relationship aspect of the event and plunging right in to business at hand can be counterproductive because it allows us to easily depersonalize each other into "the enemy." Instead, chatting about family, friends, and interests helps keep things in perspective; it helps us regard each other as essentially decent human beings with a job to do rather than as bloodthirsty adversaries about to go to war.

So although increasingly sophisticated technology, such as e-mail, telecommuting, and video teleconferencing, allows less direct and less personal human contact at work, people are stressing the usefulness of more of it.

Personal disclosure is a relationship-building tool worth learning to use effectively. Women and men, however, have widely divergent ideas about what constitutes personal disclosure and how to use it at work. This discrepancy causes them to talk about things that one considers valuable for establishing connection and mutual supportiveness and the other finds boring or pointless. So, the tool intended to bring people closer together can actually serve to further divide them. If it's to be used to construct strong mixed-gender work groups whose members trust and support each other, a lot of reframing is in order. Roll the videotape and let's get started.

❑   ❑   ❑

P I C T U R E   T H I S

Scene

Johnny's Seafood Grille

Characters

Fred Thompson, Commercial
Real Estate Manager, New
Generation Properties
Sheila Logan, Top Ten
salesperson

When the idea for these lunch dates first occurred to him, newly appointed manager Fred believed that meeting informally with each of his top ten salespeople would be a great way to get their working relationships off to a solid start. Today, he's not so sure. He's sitting beside Sheila, the only woman on the team, and the meeting isn't going well.

To get the conversation going, Fred asks Sheila what impact she thinks the new cogeneration plant will have on their community and their company. When she admits she hasn't had a chance to research the situation, Fred happily offers his own views. He likes to discuss the local economy, about which he has strong opinions, which he shares with considerable knowledge and authority.

Listening to her new boss wax increasingly eloquent, Sheila grows more and more restless. *"Interesting, what he's saying,"* she admits to herself, albeit reluctantly. *"But I thought we were here to get acquainted. How am I supposed to get to know him by discussing a new power plant? When is he going to say anything at all about his life so I can get a sense of what he's really about? Does he even have a life? Is he man or is he machine?"* Obviously, Fred doesn't like her, she thinks, or he'd certainly be more forthcoming.

Bravely determined to salvage what she can of this lunch meeting, Sheila decides to steer the conversation in another direction. Her buddy John, another salesperson, told her Fred has five children. Though she wouldn't know it from anything he's said so far today, it's a safe bet that she and Fred share an interest in family matters. She decides to tell him the saga of her daughter's acceptance to law school. But as she launches into a description of the Logan clan's current difficulties, Fred seems to visibly shrink away from the conversation.

Whenever he tries to shift the discussion to a more general topic, Sheila persists in recounting her personal melodrama. *"How do I remind her that we're in business to do business, not to conduct family therapy?"* Fred thinks. *"She's telling me more than I want to know. I heard so many good things about her, I thought we'd get along better than this. Somehow I blew it. Oh, well, you win some, you lose some."* He glances covertly at his wrist watch, wondering how soon they can end lunch. Aware of his action, Sheila smiles uneasily and thinks, *"I'm glad I spend most of my time in the field. At least I won't be seeing much of him."*

"It's getting late," Fred announces as he pushes his chair back from the table. "I think we'd better skip dessert."

❏   ❏   ❏

FREEZE FRAME Back and forth: Fred to Sheila, Sheila to Fred. Get the feeling you're watching a tennis match? But that would mean the two of them were at least playing the same game. These two people aren't even on the same court yet. What's going on here? How are the different ways men and women approach personal disclosure playing themselves out between Fred and Sheila? Can their work relationship be saved?

You Can Trust Me

Trust means knowing that people want to "do the right thing" and believing that they will deliver what they promise. Women use personal disclosure to establish trustworthiness, so they start sharing their interests and concerns immediately. *"By revealing things about my life experiences, my family, and relationships, I draw you into my circle and show you that I'm a good human being. Now let's see who you are. Then we can work together,"* women think. And they expect others to do the same. People who fail to join in with similar self-revelation risk being perceived as untrustworthy, or at least questionably standoffish.

Men, on the other hand, generally will not disclose personal information until they already trust you. *"After we've shared enough activities to prove that you'll work with me and cover my back when I need support, then I can talk about more personal things,"* they think.

Of course, what you share depends in part on what you think is personal. Men often prefer to share their views on sports, business, or politics rather than, for instance, the agony over whether to put their aged parent into a nursing home. For men, sports talk is of a personal nature because they're talking about what is important to them. Working on the military model of "if we wanted you to have a family, we'd have issued you one," many men still think family and relationship issues have little or no place at work. Men often consider women who try to draw them out about these topics as prying rather than interested. Women consider men who remain silent as distant and withholding rather than private. The results of these differences in the use of personal disclosure are often costly.

For example, Herb, a sales representative for a metal piping company, told me that he'd just lost a long-time client, owner of a small manufacturing company. "I thought we were doing fine, but she had no loyalty," he lamented. Since I know his client from a professional group to which we both belong, I had the opportunity to ask her when she'd last seen Herb. "Oh, I don't buy from him anymore," she explained. "Every time he dropped in, he barely even said hello. I don't know anything about the man. He was all business." Taking his disengaged business style to mean that he didn't really care about developing her small company as a client, Marge found another vendor.

Herb's situation also illustrates another aspect of personal disclosure: the quantity and depth of material appropriately shared in a work situation. In general, men tend to reveal "too little"; women tend to tell "too much." Your assessment of what constitutes an appropriate degree of self-disclosure and how you evaluate "too little" or "too much" is in large part a function of your gender.

How Much Is Too Much?

How much personal material is appropriate to share in the workplace? Discussing your private life can bring you closer to people, but it can also bring you grief. For example, a client told me how she confided in her boss that her husband had just lost his job. "We were really hurting for money, and I knew worrying about my personal situation was going to affect my work for a while. That's why I told Bill what was really going on in my life," Arliss explained.

One month later, she went to ask why she hadn't gotten the raise she'd been promised. "Well," Bill said, "I had to cut the budget, and I knew that with your husband out of work, you weren't going anywhere anyway. You'd be thankful you had a job at all." He felt perfectly justified in doing what he had done. She had shared some information, and he simply used what he knew.

Men can cause themselves similar trouble by telling too much. A male supervisor told me that he had been passed over for a position he thought was perfect for him. When confronted, his boss said, "You once told me that when you were in college you tried marijuana, and I thought that showed poor judgment. Since this position requires a lot of serious decision making, I didn't think you were the right one for the job."

A good general principle for the use of personal disclosure is not to share anything that you would not want spread to people other than the one you initially took into your confidence. Also, pay attention to what you communicate via e-mail because many systems have a backup you may not be aware of. Even confidential material has a way of creeping out. More specifically, think before you talk about the following:

❑ **Circumstance changes**. Even in casual conversation, downplay plans not yet final that would change your employment circumstances, such as contemplating a job change, moving out of state, returning to school full time, or starting a family.

❑ **Health issues** that could affect your medical insurance coverage or perceived promotability, such as psychiatric therapy or alcoholism counseling. Be quiet even if the event is long in the past.

❑ **Sexual prowess, sexual partners.** Keep these matters where they belong, which is definitely not at work.

❑ **Wage and salary figures; special compensation agreements.** This information should remain confidential at all times.

Take a Broad View

Taking a broader view of what constitutes personal disclosure so that you recognize it when you hear it will enable you to profit from its value in bringing people together. When men talk sports and business, women can reframe these discussions as a type of self-disclosure. Men are telling you about themselves because many men define themselves to a large degree by their work and are also seriously interested in sports. Men can reframe discussions of personal relationships not as an attempt to convert the work group into a family therapy group but as an effort to share something their coworkers consider important to them. Women don't necessarily have to discuss sports, and men don't have to discuss family, although they can do so if they wish. Still, each can recognize personal disclosure when they hear it from the other.

In order to find topics of common interest that you can comfortably share with other people, listen for "free information." Especially in casual conversation, people often reveal other things in addition to what they're saying about the specific topic under discussion. Listen for clues and then follow up on them. For example, I told a colleague, "Ray, I have to leave by 6:00 tonight because I don't want to miss my photography class." I was thinking about avoiding the local traffic jam, but Ray picked up on the free information I had offered him. "That's interesting," he said. "I was a portrait photographer for six years before I took this job, had my own studio and everything." This launched us into such a fascinating discussion that I missed my class and didn't mind at all.

Getting to Know All About You

The misunderstanding and mutual discomfort that Fred and Shelia experienced at their luncheon meeting is not inevitable. Women can control their habit of intimate disclosure, and men can talk about personal and relationship issues if they want to. They have the skills they need; they only have to decide to develop them and then choose to exercise them at the appropriate time. As with any other presentation, when you are presenting yourself, you have to know your audience. I have seen that demonstrated during my travels.

In Washington, D.C., several trainers whom I had seen around town but never actually met before gathered in a conference center's speaker lounge for lunch. The group consisted of middle-aged women and 1 man. At first, we commiserated about the rigors of air travel during the rough winter and celebrated the delights of cross-country skiing. Then Jake left. Seamlessly, the talk turned to hysterectomies, mastectomies, estrogen replacement therapy, and sex. My strongest remaining impression of that conversation is of a chorus of overlapping women's voices sharing intimate details. While Jake was part of the group, the rest of us tacitly agreed to discuss issues of a more general nature. The intimate topics were inappropriate because they would have driven him from the room.

On to San Francisco, where I met Sol. We would be collaborating on a big project, so I invited him to a get-acquainted lunch. As I nibbled on my caesar salad, Sol described in unsolicited detail how his family situation affected the job choices he'd made. I told a few stories about my own career decisions and my 3 adult children. Sol's conversation surprised me, since most men don't usually talk like that at a first meeting. But his degree of personal revelation also drew me to him. I felt as if I'd known him for a long time, and I knew at once that we'd work well together.

The next morning, Stan, our client's on-site administrator, told me he also found Sol really easy to get along with. They'd gone for a few beers after work. "We wound up having a really personal conversation," Stan said. Sol had asked a lot of questions about opportunities in the management training field as well as the internal politics of the organization we were all working for. Since Stan had a lot to say, they'd talked for a long time. *"So this is what Stan calls a personal conversation,"* I thought. *"Interesting."*

It seemed to me that Sol had deliberately engineered two very different conversations, and I wondered if he had differentiated them because of gender. So I asked him. He told me he hadn't consciously thought about what he was doing, but he'd learned long ago that "if you want to get to know somebody, you try to talk about what's comfortable and interesting for them." Clearly, Sol knew his audience. He also demonstrated a suppleness of style well worth emulating.

Mending Fences, Building Bridges

It's amazing how long some of us can work together and still know very little about each other. But it's never too late. You can tweak an ongoing relationship into a profitable new direction by telling people about yourself, even if you've never done so before.

For example, I coach an executive whose staff found him difficult to work with. Focused and hard driving, Derek didn't take time for tact, much less for personal disclosure of any kind. Morale among his staff was understandably low. During our monthly meeting, I learned that Derek is very active in his church and ministers weekly to the inmates of the local prison. "What do your staffers think about that?" I asked. "They don't know anything about it," he replied. "I never told them." Even the 2 managers who had worked with him for over seven years were unaware of his noteworthy commitment to community service.

I encouraged him to tell his team, and they were astonished. Knowing how hard Derek worked for the company, they marveled that he still found the time and energy to serve his community in that way. Both what he told them and the very fact that he had revealed something personal at all caused them to see him in a different light and to respect him more. As I continued to work with them, Derek and his staff became more relaxed with each other, in part by discussing personal interests and concerns they never used to mention.

As they began to experience him as a whole human being, Derek's people became more willing to understand the pressures that gave rise to their boss's abrasive manner and more ready to risk giving him feedback to help him modify it. He, in turn, became increasingly willing to accept their feedback about when and how his behavior had gone too far because they let him see how strongly his behavior affected their work. Although Derek and his staff have not become best friends and don't need to be, morale and productivity are definitely improved.

I'd Rather Not Say . . .

Engaging in personal disclosure doesn't require you to bare your psyche at every turn. If you believe someone is prying, consider first whether the person is simply trying to establish a comfortable connection with you. Still, no law demands that you answer every question you're asked. Instead, try offering a fact about yourself that you feel comfortable mentioning. Simply say, "I'd rather talk about . . . ," and then do so.

To deflect a question that you're not comfortable answering or a topic you'd rather not discuss, you can also try the following:

❑ **Answer with a question of your own.** Try, *"Why is that important to you?"* or *"Why are you asking?"*

Either the person will back off or say something that will make you willing to answer the initial question.

❑ **Respond in the third person general.** That is, instead of answering in the first person and revealing specific details about yourself, say something general like, *"A lot of employees these days feel pressured by the lack of available eldercare arrangements. I think the employee survey should include a question about that."*

❑ **Deflect with humor.** You can use a version of *"I don't even discuss that with the bartender,"* or *"Only my hairdresser knows for sure."*

REFRAME Let's see which reframes can help put Sheila and Fred's relationship on the right track.

Naturally Fred and Sheila want to make a good impression on each other. When Fred rattles on about the cogeneration plant, Sheila acknowledges his generous if somewhat awkward effort to start a conversation. Though what she'd really like to know is how he keeps his sanity while living with five young children, she's willing to wait until he knows her better before she asks about that. Instead, she says, "Where did you learn so much about engineering?" "I majored in it in college," Fred tells her.

At the mention of college, Sheila starts thinking about her current difficulties with her daughter's acceptance to law school. It's an issue that's heavy on her mind, and before she knows it, she's telling him about the fight they had at her house last night. *"Ouch. That's a hot button for her right now,"* Fred thinks, embarrassed by the depth of her self-revelation.

When she sees Fred shifting uneasily in his chair, Sheila reframes his discomfort not as a rejection of her but as an indication that at this time, this depth of self-disclosure is too intense for him. So she changes her tune. "I was a math major in college," Sheila offers. "And now here we are, both in real estate. So it goes. Now, I'd like to hear more about exactly how you think the new power plant is going to affect our clients."

Here's a subject Fred can more comfortably wrap his thoughts around. As he gets increasingly animated, Sheila asks several pointed questions and offers opinions of her own. Respecting her views, Fred challenges her and draws her out, and they both enjoy the ensuing discussion, which stretches their minds and stimulates their thinking. *"He's a nice guy, and he has a unique perspective on local economic conditions,"* Sheila thinks. *"I'm going to learn a lot working with him."* *"Sheila's sharp, and she certainly has a way with people,"* Fred thinks. *"I can understand how she made the Top Ten."*

"So," he says, "what should we have for dessert?"

COLLECT SNAPSHOTS
TO REFLECT ON

❑ Picture a time when you met someone of the opposite sex for the first time at work and felt you couldn't get the conversation on track. Why? Freeze frame and see if personal disclosure or the lack of it might have been getting in your way. If you could rewind the videotape and play the scene over again, what would you do the same way? What would you do differently?

❑ Picture a time when you talked with a coworker of the opposite sex and felt instantly comfortable. Why? What role do you think personal disclosure had in the discussion?

❑ Recall a time when you disclosed some information that eventually came back to bite you. If you could rewind the videotape and play the moment of revelation over again, what would you say now?

T H E   H E A L I N G
P O W E R   O F
L A U G H T E R

Since Aristotle's time, the uses and abuses of humor have received a lot of attention and psychoanalysts are still speculating today about the precise role that joking plays in our psychological well-being. Much recent research suggests that when people can laugh together in the workplace, they come to consider it a positive environment, one where you can have a certain amount of fun. Because they feel this way, job satisfaction increases and productivity improves.

Laughing with someone connects you, puts you on the same turf. Feeling more connected with your coworkers helps you become more involved with and committed to getting profitable results from your joint efforts. Sharing a good laugh does a lot to convert a gathering of people who begin by defining themselves as "you and me" into an in-group that considers itself "us." Think about the last time you told some friends about a hilarious situation that happened to you on the job—chuckling all the while at the memory of what you and your work buddies went through—and you watched their eyes glaze over in polite boredom. "I guess you had to be there," you might have mumbled, even as you continued chuckling alone.

I've heard it said that laughing together is as close as you can get to a hug without touching. Long recognized as a good stress reliever, humor has lately also become a problem-solving tool. Some companies are now showing their employees comic film clips before they go into brainstorming sessions on the theory that laughing together puts employees in a good mood, which frees their thinking and gets the creative juices flowing.

But what if humor, a potentially useful stress reducer and team-building tool, has the opposite effect? What if it pulls people apart rather than joining them together? This is more than a mere possibility when you bring gender into the equation. Solid data exists to support the theory that men and women laugh at different times, at different things, and even at different aspects of the same joke. More often than not, men and women not only fail to understand and share each other's humor, but they can even be annoyed or severely offended by it. Rather than bringing people together, then, humor has the potential for driving them apart.

Humor also has the potential to bring people into court. Jokes and stories with explicit sexual content or sexual innuendos can make some listeners uncomfortable and thereby open the door to a "hostile environment" sexual harassment charge. The many men with whom I've discussed the issue of dirty jokes freely admit that when a group of guys is sitting around, on the shop floor or in the executive boardroom, the language and the jokes generally get crude pretty quickly. Then they get dirtier, since part of the game is "if you tell a smutty joke, I have to top it with a smuttier one." Generally, the men modify their raunchy language if a woman enters the room, but still they confess to being somewhat relieved to see her leave again so the joking can continue.

❏   ❏   ❏

As part of an extended management development program, the Future Managers class has been participating in a series of workshops about diversity. Today, they're exploring the effects of gender stereotyping. To stimulate discussion, Chris distributes a checklist containing several traits, such as Humane, Foul Mouthed, Humorous, Nurturing, Self-deprecating, and he instructs the group to decide whether they think each trait is most often displayed by men, by women, or by both. "Mark your papers accordingly," Chris instructs. All 4 women in the group immediately and conscientiously set to work. They're

P I C T U R E   T H I S

Scene

Executive Development
   training room, Suburbia
   Bus Company

Characters

The men: Chuck, Fred, Axel,
   Kevin
The women: Janine, Laura,
   Virginia, Kay
The trainer: Chris

eager to finish the paperwork so they can start discussing a topic they find interesting and potentially valuable for their future management careers.

The men, however, appear less than interested in the subject and confront the training exercise less than conscientiously. "Emotional," reads Chuck. "Yeah. Tell me about it. Say one wrong word these days and women go ballistic! You better not say anything that isn't 'politically correct.' What a pain." "Tender," chuckles Fred. "Sounds like meat tenderizer. We gotta watch out, guys." And he makes an off-color remark which, although it's directed to Kevin, who is sitting next to him, can actually be heard by everyone in the room. Chris, who has many years of experience, waits patiently, and the males eventually complete the checklist under the increasingly hostile eyes of their female colleagues. Then the discussion begins.

Or at least half of it does. "What messages do you remember getting from television and popular music about how women or men are supposed to behave?" Chris asks. In response to this opening question, the women plunge into an energetic discussion; the men, however, continue laughing and joking about how useless these diversity sessions are, not to mention this ridiculous exercise, and about anything else they can think of.

No woman in the room has cracked even a smile, much less a joke. *"Good grief,"* thinks Janine, getting more irritated by the minute. *"These guys are stuck in the eighth grade! When are they going to grow up?"* Along with Laura, Virginia, and Kay, she finds many occasions to roll her eyes in shared acknowledgment of what they label the juvenile behavior of their male colleagues.

"Women have no sense of humor," thinks Axel. *"What a bunch of uptight chicks,"* thinks Chuck, as Kevin doodles on the checklist, and Fred stares at the wall. Soon the group is visibly polarized. In chorus, the women are chastising the men for behaving like bad little boys who had better get themselves together if they want to be managers, and the men are berating the women for being real downers, somber and essentially humorless. Suddenly Fred pounds on the conference table. "Why do you women always have to take everything so seriously?" he demands. "When are you going to lighten up?" "When are you going to grow up?" responds Laura. "This *is* serious!" Suddenly everyone is gesticulating angrily and talking at once. Chris decides it's time for a coffee break.

❏   ❏   ❏

FREEZE FRAME Sharing a good laugh? These people are hissing and spitting at each other! Must these women forever regard their male colleagues as hopelessly juvenile? Must the men always regard their female colleagues as uptight and humorless? Can these future managers learn to use humor to unify rather than polarize?

Who Laughs . . . Lasts

When you're in the middle of a tense situation, it's difficult to keep perspective, but that's exactly when it's most needed. A humorous remark can accomplish this. A client described how people in her company used to think Harold, the human resources manager, was completely ineffective, until the CEO started holding monthly breakfast meetings to help implement the new organization plan, and explains the severe budget cuts. "Here was a group of 50 confused and disgruntled people," Dalene explained, "but when the boss asked for questions, only Harold would raise his hand. We started noticing that in a humorous, upbeat way, he'd ask the questions that were on everybody's mind. And we'd get answers." Harold's sense of humor saved the day by lessening the emotional tension in the room.

To cultivate a humorous perspective, a kind of lightness of spirit that men and women can share without risking either social ostracism or litigation, try the following:

❑ To avoid taking yourself and any situation too seriously, try **zooming**. Imagine you're looking through a camera lens and use its zoom capabilities to move the scene far away from you. **Make a miniature**. See yourself and your coworkers as tiny little figures scurrying around in the corners of a vast gymnasium. Or go the other way. **Make a monster**. Envision all of you on a movie screen, larger than life and in extreme close-up, with every skin pore visible. It's hard to take people so seriously when you can see the hairs in their noses.

Along these same lines, change the sound portion of the event. Imagine everyone speaking in the thin voice you get when you inhale nitrous oxide. Imagine everyone whispering. Try speeding up the action so that everyone is scurrying madly around the office. Or imagine that everyone is moving in slow motion.

If you prefer, push the event out in time. Think about ten years from now: How important will this be then? What will your great-great grandchildren say when you tell them this terrible tale?

❏ **Collect in-jokes.** Look for cartoons, comic strips, or anecdotes relating either to work in general or to your business in particular to use in conversation. Designate a bulletin board where coworkers can post humorous items they want to share.

❏ **Consult references.** If you have a naturally good sense of humor, give yourself permission to let it out, and tell your own funny stories. Otherwise, take a look at *The Little, Brown Book of Anecdotes*, edited by Clifton Fadiman, and *The Executive's Book of Quotations*, edited by Julia Vitullo-Martin.

Don't Put Yourself Down

Granted, a sense of humor is a fine thing, and a lightness of perspective is to be encouraged. But whatever else you do, avoid encouraging others to laugh at your expense. Although men occasionally make self-deprecating remarks, they tend to poke fun at men in general rather than at themselves in particular; women tend to put themselves down personally. At work, it's a good idea to avoid self-deprecating humor entirely.

If you put yourself down often and well enough, people are going to start believing what you say. Tell your coworkers repeatedly how scatterbrained you are, provide enough supporting evidence in the form of funny stories about your foibles, and your listeners are not likely to fight to get you on their work team.

If you need to lighten a tense moment by making fun of something, poke fun at the situation, not at yourself. You might think about finding a home for your story in a situation comedy. Which one would be appropriate? Try leading into your anecdote with, "Oh, folks, have I got a story right out of Seinfeld!—no, Murphy Brown!—no, Star Trek!"

Quit Your Teasing

Putting others down can also be perilous. Teasing, or a verbal jab, is a form of humor with a power component. Cutting someone else down by poking fun at him, especially in public, raises you up. He shows he can take it by dishing it out in return, and the seesaw ride continues. Men find a weak spot in somebody else and hammer away at it. Nickname a short man who is self-conscious about his height "Shorty," and if you're slow-moving, he'll dub you "Pokey"; if you're corpulent, he'll call you "Slim." Men seem to work on the principle that teasing is an equalizer that helps to develop trust.

Men think it's funny and fun to tease people, and they also seem to enjoy being teased. Women hate to be teased. It's as simple as that. As you move through the company corridors, cafeterias, or conference rooms, do some freeze frames and see for yourself.

For instance, I heard a client of mine say to another member of our professional organization: "Oh, Joe, business must be getting better. This is the first time your eyeglasses have been clean since I've known you." "Yeah," Joe smiled. "Things are looking up, Boyd. Has a lot to do with the economy." And together they went to get coffee. No woman in her right mind would say to another woman what Boyd said to Joe if she expected her coworker to speak to her again in this lifetime. A man who teases a female colleague is taking a big risk.

Many women are learning to take teasing in stride by reframing a verbal jab as a signal that you're being accepted as one of the gang, instead of as a put-down. Women don't have to like being teased, much less respond in kind, but reframing helps them be less offended by it.

Instead of good-humored game playing, men can reframe teasing as potentially alienating or at least off-putting. They can recognize that their remarks might be taken literally and cause offense, even if none is intended. Men are well-advised to avoid teasing unless they know their female coworkers well enough to know they will take their remarks in good humor or tell them if it offends them, so they'll know not to say such a thing again.

Clean Up Your Act

Sexual humor has no place in the workplace, even when men are alone in the back shop or women are alone in the locker room. Simple good manners notwithstanding, it's a bottom-line issue. These days, when we are all so confused about how men and women can work together comfortably and productively and so conflicted about what constitutes sexual heckling, what constitutes sexual harassment, and what makes an environment "hostile," everybody's best bet is simply to leave sexual humor outside the office or factory door. If men want to share a dirty joke, they can do so on their own time. If women want to engage in male-bashing, they can do the same.

Managers, in particular, set the standards for how people should behave toward each other. If managers keep their acts and their jokes clean, they can help save the company a lot of future trouble. I'm not suggesting that the more enlightened among us have to become moral watchdogs or preach sermons against smut. I am suggesting that each of us, whatever our job titles, can simply choose to not join in when the jokes get dirty. At least, that's a start.

Coworkers Are Not Mind Readers

It's important to let people know when you are offended. Because most people are unaware of how their behavior affects others, you have to tell them. As a client of mine admitted, "I sometimes won't notice if I offend a woman. If I notice, I ask her what's bothering her, thereby avoiding a glacial stare. Women should tell us clearly what offends them," he recommends. Remember we're discussing a bottom-line issue here. So although they might be less likely to admit their uneasiness because they don't consider it a macho thing to do, men should express their discomfort when they are offended too.

Assume positive intentions rather than evil motives because most of the time a joke teller is not trying to be deliberately offensive or hostile but rather to be entertaining or cute. Maybe he's forgotten that you're there and can hear what he's saying. Maybe she has come to consider you "one of the gang" and doesn't think she has to monitor her language around you any more. Giving the joker the benefit of the doubt will help you be more willing to act to improve the situation rather than merely seethe with anger at the perpetrator.

If the jokes or language you hear are making you uncomfortable, or if you think they have the potential of making the environment unpleasant for others, try the following:

- **Make like a sociologist.** Reframe dirty jokes and stories as revealing more about the teller than the tale. That is, back off from the contents and consider what the joke is teaching you about the things men and women consider humorous, or what purpose the speaker might have in joking at this moment.

  The resulting degree of objectivity provided by this attitude will help you stay calm and in control. It will also make you less negative in the future toward the person now standing there smirking at a remark you find thoroughly gross and inappropriate.

- **Be explicit about your discomfort.** Say something like, *"I know you meant to be entertaining and yet I find that joke offensive. Please don't tell jokes like that to me anymore."* It's not likely to be easy to say this, but consider that you're doing your coworker a real favor because if he keeps making remarks or telling jokes like that at work, eventually he'll wind up in court.

- **Request a repeat.** Ask the speaker, *"What did you say?"* or *"Would you repeat that? I don't think I heard you correctly."* Making the remark public by calling attention to it in this way may be enough to shut the inappropriate joker up. If the joke sounded hostile, try something like, *"Why are you being so hostile?"* If you deliver the line lightly, you acknowledge the hostility but frame it as an issue not to be taken seriously. Thus, the hostility loses its power.

In general, you're well-advised to keep situations like this light and local, at least in the beginning. That is, try to deal with the situations yourself. If the hostile remarks continue, however, or if the speaker's offensive behavior shows itself in other ways, such as an inappropriate comment on your performance appraisal, it's time to consult your supervisor and a human resources professional.

❑ To get out of a tight spot, try **neutral reinforcement.** That is, ignore the remark entirely and start talking about something else. Jokers who see they're not getting a rise out of you soon shut up or go away.

If They "Can't Take The Heat," Turn It Down!

In the past, employees accustomed to using certain language and relating to each other in certain ways on the job believed that if anybody came to work among them, the newcomer had to either be able to take the heat or get out of the kitchen. "If they don't like the way we talk around here, they can leave."

In fact, clients have told me that this attitude still prevails in some instances. A group of men, for example, was relaxing in the executive lounge of an engineering design company. My client, Patti, one of only two female engineers in the building, went in search of a book from the bookcase in there, thinking she might also grab a cup of coffee and relax for a while. But when she heard the kind of jokes the men were telling and found their content offensive to her, she hurriedly took the book and went away. "It's often uncomfortable being in there. And now that I think of it," she told me, "I've noticed other women do what I did; they get what they need from the lounge and leave. I stay to myself a lot." So, at least in Patti's story, the shared humor that includes the male executives into an "us" excludes the females.

A male client described a similar circumstance that ended differently. Steve's coworkers are mostly women, and often he finds himself the only man among them. "When I join them at lunch, they're usually deep in conversation," he said. "But even if they're laughing and joking and talking 'woman talk,' they'll change the topic so as to include me in the discussion." He believes women are more willing to make this accommodation than men are.

To make humor inclusive rather than exclusive, stop telling the dirty joke and start talking about something else.

By tacitly acknowledging your coworker's existence in this way, you demonstrate that you expect and welcome their involvement in the discussion and that you're ready to make some accommodation to include them. Practice will help us get over the momentary awkwardness an abrupt change of topic can cause.

REFRAME Let's rewind the videotape and see what reframes can help our future managers become "a team" by learning to understand each other's sense of humor and by sharing a few good laughs.

As soon as they see the title on the exercise booklet, all eight future managers recognize the topic of gender stereotyping as an emotionally loaded one. To lighten her own uneasiness as well as the general mood, Virginia says, "Okay, folks. How do you think the gang on Melrose Place would handle this exercise?" Remarks fly about Alison, Amanda, Billy, and other television characters as the group slowly begins to focus on the material at hand.

When Chuck comments about women going ballistic, Kay reframes his remark as intended not to trivialize the topic but as signaling his concern with it, and she lightly asks, "Want me to be a visual aid? I'll show you ballistic. Get with the program and finish the exercise, my friend!"

To a good-humored chorus of boos and hisses, Chuck smiles and picks up his pencil. When everyone totally ignores Axel's off-color remark, which they understand as indicating his nervousness, he too shuts up and gets to work. All four women finish the checklist before any man does, and they sit waiting until everyone is ready for the next step.

Finally the discussion begins. One of the traits listed is "Humorous," and this motivates the group to discuss gender differences in humor. "I really thought you were losing it when you started talking about Melrose Place a minute ago," Fred tells Virginia. "But as soon as I laid eyes on the exercise, I expected a battle, and thinking about Billy and Alison gave me a little distance, which made me feel better." Axel also acknowledges that when everyone ignored his inappropriate comment, he was not offended but relieved. "As soon as I said it, I knew I shouldn't have," he said. "Thanks for saving me some embarrassment."

As the discussion of humor continues, Chris often hears both male and female voices saying, "Oh, isn't that interesting? I never thought of that," or "You've got to be kidding. You think that's funny?" Everybody agrees that it's a downer when a coworker tells you either to lighten up or to quit acting like a dumb adolescent. Though they are all intent on explaining their differing views to each other, mercifully nobody tries to explain why he or she finds a particular joke funny when someone else in the room "doesn't get it."

As the session ends, Janine describes a cartoon she saw where a character, beset by low self-esteem, accepted a job as a speed bump. "Boy, do I know that feeling," laughs Kevin, and all join in.

COLLECT SNAPSHOTS
TO REFLECT ON

❑ Freeze frame a time when you found a joke or story hilarious and a coworker failed to "get it." How would you characterize the humor: gross, silly, self-deprecating? What role do you think gender played in your differing appreciation of the moment?

❑ Freeze frame three different times when you were with a mixed-gender group of colleagues, and humor saved the day. What amused all of you? The small sample notwithstanding, what observations can you make about the kinds of things everyone in your workplace is likely to find humorous?

❑ Recall a time when you were either teasing someone else or being teased. Freeze frame and think about the role gender might have played in how the remark was received. What reframes would help you better understand the situation?

❑ Picture a time when you felt uncomfortable at a joke a coworker was telling because you considered its language or content inappropriate. What did you do at that time? If you could rewind the tape and play the scene over again, what would you do now?

6 ▸ Emotions at Work

Y ou spend one third of your adult life at work, where the pressure to succeed is considerable because what you accomplish there strongly affects how you organize your life in general and how you conduct it on a day-to-day basis. You work to get steady raises and bonuses, for instance, so you can build an extension on the house your family loves. If you lose your job, your family will have to live very differently. Or, your disappointment with a poor performance rating causes you to overreact when your child brings home a bad report card that same day. Since you're already under pressure to have a good job and do it well, it would be a blessing if workplace dynamics did not add their own kind of pressure.

Some of the most stressful situations you're likely to face will happen on the job, where you're expected to accomplish more and more in less time, with fewer people and fewer resources. Overworked and exhausted, you're encouraged to keep your emotions under wraps, or better yet, leave them home altogether. Of course, this cannot be done. Like it or not, emotions happen, and although you cannot control their occurrence, you can manage how you express them. Between men and women, emotional expressiveness—or the lack of it—causes problems of its own.

Historically, men have been taught to suppress their emotions, to "take it like a man," by behaving with silent stoicism. Although it's now recognized as impossible and unhealthy to do that, the notion and the habits linger on. Many men are out of touch with their own emotions, as well as unaware of how others around them are feeling. Although different emotions, such as fear, hurt, guilt, disappointment, or embarrassment, may be what's actually causing their behavior, the one emotional expression permitted and even expected of men at work is anger. So they make widespread use of it.

Women, therefore, find themselves surrounded by male colleagues who are often either inexpressive or angry and who trespass unwittingly on the feelings of others. Men consider themselves surrounded by touchy, overemotional women who besiege them by perpetually asking, "What's the matter? What's bothering you?" when they'd rather be left alone.

Although you don't need to psychoanalyze everyone you work with, you do need to realize that feelings come into play. Roll the videotape and see what reframes help to deal with emotions at work—yours and others.

❏   ❏   ❏

PICTURE THIS

Scene
Meeting room, Channel Toxic
  Waste Management
  Company

Characters
Meryl Beth Jamison, Manager,
  Finance; committee chair
Greg Peterson, Manager,
  Information Services
Cynthia Kodel, Manager,
  Purchasing
Harry Dembowitz, Supervisor,
  Human Resources
Jack Sheehan, Supervisor,
  Laboratory

Meryl Beth calls the meeting to order and reminds her colleagues that their task is to present a plan to the president recommending ways to reduce operating costs by 20 percent. Since nobody's happy about further decreasing budgets they already consider stretched to the limit, the discussion gets immediately heated. Wincing mentally as Harry, Greg, and Jack shout at each other and Cynthia tries in vain to calm everybody down, Meryl prepares for a long haul.

When Greg's frequently missed deadlines appear on the group's list of money wasters, he goes ballistic. "I don't know what you're all talking about!" he fumes. "I haven't missed any deadlines all year!" At this, Jack and Harry lose control. *"I thought Jack and Greg were good friends; I can't believe how they're yelling at each other,"* Cynthia thinks. *"I knew there would be fighting. That's why I didn't want to be on this committee in the first place."*

Because toxic waste removal is a strenuously regulated industry requiring extensive documentation, Channel managers depend heavily on the frequent long reports Greg's department produces for them. In the last year, he'd developed an interesting habit of calling internal customers, announcing he couldn't meet what he termed their "ridiculous" deadline, and unilaterally extending it for a month. Since he did meet his own deadline, he considers that he's always fulfilled his commitments!

Meryl says she understands he's very upset, but sliding deadlines out like he's been doing costs the company money. "What do *you* know about how upset I am?" Greg shouts, looking increasingly apoplectic. "You people better quit making unreasonable demands!" Scattering a few colorful expletives amidst threats to resign from both the committee and the company, Greg slouches down in his chair and says nothing more for the next hour.

Several times when Cynthia asks how he's doing, he mutters, "Fine." Finally, she stops asking. When Jack attacks him, he barely replies. Suddenly, Greg jumps abruptly to his feet, shoves his papers into his briefcase, announces, "I've had it," and storms out of the conference room, leaving his colleagues to stare after him in open-mouthed amazement.

❏   ❏   ❏

FREEZE FRAME How will Meryl Beth reunite her committee so they can produce their report for the president? Must Jack and Harry keep shouting all the time? Can Cynthia and Greg mend their emotional fences?

Bringing Emotions to Work

Though many men will acknowledge that emotions affect all relationships, they perceive the ability to get the job done despite emotional considerations as a strength. Only weaklings allow emotions to influence their thinking in any way, and nobody respects a weakling. As a male client of mine said, "Putting on a necktie or coveralls means you're supposed to be dead from the neck down. Feelings get in the way of getting the work done, so you're not allowed to have them." He claims he's not pleased about this, but he does what is expected of him.

Men ignore or deny feelings; women prefer to display and discuss them. Especially in times of chaos, women take comfort in knowing that others understand and share what they're going through. For example, Samantha, a design engineer, tells her coworker, Ted, "I can't concentrate on anything today, I'm so nervous that we're going to blow the deadline. Aren't you worried one of our competitors is going to beat us to the market after we've worked so hard to develop the prototype?" Ted replies, "We need to track down an off-the-shelf connector, that's all. We'll make it."

In a moment of crisis, Samantha expresses her fear, just as her equally fearful male colleague is battening down the hatches so as to appear cool and in control. Expecting Ted to understand her feelings and probably also to share them, she's annoyed at his emotional detachment and seeming lack of concern. He's annoyed because he considers her question intrusive and because, in addition to everything else, he has to cope with a "hysterical" woman. The feelings Samantha and Ted have for each other join the emotional stew, increasing the tension of an already difficult situation. Reframing empathy can decrease it again.

Understanding Empathy

Empathy means acknowledging what other people are feeling and understanding or willingly trying to understand why they feel that way. You become a kind of emotional mirror, reflecting feelings without judging them or explaining them away. When you say, "You seem edgy today; what's up?" you're also suggesting, *"I see you. I'm paying attention because you matter to me"* and *"I'm like you so you're safe with me."* Women reflect other people's emotions in this way, and they often look for a similar kind of understanding from their coworkers.

What they typically get from a male colleague, however, is a chorus of "do this" or "did you try this yet?" delivered in a tone suggesting he already knows all the answers. As a client put it, when his wife, a manager in a large law firm, would describe something that was upsetting her at work, "what she got from me was root cause analysis, but what she wanted was a hug."

Many men I've spoken with about revealing feelings at work have echoed the sentiments of a colleague who said, "If it's an emotion that exposes you, makes you vulnerable, shows weakness, no way." Vulnerable means weak. Replacing that word with "visible" might make the idea more palatable. That is, be willing to be visible as a human being—and humans have feelings. If men accept the fact that feelings occur at work and can be expressed out loud, even though they might prefer not to express them, several reframes suggest themselves: Reframe women who express emotion not as hysterical but as visibly human; reframe reflection of feelings as a supportive gesture rather than an intrusive one, and respond with a simple, "Thanks for your concern." Men can also add reflection of feelings to their behavioral repertoire so they'll be able to offer this kind of support when a colleague really needs it.

For their part, when men respond to an expression of feeling by offering solutions, women can reframe their response not as signaling detachment but as demonstrating a kind of empathy that signals, *"Your feelings matter to me so I want to help. I have some suggestions for making things better."*

Here are some more empathy-building techniques:

- ❏ **Verbalize your feelings.** Men generally lack an extensive vocabulary to express emotions. Using words helps them learn to understand feelings. Women who want men to reflect feelings as well as solve problems should make efforts to verbalize their feelings.

  Indicate intensity of emotion as well, either with an adverb or with another word entirely. "Happy" differs from "elated," for instance, and "slightly irritated" differs from "irritated."

Also, although feelings leak out through nonverbals, many men don't notice this form of expressiveness, so you need to be explicit.

❑ **Practice feelings reflection.** Try, "You feel (feeling word)? Ending with an upward inflection suggests you're trying to understand, but you may not have gotten it right, and this encourages dialogue. For example, you might say, *"You feel sad because Wendy's leaving?"* and your coworker replies, *"No, I'm not sad. I'm devastated! I don't see how we can run this place without her."*

Reflecting degrees of intensity helps the other person get in touch with his feelings. Your saying "sad" may help him realize he was more than sad.

❑ **Probe only once.** If your colleague seems disturbed, but isn't talking, ask, *"What's bothering you?"*— once. If he doesn't respond, let it go. You're providing an opportunity for him to share his feelings, not demanding that he do so.

❑ **Ask for the kind of empathy preferred.** If you want your coworker to reflect your feelings, try, *"I don't expect you to solve my problems. I just need to ventilate."* If you want suggested solutions, try, *"Got any ideas?"*

If you're not sure how best to support your coworker, offer a choice: *"You seem upset because you have to tell the crew we've frozen the specs. Do you want suggestions on how to do that, or do you want an understanding audience?"*

❑ **Let feelings be.** Acknowledge that emotions happen, and give people room to experience them. For instance, if your feedback about how her behavior affects you makes a coworker defensive, keep quiet and give her time to feel that way. Recognize that her defensiveness will pass, and she will have learned something from your remark.

Reframing Feelings

Labels are powerful because they carry forecasts. For instance, when you're about to give an important presentation, calling your pounding heart and churning stomach "terror" increases your chances of being frozen into immobility; label the same feeling "exhilaration," and you're forecasting success for yourself. You're also helping to bring it about because you'll give the speech energetically and confidently and even have a good time doing it.

Whether you're verbalizing your own feelings or reflecting other people's, it's useful to think about which label will lead to the most productive outcome. This may mean helping your coworker reframe what he's feeling. For instance, your buddy says, "When I think of retooling that machine, I get palpitations." "Oh, you mean you feel excited because we're finally going to get our hands on that job?" you reply.

Men often have trouble labeling the softer emotions: women have trouble with the aggressive ones. Here's where cross-gender emotional expressiveness lets us suggest reframes to each other by expanding our emotionally expressive vocabulary.

I'm Sorry; I'm Not Apologizing

You wouldn't think such a common phrase could cause such confusion. Women use "I'm sorry" in two ways. Most frequently, they use it to empathize. For many women, this usage has become a sort of verbal tic. But they also use it to sincerely apologize for an error they've made because they want to fix the work relationship. Men, however, do not say "I'm sorry" often because they only use it to mean "I blew it; I'm taking responsibility." If they had to say it often, they'd most likely find themselves out of a job. What's more, when they do apologize, they often deliver the phrase in a rote way more suggestive of "let's get this annoying ritual over with" than sincere contrition.

To reclaim the phrase, women can try using it less often and only after taking a deep breath and thinking about what they really mean. Then clarify with "I'm sorry you feel upset" or "I'm sorry I screwed up." Men can try using the phrase more often, both to empathize—because they have reframed it as a strength to admit a mistake—and to say it like they really mean it.

He's Angry, She's Angry

Anger is generally a secondary emotion. You feel hurt, afraid, frustrated, or disappointed; then, you get angry. Men and women have learned different ways to deal with anger. In general, men lash out and women repress. So we need to interpret displays of anger—or the lack of them—differently when they come from men or from women.

Men explode frequently. A man's outburst can have many possible interpretations, ranging from "I'm trying to make a point here" through "I'm just letting off steam" and "Just remember who's the boss" to "I'm really out of control." As you watch an angry man stomp around the office, it's not always apparent what his anger means. Women tend to give men's anger more extreme meanings because they interpret male anger from their own perspective. Observe a woman behaving the way you've seen many men routinely act, and you're most likely observing someone at the end of her rope.

A client described his experience at a Colorado dude ranch, where his company was holding a management retreat. One leisure activity was fly fishing, touted as a great stress reducer. Nobody had done fly casting before, and when the only two women in the group quickly got the hang of it while their male colleagues struggled clumsily to extricate their lines from the shrubbery, the men became irate. "We all started shouting at them, and it got pretty rough," Hal said, admitting he'd been yelling, too. "Then I realized [translate that to mean reframed] I was embarrassed—especially since my wife was standing on shore watching me make a fool of myself—I wasn't really angry, and so I decided it wouldn't be so terrible to admit that. So I did. Then the other guys shut up, and we all kept on fishing." In their workshop session the next morning, the group considered the different uses men and women make of anger and the ramifications of Hal's reframe.

If his realization hadn't made the shouting stop, they agreed, most likely their female colleagues would have been so intimidated by what they interpreted as real hostilities that they would have backed off and lost the chance to learn something new.

What's more, "Jean and Audrey told us they were angry too," Hal said. "But they just didn't look it." If you wait for most women to admit they're angry, you'll probably wait for a long time and eventually witness an explosion. Men can reframe a woman's display of lack of anger as not necessarily indicating a lack of anger and try labeling feelings: "You know, Jean, if some guy were shouting in my face that way, I'd get pretty pissed."

I'll Get You Later

I disagree with the popular notion that women hold grudges whereas men do not; everybody holds grudges sometimes. Maybe because they're so often angry that nothing would get done otherwise, men have learned how to be irate with people and continue working with them. They don't necessarily let go of the situation—they'll get you later—but they can work with you until payback time.

Getting past anger without holding grudges is a skill that is useful to cultivate. Learning to decode your anger and more accurately express it will help you deal with the situation that gave rise to it. Confronting the issue increases your chances of resolving it, and then you won't have any reason to harbor a grudge.

A client told me about when she and her coworkers were discussing spouse abuse, and Anthony, a new supervisor, asked, "How else do you get them to shut up?" "I was revolted," Deena explained. "He had to be joking, and I didn't think wife-beating was anything to joke about under any circumstances. And what if he wasn't joking? I knew I'd never forget what he said, and I didn't see how I would be able to work with this guy." Reframing his inflammatory remark into possibly a real question rather than a rhetorical one, she decided to ask Anthony exactly what he did mean. He explained he genuinely had no idea what skills other than physical force a man could use to make a woman stop yelling or complaining, but that he'd like to know. Rather than holding a grudge, Deena chose to confront the situation, and her reframe saved their working relationship.

Here are some additional ways you can deal with anger at work:

❑ **Acknowledge anger—your own and that of others around you.** You don't need to yell or pound your fist on the desk, but you can say, *"I'm furious because you had the meeting when I was out of town. Next time, be sure to check my schedule first."* Then people will take you seriously.

If you're thinking "No way could I be that direct," consider the alternative: You don't confront the person who made the error, but you complain about what he did to three other people instead. He knows he blew it, but he's not going to be the first one to bring his error up. Instead, he's waiting for you to do that so you can clear the air. Then he hears from the grapevine that you've been complaining about him, and he gets angry at what he perceives to be your deviousness.

Don't try to talk someone else out of feeling anger or any other strong emotion, for that matter. The last thing anybody wants to hear is *"You shouldn't be angry about that. You're overreacting."* Instead, reflect with *"You sound furious."* Then keep quiet and just listen, and you may get some good information about what's causing their behavior.

❑ **Avoid adopting other people's anger.** If someone reacts disproportionately to a situation, don't assume you've done something terribly wrong. In fact, the cause of an overreaction is almost certainly not you. Women tend to assume blame, and men tend to counterattack. Your best bet is to try talking the person down by listening, paraphrasing, and waiting until they cool off.

❑ **Suggest alternative labels.** To help decode what's behind men's anger, try asking, *"Are you angry, or are you disappointed (hurt, afraid, resentful, embarrassed)* *that we lost the bid?"* This approach can help an angry man understand himself better, and it can also change the way you deal with him.

REFRAME Click your magic clicker and let's get back to Channel Toxic Waste. Let's see how reframing can help this work group handle their emotions and effectively support each other in getting a difficult task accomplished.

Meryl is pleased when the discussion heats up quickly, because she reframes the verbal battling not as mutual anger or hostile competitiveness but as a signal of the group's commitment to their task. She observes that both Jack and Harry's frequent confrontational remarks are productive because the resulting discussion causes the others to explain their ideas more clearly and, sometimes, to improve them.

Cynthia is interested to observe that when Jack gets particularly rough, Greg deflects the attack with a good-humored "Oh, you always get loud when we're talking about anything except soil samples." Several times she expected the situation might escalate, but apparently it's under control.

Watching Greg get visibly upset when his missed deadlines are discussed, Cynthia reframes his extreme reaction as indicating a serious underlying issue. To find out what's really going on, she waits until he's cooled down somewhat and then reflects his feelings with "Help me understand why you're so furious about Jack's complaint that the Los Osos Site Report was two weeks late."

Reframing Cynthia's questions about what's bothering him to suggest she really cares and wants to help, Greg takes a deep breath and starts talking. He feels ineffective because his people are giving 110 percent and they have to work with outdated software and obsolete hardware, he explains. What they really need is a mainframe, which could cost $750,000. How was he supposed to ask for more money when they're here figuring out ways to save it?

Meryl reframes his contentious tone not as belligerence but as a request for more information. She informs him that she's seen a software vendor's advertisement describing a server-based documentation control system that can digitally store documents, including drawings. Greg gets excited: "You know, sometimes you do have to spend money to save money. A server might be the way to go!" They arrange to meet Thursday to research the system.

As Meryl summarizes the action plans and schedules their next meeting, she feels confident that the committee will do a great job on the report. She's especially pleased to see Greg and Cynthia talking amiably as they head for the cafeteria and lunch. "Hey, folks," she asks. "Mind if I join you?"

COLLECT SNAPSHOTS
TO REFLECT ON

❏ Freeze frame the last time you asked a colleague who looked upset what was bothering him and got little or no response. What role might gender have played in that situation? If you could play the scene again, what would you do the same way? What would you do differently?

❏ Recall a time when a coworker asked you what was bothering you. How did you feel? How did you express your feelings? What role might gender have played in your reaction?

❏ Picture a time when something happened at work to make you very angry. Freeze frame and think about how you displayed your feelings. How did your coworkers respond? What role do you think gender played, both in your expressiveness and in your coworkers' reactions?

❑ Picture a time when you were trying to be supportive of a colleague and your efforts were rejected. Freeze frame and see if you were reflecting feelings or offering solutions. If you could rewind the videotape and do the conversation over, assuming you still wanted to be supportive, how might reframing help you change your behavior?

❑ Recall a time when you felt a strong emotion at work. Freeze frame the scene and label the emotion. How many other labels can you think of for that emotion? If you could play the scene again, would you reframe the emotion? What would you now label it? How might doing so lead to more productive results?

7

NEGOTIATING FOR YOUR WORK LIFE

Whether you realize it or not, you're negotiating throughout your life, at home and at work. You negotiated to get yourself hired in the first place. Now you negotiate to get ideas accepted, resources allocated, products and services bought, contracts ratified, and conflicts resolved. You negotiate with colleagues in other departments about deadlines and with coworkers about where to have lunch that day. You negotiate with union or management employees, suppliers, and customers. You negotiate one-on-one, and you do it in teams.

But doing something often does not necessarily mean that you do it happily, are as good at it as you'd like to be, or are always completely satisfied with the outcome. Complications increase when gender enters the picture, because men and women bring different strengths and styles to the negotiating table, and these differences are sources of potential confusion. But these same differences can also be profitable at different stages of the negotiating game. Roll the videotape and see how reframing can help you learn to overcome the confusion and capitalize on the differences in men and women's negotiating styles.

❏   ❏   ❏

"I know it's late, but I wanted to tell you what's going on before I went to Human Resources to give my notice," Rosalie Coolidge says to her boss's receding back. Although it's hard to get private time with Sam Howard because he's always so busy and moving so fast, this statement gets his attention. He turns on his heel, takes one look at her face, and invites her into his office, instructing his office support staffer to hold all calls and allow no interruptions.

Moving her chair to a position beside the desk, Rosalie sits down confidently. She explains that she likes working with the folks at SCI very much and appreciates the challenges and opportunities Sam has been offering her. But her former employer, whom she left when her depart-

P I C T U R E   T H I S

Scene

Corporate offices, Science
Consultants, Inc.

Characters

Rosalie Coolidge, Executive
Assistant
Sam Howard, Vice President,
Engineering

ment was downsized, wants to hire her back at a considerable increase in pay, and Rosalie explains that she needs the money. "I'd rather stay here," she reiterates, "but as things stand, I can't afford to. I'd like to see what options we can come up with, and I have a few suggestions."

Although she is nervous, Rosalie has done her homework and feels well prepared for this meeting. First, she ran the numbers on her monthly bills to be sure she knew exactly what her economic bottom line was. Then she spoke with David Paul, Sam's second in command, who had worked with him for over five years.

Not interested in gossip or conjecture, she asked David for facts about Sam that might give her a handle on how to approach him. She learned, for instance, that he'd had four different assistants in the last five years, which alerted her to expect a strong reaction when he discovered he might be losing another one.

Knowing that Sam valued his new assistant and would most likely prefer to keep her, David willingly helped Rosalie plan her strategy. "Bring whatever documentation you have, avoid the small talk, and be prepared to make a deal on the spot," he advised. "Also, don't get upset if he starts to yell. He'll probably try to intimidate you. You've got to show him you can take it."

When Rosalie finishes her announcement, Sam sits staring at his desk in utter silence. Rosalie waits quietly for Sam to speak, coaching herself to stay calm. *"Let him take as long as he needs to decide whether he wants to keep me and what he can offer,"* she thinks. *"After all, I did take him by surprise."* Rather than allowing the protracted silence to make her nervous, she uses the time to rehearse some points she plans to make later in the meeting.

Finally, Sam says, "Exactly what would it take to keep you here?" Rosalie is ready for this question. Though her voice falters at the start, she gains fluency as she explains her situation. Sam begins negotiating salary instantly. When they get down to details and the dialogue becomes intense, Rosalie concentrates on listening carefully to uncover Sam's primary interests. She has a hunch something's bothering him that she doesn't yet know about, so she probes with a few carefully constructed questions, such as "What's the most important attribute you want in an executive assistant?" and "If I were to stay, what would you want me to do more of? And what would you prefer I do less of?"

She learns that Sam finds adjusting to new people a real hardship. Not only does he find it difficult getting to know them but also each one tries to organize his disorganized office in a different way. When he finally figures out one system, its designer leaves, and he has to adjust to a new person and a new system. "I don't want somebody who's always going to be looking over her shoulder for a better job," he asserts. "I want loyalty." She reassures him that as long as she can pay her bills and grow in the job, she wants to work with him and she'd prefer to stay put.

The negotiation continues. "You divorced women are all alike; you expect special favors because you have kids to take care of," Sam says. "That's not going to happen around here." *"He's trying to bait me,"* Rosalie thinks, drawing a deep breath. "Staying overtime isn't a problem for me," she assures him. "Remember last month when we worked till midnight on the Geneva conference paper?"

She is especially proud that she doesn't lose her cool when Sam pounds his fist on the table and threatens to make a few phone calls that he insists will definitely destroy her credibility and her employability in the entire state. "If that's what you think you have to do. . . ," she says. Uncomfortable as his threats and shouting make her, she waits him out, and he cools down. *"I thought that little display would make her give up on the insurance plan increase, but apparently she's tougher than she looks,"* Sam thinks in admiration. *"She'll keep my office running the way I like it. We're going to make a great team."*

Finally, they settle on a slightly lower salary than Rosalie has asked for, but it's augmented by a transportation allowance and an upgraded health insurance package. As Sam and Rosalie shake hands, they're both smiling. "See you Monday," says Sam. "Sure thing," Rosalie replies. "Have a great weekend."

❑   ❑   ❑

FREEZE FRAME Nice work! Rosalie and Sam have negotiated an agreement they both can live with. How did they manage the negotiation meeting so successfully?

Beginning with Basics

Negotiations have a basic shape that can be separated into four stages:

1. Preparing—researching goals, opponents
2. Exploring—discussing issues and interests, yours and theirs
3. Proposing—presenting proposals
4. Agreeing—settling on solutions

At each stage, women and men have special strengths to offer. We'll see what they are and how we can use them advantageously. But first, let's do an attitude check.

Attitude Adjustment Time

If you start a negotiation with the attitude that you're fighting a war, then you behave as if the best defense is a good offense. Feeling attacked, your opponent fights back, and the battle rages. If you go in expecting a rout, you give in too easily and give up too soon. Sensing a victim, your opponent moves in for the kill. Although men generally go in determined to win and women expecting to lose, both genders are still fighting a war. Let's reframe this adversarial attitude into a more productive one.

If you go into any negotiation believing in the process, believing unequivocally that you can do something valuable and work something out, you increase your chances of a successful outcome. Cultivating a "let's build a bridge" or "let's get together on a workable solution" attitude is likely to be more productive than either "win at all costs" or "haven't got a chance." A good place to begin the attitude adjustment process is to reframe your "opponent" as an individual holding a view that in some way opposes your own, not as an adversary going for the jugular.

That's not to say that negotiation situations never get adversarial or that all involved are amenable to joint problem solving. In fact, you increase your chances of a successful outcome when you're flexible enough to use the approach most appropriate to the particular circumstances. But let's distinguish attitude from behavior. If your attitude is "we can achieve something good here; we can do this," you'll be able to tailor your own behavior to the circumstances, use all your skills, deal with whatever tactics your opponent tries, and persistently work toward an acceptable outcome.

Invest in Intuition

At every stage of a negotiation, intuition has its uses. It can be a valuable source of information, if you pay attention to it. Intuition means knowledge you've gained without rational thought—a hunch, a gut feeling. Actually, it's composed of trace elements of every direct and vicarious experience you have collected in your lifetime. Stored in your subconscious mind, these trace elements combine with what's currently going on to suggest a course of action to you. In a negotiation situation, information from any source is not to be summarily dismissed.

Although everyone has an intuitive sense, women, more than men, in our culture have been allowed to develop their intuitive sensibility, and negotiating teams can profit from a well-developed gut instinct. One of my clients had a strong intuitive dislike of her new CEO and told a male colleague about it. When Barbara couldn't pinpoint any specific reason for her uneasiness, David dismissed her concerns, muttering, "Who pays attention to women's intuition?" Then, the CEO reneged on all promises to the contrary and laid off 20 percent of the staff, hired his son as chief financial officer, and was ultimately indicted for fraud!

Perhaps because we've historically labeled it "women's intuition," intuition has not been taken seriously, either by men or by women. I'm not saying you have to take gut instinct as gospel, but don't dismiss it as frivolity or madness. Reframing women's intuition as at least thought-provoking and not to be overlooked or ignored gives negotiators another helpful tool.

Homework Counts

The most important part of any negotiation takes place in Stage 1 (Preparing), before the talking begins. Eighty percent of the game is in the pregame planning. If you don't know your stuff cold before you enter the meeting room, you won't be able to give your full attention to what's going on there. You'll miss the subtleties, and you'll have trouble making mid-course corrections to your approach in response to what's going on.

It's important to research your issues and your opponents as thoroughly as possible. You can start by writing down exactly what you want; then ask yourself why you want it. That way, you'll pinpoint your underlying interests or what you're really after. Then you can decide what you're willing to give up to get your interests met and start gathering evidence to help you argue your views more forcefully. Also consider what you know about your opponents' interests and their negotiating style, so you can prepare yourself to counter whatever moves they might make. Review previous negotiations you've had with them or, if possible, consult others who have dealt with them before.

Although this kind of careful preparation serves everybody well, women are generally more willing to do it than men. Maybe because they're relative newcomers to the negotiating game, women tend to take it more seriously and therefore often prepare more conscientiously than men do. Men often prefer to "wing it," relying on past successes, quick thinking, and fancy footwork to get them through. This can be problematic for a man facing a woman who's done her homework because she may destroy his arguments with information he knows nothing about. But it can be advantageous when she's part of his team, so long as she briefs her male colleagues thoroughly.

Men have been at the game longer and know more people, both by reputation and by experience. These network connections can provide vital information-gathering opportunities in Stage 1. Also, men can brief the women on their team about an opponent's tactics so they will know what to expect.

Listen Your Way to Agreement

Everyone wants to be listened to and understood. Effective listening is crucial in negotiations because you can learn a lot of useful information and because good listening helps you know how to position your arguments for the best results. While good listening is necessary throughout a negotiation, it's crucial in Stages 2 (Exploring) and 3 (Proposing).

Research tells us that women tend to be more skilled listeners than men. This generalization is mutating somewhat, as companies recognize the importance of listening and send more men to communication skills training courses.

Still, while men are learning to listen better, including women on negotiating teams makes practical sense because they can exercise their skills to their team's advantage and, by modeling good listening, help the men working with them develop their own skills. Since half the time people spend involved in any form of communication (listening, speaking, reading, writing) is spent listening, refining your skills in that area is a good investment. Here are some key points to consider:

❑ **Avoid rehearsal drop.** When you start planning your rebuttal before your colleague has even finished speaking, you're not listening any more, and you might miss something important. Though men coming in with a "win at all costs" attitude tend to do this more frequently, it's problematic for everybody. Listen to the other person's complete message before you start constructing your reply.

❑ **Use jotting as a memory jogger.** If you rehearsal drop because you're determined to remember what you wanted to say, try jotting instead. Scribble a key word or two on the pad in front of you—with a little practice, you'll be able to do this without even lowering your eyes. And keep listening. When it's your turn to speak, look down and let your jottings jog your memory.

❑ **Listen past the delivery.** If a speaker has a weak voice or annoying or unfamiliar mannerisms, discipline yourself to listen past the ineffective style. Pay attention to content, not manner or appearance.

❑ **Capitalize on thinking time.** We speak at 125 to 175 words per minute but can think four times that fast. As you listen, use your additional think time to weigh verbal evidence, speculate on where the argument's going, summarize main points, and "listen" to what's not being said.

❑ **Desensitize hot buttons.** Emotional words or hot topics will throw you if you let them, and wise negotiators will quickly discover your touchy areas.

Women tend to get flustered and men lash out angrily, but once a situation becomes emotional, everybody's likely to say things they'll regret later on. Start by identifying your hot buttons so the intensity of your own reaction won't take you by surprise.

❏ **When someone pushes your buttons, breathe deeply,** count to ten, and then decide whether and how you want to respond. You can also try envisioning a supergraphic "Stop" sign in your mind's eye or hearing an echo chamber version of "Stop." One of these images will slow you down.

❏ It's a good idea to **desensitize yourself to sexist behavior** because it's often done deliberately to unhinge you. Then the next time your opponent says, "Why did you guys bring a *woman* along to do a *man's* job?" you'll be able to remember that your goal during the negotiation is to gain what you want, not to argue about someone's attitude toward men or women—and you'll stay cool.

Reframe the Rituals

More experienced in workplace negotiations than women, men are so familiar with certain rituals that they barely notice them as anything that might have to be explained to a newcomer. Their knowledge of playing the game can be an especially valuable asset in Stages 3 (Proposing) and 4 (Agreeing), but it doubles in value when they teach it to others.

Susan, a client who is director of research at a major university center, told me about the statewide meeting she and her boss Ben attended. He invited her to join the gang in the hotel bar for drinks at eleven o'clock that night. "I didn't understand that much of the negotiation actually takes place over drinks rather than in the regular meeting room. And he didn't know how to teach me in a way that wouldn't offend me or my sense of morality. I don't drink, so I didn't go. And he was furious because he had nobody to cover his back."

Reframing would have helped both of them. Susan could have reframed the invitation for drinks, not as a social event of possibly dubious intent but as the business requirement it actually was. Knowing that she might misunderstand, Ben could have been explicit about the evening's business nature and then, justifiably within his rights, insist that she attend.

Some rituals need to be taught; some need to be changed. A frequent locale for doing deals used to be the men's washroom. When you're negotiating as a team, you have to function as a team, and the team's composition has changed. Do not discuss the topic under negotiation in either the men's room or the women's washroom, for that matter, because doing so excludes some of your teammates and makes you vulnerable to the divide-and-conquer strategy. If your opponent should raise an issue, ask him to wait until your gang is together because that will be easier than repeating the dialogue for them later on. Keep your team intact.

Here are some ways you can all become better negotiators:

❑ **Collect yeses.** Saying "yes" reduces tension by bringing an atmosphere of agreement into the room. Simply say yes to your opponent whenever possible: *"Yes, I understand,"* or *"Yes, that's an interesting point."*

Also, collect your opponent's yeses. By the time he's said yes to you three times in quick succession, he's in an agreement mode. Try paraphrasing something he said and then ask, *"Is that what you meant?"* Most likely he'll say yes, and you're on your way.

❑ Men with a competitive mindset might have a harder time using this technique than women; the point, however, is not to concede anything but to encourage a more "agreeable" atmosphere.

❑ **Label tactics.** Tears, threats, silence, "pity poor me," intimidation, good cop/bad cop, and take-it-or-leave-it are all tactics. Name them in your own mind, and they lose their power over you. You can also name them out loud. Try calmly saying something like, *"Is that a threat?"* or *"Do you expect me to pity you and give you what you want?"* Or simply wait and see what happens. The other person will eventually get the ploy out of his system and work himself into a more reasonable position.

Women are more likely than men to react to a tactical ploy by thinking they've made a mistake of some kind or are in some way doing poorly. Men are more likely to counter an opponent's tactic with one of their own and, by fighting fire with fire, wind up standing in a pile of ashes. Reframe tactics as an interesting part of the game, a "nice try," and wait them out.

❑ **Buy percolation time.** If you're quick on your feet, by all means, use the skill. If not, it's not productive to berate yourself for failing to do so. Although it's nice when you can do it, no rule book says you must come up with a brilliant remark the moment the situation calls for it. Try something like, *"Good point. We'll get to that in a minute. First, I want to discuss. . . ."*

You're buying time for your unconscious mind to percolate with the idea, and often the response will pop into your mind in a short while. Then you can say, *"Getting back to what you said earlier. . . ."*

❑ **Pay attention to nonverbals**. Nonverbals can be carefully calculated to deceive, and you may not know if you're negotiating with a sincere person or a consummate actor. So take nonverbal signals with a grain of salt, but don't overlook what they can reveal.

❑ Don't observe only the speaker; **focus on the other members** of the negotiating team. People who are not the center of a group's attention for the moment often forget to monitor their nonverbals. For instance, watching an opponent's foot begin to tap nervously as his teammate is making a proposal might well encourage you to ask more questions than you might otherwise have done.

❑ **Put personal affinity aside.** When negotiating with someone you like, back off more often from what's transpiring and freeze frame to take stock of the situation because your natural inclination will be to do it less. Men have more practice in separating the personal from the professional, so they are not as vulnerable to being sidetracked because they like somebody, but it still happens.

Harness the Power of the Unexpected

When dealing with someone whose personal style is unfamiliar, most people resort to stereotypes; they expect men to be tough and women to be pushovers. At every stage of the negotiation, these stereotypic expectations can be used to advantage.

Men reacting with traditional gender expectations are likely to underestimate the women facing them. For most men, competing *for* women is familiar, but competing *with* them is new. You can capitalize on the unexpected by making a woman the head of your negotiating team. Your male opponents won't know what to make of that, and it will unsettle them, giving you an immediate psychological advantage. They'll expect her to be a weak link, and when she holds her ground and also helps the team gain it, they'll be taken by surprise.

Throughout Stage 2 (Exploring), for instance, an adroit woman can augment her power by crossing gender expectations. She can deliberately pound on the table to demonstrate the kind of behavior she's capable of if pushed. Or she can raise her voice to make a point. Men sometimes actually do not hear a woman's voice in a group, and they do not expect to hear a loud one, so a woman deliberately raising her voice is likely to get their attention. Of course, this approach only works for a little while because soon your female colleague's reputation will precede her.

Women who cannot see past gender stereotypes are likely to wrongly estimate the men facing them. Believing that all men have poor listening skills, they might let their guard down and reveal more information than they intend to or than they're even aware of conveying. In such circumstances, a man who knows how to listen effectively and ask probing questions can be at an advantage.

REFRAME Let's return to Rosalie and Sam. Rewind the videotape and let's see which reframes helped them negotiate a deal that promises to be the start of a long and productive working partnership.

Going in to the meeting, Rosalie feels confident she and Sam can come to terms. Because she has prepared carefully, she knows what her bottom line is and what to expect from Sam as well. When following a hunch leads her to discover how important loyalty is to him, she can assure him she'll deliver that willingly.

Rosalie recognizes Sam's threats, sexist remark, displays of anger, and prolonged silences for the tactical maneuvers that they are. She reframes them not as signals that she's playing the game badly but as relating more to Sam's negotiating style than to anything she might or might not be doing. This reframe allows her to face his tactics with relative calm. If she had risen to the bait of his sexist remark about divorced women, for example, with a response such as, "All you men are alike. You think only about your own needs . . . ," she'd have blown the whole deal.

Sam recognizes when he's sliding into a competitive mode, reminds himself that doing battle, however bravely, will most likely cost him an executive assistant he'd prefer to keep, and reframes the negotiation not as a contest of wills but as a problem-solving opportunity for both of them. He's interested in seeing how Rosalie responds to his tactical maneuvers not because he wants to win the game but because he needs an assistant who can handle herself when the going gets rough. Apparently, Rosalie can. He admires her thorough preparation and her courage in initiating the dialogue in the first place, and later on, he'll tell her so. He reframes Rosalie's periodic silence and controlled demeanor as tactical maneuvers he can understand and respect.

Both Rosalie and Sam leave the meeting feeling like winners.

COLLECT SNAPSHOTS
TO REFLECT ON

❑ Freeze frame a recent negotiation and do an attitude check. What did you expect going in? How do you think your expectations affected your behavior? What role might gender have played? If you could rewind the videotape and start the negotiation again, what reframes would you use to adjust your attitude?

❑ Recall a negotiation where an important issue hinged on careful preparation. Freeze frame and see whether you prepared as thoughtfully as you should have, carefully pinpointing your interests and researching your opponents and their interests as well. If you could rewind the videotape and play the situation again, what would you do the same way? What would you do differently?

❑ Picture a time when an opponent pushed one of your hot buttons. Freeze frame and see how you handled the situation. Did you lose your pacing or your poise? Did you label the tactic and calmly say "Nice try?" How did you feel about your opponent's use of a tactical ploy? How might you now reframe his behavior?

❏ Picture a recent negotiation that went well. Freeze frame and see what made it work. If you had to pinpoint the most important thing you did right, what would that be?

THE IMPACT OF NONVERBAL MESSAGES

When you're at work and, therefore, among other people, you are never *not* communicating. Though you may not be speaking any words, you are still sending messages with your facial expressions, gestures, and posture. Even if you are alone in your office, you send messages. Door closed? Obvious. Door open? What if people see you hunched over your desk, hugging your body, and scowling at a piece of paper in front of you? You are communicating in boldface. You may be unaware of the messages you're sending, and what you transmit and what other people receive don't necessarily coincide. But you communicate *something* nonetheless. Nonverbal messages are inevitable. They can also be surprisingly loud and enduring.

Nonverbal messages deal not with *what* you say—the literal and symbolic components of the words you're using—but with *how* you say it. They comprise body language, or the physical cues you use to express yourself, such as eye contact, facial expression, posture, gesture, rate of speech, volume, and tone of voice, along with other means of communication, such as manipulation of space and type of dress. Nonverbal signals combine with words to convey meanings.

Just as we transmit nonverbal messages without being aware that we're doing so, we often respond to them unconsciously as well. Remember the last time you said something like, "He talks a good ball game, but something tells me . . ."? The "something" was most likely nonverbal, and you'll be able to pinpoint many of its components in the material that follows.

Nonverbals "speak" loudly. If they harmonize with the words you use, you're sending a strong, unified message. If they do not, it's almost impossible to conceal the meaning of your body language with your words. For instance, you tell someone, "No problem, I'll be happy to take care of that for you," and you deliver your perfectly polite words through clenched teeth with your face averted. Or you carefully keep your tone of voice neutral, and you don't even realize that your hand has clenched itself into a fist. Most people would recognize that you do indeed have some kind of problem, though they may not be inclined to confront you with it at that moment. What you transmitted was a mixed message: The words you used and the way you delivered them contradicted each other.

If your nonverbals contradict your words rather than underline them, people tend to believe the nonverbals as more trustworthy indicators of what you really mean. They do so in part because they know that many of us have become very glib, and unless you're a trained actor, it's easier to consciously manipulate words than body language. In fact, even if you attempt to conceal it, your attitude often leaks out via nonverbal signals.

Nonverbal messages can also be enduring. Unless there's a special reason to videotape the proceedings, the actual signals do not remain after the event that elicited them because they cannot be captured in a memo as words can. But the impression they made lingers on, and it can give rise to a reputation that affects future workplace relationships.

For instance, in the interest of securing his cooperation on another matter, you may have graciously conceded a big point to a coworker whom you met with last week. But your accommodation will go unrewarded because he doesn't remember your generous words. Rather, his strongest and most lasting impression of that meeting is that you fidgeted with the papers on your desk the whole time he was talking with you, and in a heated moment, you actually wagged your forefinger in his face. As a consequence of what he took to be your inattentiveness and condescending attitude, he did not nominate you for the high visibility task force he's chairing. What's more, he's already told five other people how difficult you are to work with, and you're on your way to getting a reputation you'd rather not have.

Communicating across genders further complicates an already complex issue. Though many nonverbal signals are universal, women and men differ in several of the signals they use and in how these should be interpreted. What's more, although everyone responds to nonverbal signals, women tend to be more aware of them than men are, causing women to sometimes overestimate their impact, and men overlook it. Start the videotape and see what reframes will help you recognize and control your own nonverbal signals and learn to understand the nonverbal messages of others.

❑   ❑   ❑

"Ms. Brown, Mr. Hsieh, I'm glad you both could join us today," says Sal. *"You sure don't look it,"* thinks Lily, noting his somber expression and subdued voice. She smiles broadly at the group, and Tony, seated beside her, nods briefly. They want to discuss linking the college with two big local employers by

---

PICTURE THIS

Scene

Dean's Conference Room,
Parkwood Community
College

Characters

Sal Vasquez, Director,
Cooperative Education,
committee chair

Frank Witmer, Dean of
Instruction

Phyllis Guttierez, Provost of
Cooperative and Extended
Learning

Jay Kesselman, Faculty,
Computer Information
Systems Department

Lily Brown, Manager, Training
and Development,
Computech Inc.

Tony Hsieh, Manager,
Community Services,
Aquadyne Corp.

---

establishing internship programs for students as well as in-company college courses for employees. It's a project close to Tony's heart.

As Sal guides the discussion, Frank Witmer leans back in his chair, face impassive. For the next hour, he hardly moves at all, save to glare occasionally at Jay, who glares intrepidly back. Phyllis, however, is a ballet of perpetual movement, rearranging her pad and pencils, fiddling with her earrings, leaning forward in her chair and then back again, but never once leaning closer to Jay, who is seated on her left.

When Lily questions the value to Computech of investing fifteen weeks to train people who are then going to leave, Frank says it's worthwhile because they're educating the next generation of workers, and everything cannot be learned from books. This leads him to explain at length the educational value of his two months clerking in an insurance agency before he earned his master's degree. *"This makes him an expert on corporate America?"* thinks Lily. As he drones on, Phyllis doodles in her notebook or taps her pencil; Jay stares out the window, Sal smiles and nods his head, and Lily quietly begins putting papers into her attaché case.

After the meeting ends and as they walk to their cars, Tony tells Lily he's going to commit Aquadyne to the program because the college folks seem like an enthusiastic, energetic group who can certainly make it work. "I'm glad you're going to be working with me on this," he says. "I don't know what you're talking about," Lily replies. "Phyllis and Jay have to work closely on curriculum development, and they can't stand each other. Sal's a typical 'yes' man, so who knows what he thinks. And Frank doesn't seem to think about anything but himself. I see trouble ahead, and I'm advising Computech to pull out."

❑   ❑   ❑

FREEZE FRAME   Is the project blown? Where did Lily and Tony get such different impressions of the meeting at PCC? Is Tony ignoring important nonverbal signals? Is Lily making too much of them? What will get this project back on track?

Check Them Out

The art of decoding nonverbals involves *noticing* and dealing with them at a conscious level. First, *examine your perception in the context* of other nonverbal signals and the total situation. Nonverbal signals appear in clusters, and decoding a meaning from only one of them is like trying to understand a paragraph by reading only one word. What's more, although you observe the signal, you may not be aware of the real reason behind it.

For example, while you were in the middle of explaining your pet project to him, your coworker suddenly crossed his arms in front of his chest with the classic gesture of someone no longer receptive to an idea. Rather than assuming that you've lost his attention, examine your perception in the context of other things that may be going on. He is still looking directly at you, which suggests all is not yet lost. In fact, your colleague may simply be physically cold—is the room getting colder? Or, his back may hurt—do you recall his having back problems in the past? Then ask a question like, "How does this strike you so far?" or "What questions are coming up for you?" This technique provides a conversational opening to discuss what you thought the nonverbal signal meant. Your colleague's answer will tell you whether your perception was on target or not.

Second, *bring the signal up and out*; that is, explain what the signal you're sending signifies or does not signify, or ask what a signal you're getting might mean. In so doing, you can encourage cross-gender understanding. For instance, a male using volume to emphasize something he's saying might explain to a female colleague, "I'm not yelling—I'm trying to make a point here." Or, she might say, "When you raise your voice like that, I think you're angry. Are you angry, or are you just trying to make a point?" Whatever his answer, they've both learned something.

If he had raised his voice without explanation, she might have wondered what could be upsetting him, been unable to pinpoint anything, and decided he was just being unreasonable. If she hadn't given her colleague "reaction" feedback but simply acted from the premise that he was unreasonable, she might have gotten annoyed in return. Or, if she didn't want to fight, she might have recoiled from his anger. He would then have sensed her rejection but would've had no idea why she'd suddenly backed away. This might have caused him to consider her uncooperative, not a team player, which might have led him to be less than cordial during the rest of the conversation. His behavior would then have given her ample justification to regard him as a boor. Consequently, they would have had neither mutual understanding nor the chance to repair their working relationship for the future.

The Eyes Have It

"Watch out for him; he's got shifty eyes." "She never looked me straight in the eye; what's she trying to hide?" "Pay attention, Johnny. Look at me when I'm talking to you!" These familiar phrases testify to the importance that our society places on eye contact. Direct, clear eye contact signals attentiveness, interest, and concern, which, oddly enough, can cause difficulties for women and men at work.

Women tend to look more directly and for a longer time at the people they are speaking with. The signal means "I'm interested in you; I want to connect with you," and other women recognize it as such. Men, however, find prolonged eye contact from a woman disconcerting and confusing. Men habitually look away from other people and into the distance often, when both speaking and listening. This is especially but not only true when emotional issues are being discussed.

Men experience prolonged eye contact with another man as aggressive and usually avoid it unless they're "squaring off" for a fight. Men perceive women who look intently at them as uncomfortably intense and ready to jump down their throats. Or, they experience women as flirtatious because in a social setting, prolonged eye contact between a man and a woman usually suggests more than polite attentiveness and a passing interest. Rather than feeling uneasy and withdrawing from a female colleague or being confused by her message and making an inappropriate social advance, men should bring the signal up and out. Try saying, "It feels as if you're staring at me. Are you?"

Women perceive men who look away often as uninvolved, arrogant, or simply rude. Before deciding that your male colleague is arrogant or obnoxious, examine your perception in context. Has he been asking good questions about what you're discussing? Has he made helpful suggestions? Is his body generally relaxed? If so, he's probably still interested. Then you can bring the signal up and out: "Would you rather discuss this another time? You're looking down the corridor; does that mean you have to leave?"

To understand and control eye messages:

❑ **Look into the "third eye."** If you want to increase your eye contact but doing so makes you uncomfortable or you don't want to be perceived as invasive, focus on a spot between the listener's eyes and about a half inch above the bridge of her nose. She will still perceive that you're paying attention, and you'll both have a comfortable, if slight, degree of distance.

Distance has the advantage of making you less vulnerable to intimidation by another's glare. For example, when you are receiving a compliment and you're uneasy about it, rather than lowering your eyes and thus nonverbally discounting the compliment, focus on the third eye and say, "Thank you."

❏ **Learn to look away.** Recognizing that men may experience direct and prolonged eye contact as confrontational and even hostile, women can reframe a man's looking away as possibly an invitation to continue talking rather than a signal to stop because he's no longer paying attention. Glance at him, look away, and glance again—and keep talking. See what happens.

❏ **Don't look down.** Doing so suggests timidity, submissiveness, or acquiescence.

❏ **Watch the responses you get.** Experiment with eye contact, and carefully observe others' reactions. Then you can decide the degree of eye contact that best communicates interest, and you won't inadvertently convey a lack of it.

Understanding Face Talk

Since more than half of nonverbal communication occurs with the face, it's important to interpret and control facial signals. An animated expression that harmonizes with your words increases your persuasiveness because it makes people want to hear what you have to say, and it holds their attention. An expression that contradicts your words can wreck your credibility.

Inappropriate or excessive facial expressions confuse and annoy people, but a lack of facial responsiveness is also unsettling. During a sales pitch or a negotiating session, a severely controlled face serves you well. But in general, blank faces are detrimental to effective communication. Men in conversation tend to have less animated facial expressions than women and give few if any visible signals that can be interpreted as responsive interest in or encouragement of the other person. This causes many women to regard them as bored or emotionally and intellectually unresponsive. Rather than aborting or escalating your presentation in response to a male colleague's bland face, which suggests that you haven't yet captured his interest, bring the signal up and out with, "You look uninterested. How is this working for you so far?" His answer will reveal whether it's time to continue talking or time to leave.

A lively face adds impact to your message. Such affirming animation as smiles and nods visibly encourages other people to smile and nod. To increase your facial vocabulary, try the following:

- **Study face talk.** To develop your conscious awareness of how different feelings look on a person's face, tune your television to a talk show, an interview, or a dramatic presentation, and videotape a 15-minute segment. Then play it back without sound. Look at the faces and decide what feelings you think they're trying to convey. Are they discussing something serious or frivolous? How do they feel about their topic? About each other? Then rewind the tape and play it again to hear the actual voices so you can check the accuracy of your perceptions.

- **Practice face talk.** To practice using your face to add impact to your words, sit in front of a mirror so that only your face is reflected. Tell the same brief story six times, trying each time to convey a completely different emotional atmosphere with your face: enthusiastic, bored, furious, restless, confident, confused, contemptuous. As you speak, watch your face and ask yourself, "Would another person understand the emotion I'm trying to convey?" You might even want to try this exercise with a partner.

❑ **Increase facial control.** If your face reveals your every thought, sit in a chair in front of a full length mirror and discuss a subject you are passionate about. Keep your entire body quiet, face lifted and completely still, hands resting on your knees, legs loosely together. Use only your voice to convey your emotions; move nothing but your mouth. As you speak, observe your face in the mirror and concentrate on keeping it still.

With practice, you'll become increasingly aware of your body language in general and your facial expressiveness in particular, and you'll learn how to control your face.

When You're Smiling . . .

Generalizations about perpetually smiling women and stone-faced men are changing as more men are loosening up their smile muscles and more women are smiling only when they want to, rather than when they think they should. A sincere smile that indicates genuine warmth, amusement, or pleasure can be motivating; not smiling when you feel like doing so deprives your coworkers of a shared pleasant moment. But a mechanical smile, one intended to conceal an emotional state, not to reveal one, or to please others—or at least to not displease them—dilutes the smile's value.

I've heard it said that women smile *to* please, and men smile *when* pleased. Be that as it may, women tend to smile more at work than men do, even when that facial expression seems at odds with the situation. This can be confusing. For instance, Gupta promised Melody that he'd locate a critical machine part, but he forgot. Hearing his confession, she smiles and says, "Oh, that's okay." But is it really? Gupta can examine his perception in context: Was the project relatively important? Does she care about doing a good job? Will his failure increase the pressure of an already critical situation? Doing so causes him to reframe Melody's smile as probably signaling anxiety rather than pleasure, and he asks what he can do to help her now. If he had not thought about it, he might have taken her words literally and walked off down the hall, leaving her to rage at his unreliability.

Posture Points

Posture broadcasts overall mood. Slouch down (shoulders hunched, head lowered, stomach protruding) and you seem demoralized; sit or stand straight (head up, shoulders back) and you seem confidently in charge. This holds true for everybody; a perpetually lowered head (women do this more often) or a too-rigid spine (men do this more often) does not do your image any good. To improve your posture, whether sitting or standing, imagine a metal loop on top of your head, through which a string pulls you gently toward the ceiling. Your body will align itself in its most comfortable upright position.

Men and women differ considerably in their listening postures. When sitting at a desk or around a conference table, men lean back in their chairs to listen, often actually tilting the chair away from the speaker; women lean forward much of the time, sitting on the edge of their seats and resting their forearms on the table. At the next meeting you attend, do a freeze frame and you'll see what I mean. Before labeling your female colleague hostile or your male colleague uninterested, bring the signal up and out: "When you sit that way, does it mean you're listening?"

Pull Yourself Together

Though women and men use many gestures in common, men tend to gesture away from their bodies; women gesture toward their bodies. So, in the extreme, women experience men as overbearing bulls in china shops, imposing on everyone else's space and acting unintentionally rude or aggressive. Men experience women as relatively nonassertive, insignificant, small.

To increase control of your gestures, imagine two rectangles outlining the perimeter of your body, one from side to side, the other from front to back. Women's gestures tend to stay within their own frames; men's protrude more often through theirs.

To appear strong and assertive, gesture past your perimeters. For example, bend one elbow on the arm of your chair or over the chair back to look relaxed and confident, or fling your arm straight out to the wall to strongly emphasize an idea. To avoid appearing overbearing or intimidating, pull into your frames. Pull your elbows nearer to your sides, for instance, remove your arm from the back of the chair, or bend your leg at the knee when you're seated rather than thrusting it straight out in front of you.

Becoming more aware of the signals that your body parts can send helps you use them to support your words. For instance, if you're excited and talking loud, pull in your arms so as not to seem overbearing. If you're speaking softly, lower the risk of seeming nonassertive by bending your elbow over the chair arm.

Stop Fidgeting!

We all fidget. Women twirl their hair and their jewelry and adjust their clothing. Men tap pencils, rock back and forth in their chairs, or jiggle the coins in their pockets. Everybody picks their cuticles and shakes their legs, with equal frequency.

Fidgeting not only annoys the people witnessing it but it also broadcasts uneasiness and uncertainty, so it can call your credibility into question. People start wondering what you're so nervous and restless about or what you have to hide. If you are nervous, you'd most likely prefer others not to know it. Because much fidgeting is unconscious, the trick is to become aware that you're doing it and then to stop it.

When you witness fidgeting, bring the signal up and out with a question like, "You've started doodling, Dave, so does that mean the meeting's over?" Say this in a good-humored way, but find out what the signal means before acting on an erroneous assumption.

To stop yourself from fidgeting, try the following:

❑ Cut your hair short, remove your jewelry, and empty your pockets. If you're not sure about your type of fidgeting, **ask others for feedback** about when and how you do it.

❑ **Belly breathe.** Breathe deeply three or four times, being sure to expand your diaphragm fully. Check that by putting your hand unobtrusively on your belly; you should feel it bulge out as you inhale. This deep breathing will calm you down enough to stop fidgeting.

❏ **Try steepling.** Avoid flailing arms at all costs. Relaxing your fingers will help you relax your hands and arms and keep them quiet. If you don't know what to do with your hands, hold them in front of you with your fingers lightly together and resembling a church steeple pointing outward rather than upward. Keeping your steepled hands close to your body and at a level somewhere between your waist and your chin signals confidence and authority.

Get a Grip

Touch creates an instant connection metaphorically and literally, and shaking hands is the only thoroughly noncontroversial way of touching each other in a business setting. The handshake is an important ritual that signals a simple greeting or a deal concluded. Men shake hands with each other all the time. They shake hands with men they saw two days ago. But cross-gender handshakes can be confusing.

Men are confused about whether a woman expects a handshake and will accept it. Women wonder if they will appear pushy by thrusting their hand out and whether they should shake hands with other women, too, or only with apparently high-ranking ones. The rule of thumb is "when in doubt, put your hand out." Framing the gesture as a valuable signal of mutual acknowledgement, women can end the confusion by extending their right hands, and men can reach out as well.

Shaking hands symbolizes somewhat different things for women and for men. When men greet women with handshakes, it suggests "I accept you—I'm ready to work with you." When women shake hands, it means, in part, "I know the drill—I know how to play the game." Because handshaking is an important ritual, it has to be correctly done.

A lot of inferences can be drawn from the way people shake hands. A short, firm handshake signals competent self-assurance; offering only the front half of your fingers suggests that you prefer to remain uninvolved: and a bone-crunching shake transmits macho aggressiveness. Under any circumstances, a wimp shake is not okay. It makes other people uneasy, and it signals weakness.

To encourage a good, firm grasp, when you offer your hand, don't point your thumb skyward; instead, turn your palm up slightly and tilt your hand at a 45-degree angle, as if you were about to grasp an item someone was handing you. That way, it's hard for the other person to grab just the tips of your fingers. He's more likely to slide his hand into yours until the web between your thumb and forefinger touches the web between his, and you clasp hands in a good, solid grip. One or two shakes of your forearms for a total of three seconds, and the job is done.

Also, remember that wearing bulky rings on your right hand can bring you pain, and wearing sharp, pointed ones can cause it to others.

Nod Once If You Mean . . .

For men, nodding their heads means assent, so they do it infrequently and with deliberation. Women nod their heads more often than men do, and often it's an unconscious gesture. That's not surprising because women's nods generally mean "I'm listening; I hear you," rather than "I agree." Women may be indifferent to what you're saying, as yet undecided about it, or in violent disagreement, but announcing their position is the second step; the first step is acknowledging your viewpoint and encouraging you to express it.

Unfortunately, men tend to interpret a woman's nodding as agreement, especially since it's usually accompanied by vocal encouragements such as "Um hmm" or "Ahh hah." In fact, this cross-gender confusion may be where women got the reputation of always changing their minds. No study of decision making proves that women change their minds more frequently than men, but if you interpret nodding as agreeing and then come to find your listener disagrees with you, you're going to lament her inconsistency.

A client described how she and her female partner were shopping for a color photocopying system. A hopeful sales rep spent nearly 2 hours explaining the intricacies of his product, watching them nod all the while. When he requested they sign the contract so he could begin processing the paperwork, they explained they still had 2 other salespeople to meet with. He was infuriated that they had wasted his time by turning what should have been a 15-minute introductory pitch into what he thought was a 2-hour new owner orientation. He might have said, "I see you nodding, so I assume you're buying." She or her partner might have said, "Nodding for me means I'm listening. I haven't made up my mind yet." Bringing the signal up and out would have saved everybody a lot of time.

How Fast Can You Say This?

Your rate of speech strongly affects whether people understand what you're saying or bother to try and what they think of you as well. Speaking too slowly makes a fascinating topic boring, so people lose interest or start mentally finishing your sentences for you. Also, they wonder why you're hesitant and uncertain. Speaking too fast makes your topic sound trivial, and because it's difficult to follow machine-gun delivery, people get annoyed and stop listening. They think you're impatient or insecure, and they also may wonder whether a "fast talker" can be trusted.

Regional differences aside, men tend to speak more slowly than women. Maybe that's because they're used to being listened to, and so have come to believe they can take their time. Maybe women speak more quickly because they expect to be interrupted and want to make their point before that happens. Try bringing the signal up and out and say, "You're talking so fast, I wonder what you're anxious about."

If you have to do one or the other, it's preferable to speak quickly because then at least your lively pace keeps your listeners awake. A smooth, measured delivery, with a pace that varies to match what you're talking about, makes you a more authoritative and persuasive speaker. To develop a rhythm that works for rather than against you:

❑ **Record yourself.** To increase control of your speech rate, read a passage from a book into an audiotape recorder for at least 3 minutes. Read at your usual tempo. Then read again, slowing yourself down. Do it again, even slower. Read again and speed yourself up. Do it again, even faster. Review the tape and listen to the effect of your rate of speech.

❑ **Lose vocal ticks.** If you speak slowly, and you have a habit of protracted "ahhhhs" or "ummms," it's going to cost you. Your listeners are likely to start counting the "ahs" or finishing your sentences for you—or both. Either way, they're not paying attention. Speaking fast makes the ticks less noticeable, but they still can be intrusive and should be stopped.

Start by diagnosing the issue. Tape record a 5-minute segment of yourself speaking with someone else or giving a presentation. Then count the number of times you say "ahhh," or whatever filler you hear. Thereafter, whenever you start to use the filler, cut it off immediately and draw a breath instead. Hold the breath for a second. Then continue speaking. With a little practice, you'll become more fluent.

❑ **Fiddle with a prop.** If you speak quickly, remove your eyeglasses, for instance, or take a sip of water. This gives listeners time to absorb your remarks.

❑ **Pause in midsentence.** This is helpful for both slow and fast talkers. It's unexpected so it gets people's attention and it adds force to your words.

Where's the Volume Control?

Speaking too loudly can annoy everyone around you, even people you've never met. They're trying to concentrate, and all they can hear is your voice booming down the corridor. Believing that you're always angry or at least inconsiderate of everybody around you, they turn off and tune out. On the other hand, if you speak so softly that people have to strain to hear you, they won't want to be bothered, and they'll soon stop listening.

Men use volume to emphasize. Enthusiastically presenting their views, they don't realize they're shouting. But their coworkers do. To avoid annoying people with your volume, pay attention to your listeners' nonverbal signals. If you observe averted eyes, facial grimacing, or pulling away, bring the signal up and out: "Are you turning away because you disagree with me, or because I'm talking too loudly? I'll try to lower my voice."

Women often experience an emphatic male speaker as angry rather than enthusiastic and may tend to avoid dealing with him. Instead, women can examine their perceptions in context and bring the signal up and out by asking one question: "It sounds like the Harrison project really annoys you. What are you so angry about?"

If you notice that people often ask you that, it's time to do something about it. To lower your volume, work with a tape recorder that has a volume meter. As you speak into the recorder, watch to see that the meter's pointer stays on the midline. Concentrate on the meter's needle, rather than on what you're saying. You'll soon learn volume control.

Many women speak softly and undercut their credibility by sounding timid and uncertain. What's more, some men literally do not hear a woman who is speaking softly. To increase your volume, bear down on your stomach muscles as you speak. To be sure you're doing this, place your palms on your stomach so you can feel your muscles tighten. Also, try visualizing your voice as an arrow emerging from your mouth and aiming through the listener's face to a point at the back of his head. Doing this will help pull your voice from your throat and increase your volume.

Bringing the signal up and out can help here. For instance, a man might say, "You're speaking so softly you sound uncertain to me. How convinced are you that your proposal works?" A woman might say, "I feel I'm being ignored. Is it because I'm speaking too softly?"

Tone

Your tone of voice can win people over or alienate them entirely. Although trained listeners can listen past an annoying voice to what a speaker is saying, most of us cannot. Men use fewer vocal tones than women do, which can make them sound monotonous and unsure of themselves. What's more, a boring monotone frustrates other people, who don't know how to interpret the emotional content of your message. For instance, say, "I had a great weekend" in a monotone. The emotional component of that simple sentence can range from sincere to ironic to anywhere in between, and a monotone offers no clue. Bringing the signal up and out helps: "You sound like you're being ironic. Did you mean to be?" To expand your range of vocal expressiveness do what I do: turn on your car radio or your CD player (when you're alone) and sing along with your favorite songs!

Women use intonation to emphasize. So men often hear a woman as whining when she's trying to be emphatic. Men tend to avoid whining women. Before you do that, try bringing the signal up and out by asking, "You sound like you're upset about something. Are you upset, or are you just trying to make a strong point."

"Did I Say Something to Offend You?"

When someone reacts to what you've said in a way that takes you by surprise, you may be experiencing what I call an *affect-disconnect*. That is, what you meant to sound like—the attitude you meant to convey—and what the other person heard are disconnected. Sometimes as you speak, you recognize that you sound nasty or condescending or in a way different from what you intend. When that happens, bring the signal up and out immediately with, "I didn't mean to sound patronizing. What I meant was. . . ."

But sometimes you don't hear the music you're making. If you stay mindful of other people's reactions to you, and you're puzzled by what you notice, suspect an affect-disconnect. Bring their signals up and out and find out what's going on. For instance, having said something you considered relatively innocuous, you see your listener turning away. Bring the signal up and out by asking, "You seem offended. Was it something I said?"

REFRAME Let's get back to Parkwood Community College. Start the videotape again and see how reframing nonverbal communication by examining perceptions in context and bringing signals up and out can help save the internship program.

Though neither Sal nor Frank seems enthusiastic to her, Lily decides she needs more information before determining how committed they are to this joint project. Examining her perception in context, Lily notices that although Frank's face and voice are not animated, he does look intently at whoever is speaking, and the few questions he does ask are pointed and helpful ones. She reframes his demeanor as a signal that he is paying attention, although in a style different from her own.

When Phyllis's fidgeting begins to irritate Tony, he brings the signal up and out by asking, "Something seems to be bothering you. How do you feel about our plans so far?" Phyllis explains that she's worried about her three o'clock meeting, where she has to deny a student committee's funding request. "They're going to be so disappointed," Phyllis says. "Jay's the faculty adviser, so we're both in for a tough afternoon. We talked about postponing this meeting because we knew we'd be distracted, but we wanted to get this project going and we didn't want to wreck your schedules." "This is going to work, after all," thinks Tony, congratulating himself for paying attention to nonverbals.

Wondering why Sal's perpetual smiling and nodding so strongly affects her when his behavior is not any different from hers, Lily recognizes that he's crossing a gender expectation and nodding in encouragement rather than agreement. Reframing his behavior, she examines her reframe in context and acknowledges that Sal often disagrees with what someone is saying but still helps them express it.

Standing in the parking lot, Tony says, "I think the meeting went well. I'm committing Aquadyne to the program." "Yes," agrees Lily. "Computech's in, too. I admire your enthusiasm, and I think we're going to have fun working together. See you at next week's meeting." They shake hands and walk away smiling.

Taking Up Space

Space is another form of nonverbal communication. At work, space relates to status, so it's a nonverbal cue people notice; the higher you are on the organization chart, for instance, the more floor space you command. A colleague described how she used space to communicate a forceful message.

The first female regional director of a state agency, she frequently mediated disputes between opposing attorneys. When the lawyers, all male, had difficulty acknowledging her position, she used space to establish her authority. She had the lawyers shown into the conference room, where she joined them. "No matter where they were sitting," she explained, "I would rearrange them. 'Who is the complainant attorney?' I would ask. 'Please take your party and sit on that side. The respondent attorney? Over there, please.' I sat at the head of the table, and wherever they had started out, they wound up in a different place, where *I* had put them. This told them right away who was calling the shots," she said. "It was easy after that."

In general, men claim more space than women do. They spread their possessions over every available horizontal surface. Women often experience that expansiveness as inconsiderate, which it well may be, or even as aggressive. Before deciding your colleague is obnoxious, try examining this perception in context: Did he shake your hand when you entered the room? How attentive is he to what you're saying? Is he monopolizing the conversation? Then try "I need to share this table" (said while moving items around to claim some room).

Women at work tend to gather their possessions close to themselves, which makes them somewhat less visible in the environment. Men experience that contracting as hesitant, tentative. Examine this perception in context: Does your female colleague also speak in a low, quavering voice? Is her data on your joint project solid? Could she merely mean to be polite? Then bring the signal up and out with, "I'm taking up the whole table. Here (said while consolidating possessions), you can put those folders over here."

Clothing Makes the Person

Clothing is very important because it contributes greatly to the first and lasting impression you make.

Dressing for success notwithstanding, clothing sends different signals for men and for women. For men, clothing primarily signals status (as in "white collar" versus "blue collar") or three-piece suit versus coveralls. If an executive man wears slacks and a sports jacket rather than a suit to work, it's assumed that he doesn't have any client contact or important meetings that day. Other than that, people generally pay little attention to men's clothes. Women may say, "Loud tie," but that's about it.

For women, however, clothing signals sexuality along with status. If a woman wears a short skirt or a low-cut blouse, men notice. Many men have told me they always notice what women wear, and they make judgments about it. "If a woman wears conservative clothes, you think she knows a little more about what's going on," a client said. "You think she's more savvy about the business world. She knows how to blend in."

Companies tend to have their own clothing culture, and you're well advised to stay within its accepted boundaries unless you want to call attention to yourself. If you want to express your individual style by wearing a special tie or a brightly colored blouse, fine. But if you can't decide whether to wear something to work or not, a good rule of thumb is "if in doubt, don't."

COLLECT SNAPSHOTS
TO REFLECT ON

❑ Page through your album of snapshots and zoom in on the nonverbals depicted in the various scenes and think about how gender differences might have led to misunderstanding. If you could rewind the tape and play each scene again, which perceptions would you examine in context? Which signals would you now bring up and out? Which reframes would improve cross-gender understanding?

❑ Recall a time when you formed a strong impression that seemed to contradict other information you had, such as believing a job candidate whose résumé was incomplete would nevertheless do well in your group, and events proved you correct. Freeze frame and think about how nonverbals might have helped you form your initial impression.

❑ Freeze frame the last time you were astonished at someone's reaction to what you were saying. Might affect-disconnect have been the cause? Which signals would you now bring up and out? Which reframes could have saved the situation?

Frames of Reference is about paying attention—about staying open to differing points of view as well as new information. It's about recognizing that communication skills deserve your conscientious attention in the first place. By reading *Frames of Reference* you've already taken the important first step of acknowledging that consciously studying communication skills and learning different techniques are worthwhile pursuits. There's no magic formula that will ensure effective workplace communication—but that's exactly the point. We have to keep paying attention because the process is perpetually evolving. Changes in the generalizations I've been making about how women and men communicate will come from the efforts of a lot of individuals who are staying tuned and trying to figure out how to work more productively together.

Staying tuned means noticing not only what people are saying but *how* they're saying (or not saying) it, and actively working to understand what they mean when they use certain words *and* make certain moves since their verbal and nonverbal meanings may differ from yours. Along with working to understand others comes a willingness to understand and reveal yourself *to* others. I don't mean the intimate details of your private life but your communication patterns, your habitual frames of reference, how you define certain words and concepts.

It becomes acceptable to talk about *how* you communicate, process as well as content. It becomes habitual to try different techniques and see how they work, with an eye toward reframing your message so as to get the best results. The gender divide is a good place to begin, but finally, the three-step approach you've learned here will work for you in all the communication circumstances you encounter.

As you start taking more control of how you communicate at work, as you start discussing the communication process in ways that are descriptive rather than aggressive or defensive, you'll be amazed at how forthcoming your coworkers will be. Try it and see what happens. You'll be doing good things for your company and your career. So grab your magic clicker and roll the tape!

INDEX